The Big Book of Yes

17 Short Adventure Stories

Edited by Jon Doolan

Contents

Foreword

It wasn't until I was twenty five that I first understood the true thrill of a big, fat yes. This wasn't an 'okay, I'll go to the cinema with you' yes. Instead, it did exactly what the best yeses do. It opened up a whole new path, a different way of thinking and, subsequently, an appreciation of how chasing curiosity can create a magical, impactful life.

The YesTribe was born from that same curiosity. Nineteen strangers gathered beneath a train station clock in response to a single Facebook post, their rucksacks snugly filled with sleeping bags, hammocks and midnight snacks. Hugs instead of handshakes. Strangers became friends. And then, after a night beneath the stars, a little community was formed of just the type of positive people you'd want around whether times were good or hard.

Since that evening in June 2015, the YesTribe has grown to thousands. Our members have embarked on countless adventures and created projects and charities and initiatives that have had an impact around the world. We've held hundreds of events, three annual Yestivals and created all kinds of amazing spaces designed to bring people together in the real world, where a culture of creativity, confidence and audacity can blossom. And, of course, we built an HQ for the tribe out of an old London bus, which now lives in the middle of a beautiful solar-powered countryside landscape waiting for the next group, team or individual to come and enjoy the fresh air and campfire.

Much to the chagrin of the more structured core team members of SayYesMore, I've always refused to set targets and goals for our work. My favourite times to be alive have been those weeks without restriction where the open road or river has been the signpost, when opportunity and recommendation and sometimes just the direction of the wind dictates the next choice. Waking up on a Mississippi sandbar or beneath the canopy of a beech forest in England without a clue where the next night's 'bed' will be yet still knowing it's all going to work out.

Too much certainty, of course, removes the adventure. And while adventure is so often prescribed as a long, hideously exhausting self-propelled mission into the unknown, for me it's at its most powerful when embedded behind enemy lines. A cunning smile at a plan hatched on a commuter train. The clink of pints in salute to a zany idea that will not die stagnant in that same pub. That glorious surge of certainty in the gut that tells you there is no choice but to chase the adventure that is going to make your lifelong friends look at you funny. The same adventure which will change your life and have those same friends respectfully salute you before they settle down to the next episode of Love Island.

So, that's why we wear Say Yes More on our shirts and why the YesTribe grows through word of mouth. To be that ready-made cluster of positive angels on your shoulder to whisper encouragement and offer support. The cheerleaders from near and far, pulling and pushing as you do your thing, all brave and epic, but actually just sensible and full of life.

If you're holding this delicious book in your hands then you're already a yes person. Please don't just enjoy the tales here, but share them with others. Do justice to the effort behind these chapters, the decisions and determination and inspiration. With every 'yes' we gain another story and life becomes a little more interesting. Good stories make us think, but great storytelling leads us down a road we'll never regret. And maybe, just maybe, it'll end up with you writing a story in the next edition of this book. That, my friend, is totally up to you.

Keep being you. Say Yes More.

Dave Cornthwaite

SayYesMore and YesTribe Founder, July 2018

Thank You

This is a collection of 17 incredible and inspirational adventure short stories. Some of the stories are epic adventures to faraway lands involving great heroics of endurance. Some are more modest and took place close to home.

Each of the stories involved the author saying 'Yes' to something, whether that is launching themselves into a hair-brained adventure or simply making a positive change in their life.

But this book is more than just a collection of stories. Simply by buying this book you are making a difference. 100% of royalties are going to the Teddington Trust, a charity set up to support people with rare and misunderstood illnesses.

Each of the authors has dedicated their time and effort for free. If you like their writing, please reach out to them on their social media and/or their websites which you will find at the end of their chapters.

Our incredible cover designer is Harkiran Kalsi. Please check out her stunning designs at **www.harkirankalsi.co.uk**.

Thomas Marmoy drew the beautiful illustrations that you will find throughout the book. If you would like to find out more about Tom, he'd love it if you'd drop him an email at **tom.marmoy@gmail.com**.

All of us (authors, designers, editors and charity founders) are members of the YesTribe, a group of individuals who inspire each other to live full lives by saying 'Yes' to the things that we truly want to achieve. If you want to Say Yes More then join the YesTribe on Facebook.

Thank you for buying this book. You're an absolute legend!

Read, be inspired and SAY YES MORE!

Jon Doolan

Editor

jondoolan.com

Chapter 1

The Arc of an Alcoholic

by Paul Parrish

The Channel Part 1

This will never end. It will never end. I have been swimming for 17 hours. I don't know for sure that I have been swimming for that long. In fact, I think I have been swimming for much longer. No one on Gallivant, the pilot boat that shadows me on my left hand side, is allowed to tell me anything. It has been dark since 7pm the previous evening. I know it must be dawn soon and the fact that I can't see traces of light in the sky is confusing me. Everything is confusing.

Stroke, one, two, three , head out. Stroke , one, two, three, head out. The same mantra repeated for many hours. Back then, it had been relaxing to repeat. As my initial nervousness had subsided the mantra had been a comfort. I had felt strong. The adventure had seemed possible - probable, even. There was confidence in me, back then. But now many, many hours down the line it is over. I have failed. I know from all the things that I have read and from all that I know about my own ability that I should have finished this swim hours ago. The fact that I haven't reached dry land means something has gone horribly wrong. Something going horribly wrong on a Channel Swim preceded by an 87 mile run will mean a compounded disaster that the human body won't have the resources to deal with. Every store of energy in my body must be used up now. There can't possibly be anymore left. It's gone now. All possibilities of success have evaporated.

It was light when I had left Dover. Back then, hours ago, I had visual references. I could see the bright white superstructures of the ferries trawling between Britain and Europe. I could look up to the left from the water every six strokes and see the faces of my support crew on the pilot boat. Early on I had imagined that they might be admiring the power of my stroke, but as time had dragged on I began to read concern and criticism in their expressions. This was the beginning of the paranoia that fatigue brings.

Then the light had faded. By seven it was dark. At that point I had been excited. I'd never swum in darkness before and it seemed like another part of the adventure. I believed that I could be at the French coast by midnight. But now so many hours have passed. Far more time than I believed I could carry on swimming for has elapsed and there has been nothing but darkness. Nothing that gave me a visual fix on anything other than the lights on the boat, and the shadow shapes of my crew.

A while back there had been a bright light. It had seemed to float a few metres above the water. My mind had been telling me for some time that I was somewhere off the entrance to Calais Port and this light had been a navigation buoy. But it had disappeared what seemed like a lifetime ago and now there was nothing but deep, deep blackness all around. To my right the dark of the sky met the dark of the sea and now, out ahead of me the same darkness both above and below water engulfed me and with it any hope of finishing this godawful swim.

How could I have been so stupid, so egotistical to believe that I, a frightened, worthless drunk, could do this? The mind has taken over and, battered by fatigue and extreme fear, the lurking addict, never far below the surface, has reappeared. All those people watching me, all those people who I had told to watch me. They are going to laugh at me. The paranoia is rampant and bit by bit the strength of will is being chipped away. Blocks of resolve, like the edges of the ice shelf, are falling into the sea around me. The doubts flood in now. How could someone like me believe themselves capable of swimming the English Channel? It is the swim of swims: the jewel in the crown for all endurance swimmers. The best swimmers from all over the world come to Dover to attempt this crossing. *The best swimmers in the world!* The age old cliché amongst the swimming community is that The Channel is the Everest of swimming. They will then add to this by telling you that far fewer people have swum the Channel than have successfully summited Everest. So what am I doing here? Fourteen years ago I couldn't touch a drink without wanting to send myself into oblivion, chain smoking as I sank. What makes me think I can dine at the top table with the best swimmers in the world? For Christ's sake, I couldn't even swim ten years ago! Correction, I could manage some slow approximation of breaststroke but that barely got me across the width of a swimming pool, let alone one of the hardest sea swims in the world.

There is now an overwhelming feeling of hopelessness and helplessness. This is so frightening. In the middle of a sea, with no knowledge of where I am. My crew are not allowed to tell me. They are under orders to say nothing. All they are permitted to say is "keep swimming", and that phrase has run thin and I hate them for their false encouragement and their forced optimism. I can see Zara now, sitting on the steps leading up to the bridge, her robe wrapped around her and her head down. Probably trying to grab some sleep and not even watching me. Alex is slumped on a deck seat in a similar pose.

So I am alone and I have failed. I am still swimming but for what reason? I can stop now and in a few seconds I will be fished out of this hateful place, onto the boat, where, within minutes I will soon be warm and dry and fed and feeling normal. But, it is that phrase "within minutes I will be feeling normal" that propels me onward. I am too far into this and know the regrets that come with "feeling normal". To give up at this stage, after so much, to return to a comfortable state changes my resolve. I cannot give up now.

It is at that moment, thinking that thought, that the swim changes. From within the deepest cortex of my brain, plucked from so far down within, my mind shifts and it ignites. It feels like it is on fire and within seconds all I can visualise is my mind as a furnace. In the space in my skull where rational thought lay there is fierce light and this light is magnesium white and burning in the very core of my consciousness.

I am lost but I swim onwards.

Lost

14 years earlier I was lost.

I am coming back across the fields on a cold autumn day. It's Sunday and my wife and I have taken our little ones out into the fields for some fresh air. It's been hard getting them to walk but once outside there are always distractions and the change of scene will tire them and they will eat well. Low clouds scud across the sky and as I turn around to look at where we have walked and the simple beauty of the trees, their leaf covering almost all lost, I am filled with dread and a sadness seeps into every pore of me.

On afternoons like these I can feel my addiction expanding inside me. It is taking over my brain and dominating my thinking. I am beginning to plot and scheme. My wife will be horrified if I say I am going to the pub. She knows that I will come back drunk, clutching a plastic bag containing more booze which I will then drink into the early hours until I render myself insensible. There is no rational reason for this behaviour and she will plead with me not to do it, but I will be powerless. I will drink to oblivion. I will wake the next morning, full of shame and regret, but I will then repeat the process. It never changes. I am caught in a circle of destruction and as I head into my 36th year I have given up. I know I will die. I imagine my funeral and my children mourning a father that could never quite connect.

What I don't know is that there is a date that is looming on the horizon. That date is November 22nd 2000. My life will change on that date. I still have my work diary from that time and I can look back at my whereabouts. At no point is there even the slightest hint that I am going to undergo a vast psychological change that will send me down a new pathway that I could never have imagined before.

I arrive home from a business trip on November 22nd. I am already very drunk and I have even more booze to consume. It's a rare occasion, but I am alone in the house. The family are away. I would always see this as an opportunity to find new depths of oblivion. Recently, these opportunities have begun to scare me. The drinking has become so crazy that I am scared that I won't wake up, or that if I do wake up, it will be in a place that is unfamiliar that will betray a trail of humiliation and shame.

I take the booze into the kitchen and suddenly it hits me. I am finished. I cannot do this anymore. I am at the jumping off point. I cannot drink any more. But I cannot stop, either. My personality is ripped apart. I am hung out, crucified by my addiction and the pain is insufferable. On that night I call for help and anonymous people rush to my aid. On November 23rd I pour my last alcoholic drink down my throat in some kind of pathetic, self-pitying, symbolic gesture (I want to hospitalise myself). To this date I have not felt the need to drink alcohol again.

Sober

The journey to sobriety is an astonishing and confusing ride. I hate these people who take away my choice to drink. How dare they suggest that I cannot run my life according to my will? I am livid with them, but there is some part of me that seems to know that they are right, no matter how terrifying the prospect of a life of abstinence seems.

The sober days pass into sober weeks which become sober months which, and - this is a miracle - become sober years. I now see that this choice, whether to drink or not, was never a choice. I am an alcoholic, and by definition, can never drink safely. But if you take away this choice you are given a new choice: the choice to live. The choice to inhabit a varied and exciting existence. I knew none of this back in November 2000. All I knew was that I was full of shame and, although it was obvious to everyone that I had a problem, I wasn't brave enough to be honest about it. In my attempt to clumsily explain why I wasn't drinking I cast around for an excuse and alighted on a great idea: I would say that I was going to run a marathon...

I signed up for a charity place to run the London Marathon. The following week, I set out on my first three mile run. By the end of it I was in tears. I couldn't run for more than a mile at a time. The past twenty years had stripped me of any fitness. Coupled with that, I was now much older than when I had last applied myself to any serious sport. These are the moments of truth in a life. The obvious choice was for me to throw up my arms in despair and walk away from this. A life drinking was much easier, as was an existence left to play itself out on the sofa of apathy. At this point, I used a level of intuition that had previously been hidden from me. It dawned on me that the steps I was taking to stay sober could just as easily be applied to marathon running. As an alcoholic I wasn't told not to drink for the rest of my life – that was the quickest way to get a drinker back to the bar. Instead, I was told not to drink just for today. By starting afresh each day and chunking up my life into manageable proportions, I could get sober days to become sober weeks. Similarly, I realised that I had run a single mile and that if I could run one mile, well maybe I could run another mile, and gradually build up my exposure to long distance running in this way.

Over the course of the winter I did just that and just as the sober days built up, so did the running miles. I had inadvertently discovered a simple life rule that would open up a world of adventure. When a task was looked at as the sum of its smaller parts, nothing seemed too big. Within a few months my body had begun to develop a runner's physique. My clothes became too big for me. My mind became focused. Best of all, I began to fall in love with the outdoors. In those formative months I ran hundreds of trails around my village, sometimes in hard rain, sometimes in snow, sometimes under glassy blue skies with air so cold that it felt like my breath would shatter. And then at the end of March the days lengthened and it seemed as if the world was laying on a celebration. The gorgeous yellow daffodils gave way to luxuriant bluebells that dominated the paths and trails creating wondrous azure carpets that would frequently make me cry with gratitude. I now understood that I had been given another chance to live and that these were the rewards should I keep moving along this pathway. I was handed a gift.

In April 2001 I crossed the finish line at the London Marathon. Friends waited to see what I would do next. There were some who thought aiming for a goal was a dangerous idea, and that once that goal had been achieved I would be in danger of slipping back into my old ways. Afterwards, I sat in one of the hospitality suites at the marathon finish and said to a friend, "I think that this is just the end of the beginning". It was one of those times in my life when my insight was totally correct.

The Channel Part 2

It's Midday on the 15ᵗʰ September 2014. I am standing on the pebbles of Shakespeare Beach to the west of Dover. I am about to wade in and attempt to swim the English Channel. I have been sober for nearly 14 years and now I am facing one of the hardest swims in the world.

14 years ago I couldn't swim. 14 years ago I could only drink. Time changes everything if you will only let it. Give time time. Add to your dreams little by little. Give them time to germinate.

I am standing amongst a small gaggle of well-wishers on the pebbly beach staring out at the pilot vessel that will stay by my side and direct me across the Channel. The pilot, Mike Oram, is the most experienced Channel swimming pilot in the business. When he welcomed me aboard this morning he laughed and asked me if I had crampons with me as the waves were forecast to build up during the day. I am not sure if he was being funny, but it makes me feel sick with fear. I need every bit of luck that I can find to accomplish this swim. Big waves are not going to help.

My crew wave at me from the boat and then Mike blasts the air with his fog horn which is my cue to begin the swim. Looking back on this moment I believe it shows that fear is finite. It has a limit and I think at midday on this day I had reached that limit. Successive challenges had shown me that it was possible to move through the veil of fear and walk through to the other side. When that horn sounded the most natural reaction would have been to hold my hands up, admit defeat and give up. But I walked into the water, stumbling over the uneven pebbles and when it was deep enough I shallow dived and began to swim. As I swam my mind did what it had done many times before and slowly began to loosen the asphyxiating noose of fear.

And as I swam and I felt the chill of the water encase me, I still had doubts. I didn't really know how my body would react to a swim that, on its own, was a lifetime's challenge, but I had also a further doubt about how it would react because eighteen hours earlier I had arrived in Dover having run the 87 miles it takes to get to the coast from Marble Arch.

The Arch to Arc

My philosophy of "running one more mile" had led me to complete a number of eye-wateringly long triathlons, raising money along the way for the various charities I have worked for in sobriety. In recovery I learnt that I could keep going forward and that discomfort would always pass. This outlook has kept me going both in my personal life and in my physical life. It has also led to expertise in coping with extreme endurance events. The marathon led to triathlon, which led to Ironman triathlons, which led to ultra-running, which led to double and even triple ironman distances. None of these events were ever comfortable and every single one of them was preceded by fear and self-doubt. All, ultimately, were completed. Success did not teach me arrogance. If anything, I learnt the opposite; I learnt humility. Every event was far larger than me and I came to believe that if I treated them with respect then they might allow me to dance with them for a very brief time. Treated without deference, they would spit me out with little ceremony.

During this time of development, I became aware of a preposterous event that was whispered about with incredulity by some in the endurance world. It was a "triathlon" in the loosest term of the definition only because it consisted of the three component disciplines of triathlon: swimming, cycling and running. Its name was The Arch to Arc. The premise was as follows; starting at Marble Arch the participant must run an 87 mile route down to Dover. Within 48 hours of starting the run the participant must begin to swim the English Channel – a 22 mile crossing at the closest point between England and France. If that was completed the event finished with a triumphant 182 mile cycle ride from Calais to the Arc de Triomphe in Paris.

When, against all rational thought, I signed up for the event, only eight people had completed it; fewer people than had walked on the moon. Nearly all the unsuccessful candidates, of whom there was a growing number, had failed in the English Channel. The Arch To Arc was the brainchild of an ex Royal Marine, named Edde Ette, who had finally completed it in 2000, on his fourth attempt. "Royal Marine" and "four attempts" should have acted as enough to dissuade me, but there was that willpower within me that refused to listen to reason (there is a badly informed presumption that addicts lack willpower. Totally spurious. Addicts have vast reserves of strength. After all, who could possibly force a drink down them at 11am when they have woken up terminally hungover and gagging with nausea? That takes real willpower!). Having had a second chance at life, I decided to sign up in 2012 and having done so, promptly filed it in the "this will never happen" compartment of my brain, and got on with my life.

September 13th 2014 saw me standing under Mable Arch with another group of well-wishers as I prepared to set off on my own Arch to Arc attempt. Rather like an important exam the spectre of this immense event happening had loomed larger on my life's horizon filling me with ever increasing panic but I still placed myself in a position of denial and thought that it would never happen. A year away it was obvious my swimming was so poor that I wouldn't have a chance of getting across to France. I had had to have a crash course in swimming whilst at the same time conditioning myself to be able to run 50 miles without batting an eyelid. I learned that it's sometimes impossible to be fully prepared for something, but that you may as well give it a go and see what happens, which is why I was now about to attempt this outrageous feat of endurance. No amount of training could prepare anyone for what was to come.

At 8pm on a warm September evening I left the bright lights of Central London and began to pick my way through the London streets led by the eccentrically named Dan Earthquake, who was to be my guide and race director; a grand title for a man who was leading a solo participant on an event that clearly wasn't a race of any kind. The only race benchmarks I had were the times that the previous successful attempts had taken, but comparative timings were furthest from my mind. Even the thought of finishing seemed too much to hope for.

The route took me across the Thames and into South East London. It was whilst passing through Camberwell that I ran past a pub called the Hermit's Cave. This had been my 'local' when I first moved down to London in the late 80's. Back then (and it may be the same today), it was a real dive bar where the low life of the area drank. One evening, at the age of 22, I was in there, drinking on my own. I liked these kinds of pubs, because the tragedy of a young man, starting out on his adult life and already struggling to cope, went unnoticed in the Hermit's Cave. Everyone in here had some sort of troubled existence. It was as I was taking a draw on my cigarette that a woman staggered up to my table, scooped up the contents of my ashtray in her fist and stuffed the ashen filth into her mouth. Instead of being horrified, I remember accepting her actions and making a mental note that 'at least I wasn't that bad, yet'. Now, 28 years later, I was running past the same pub - a different person. At this point I was finally able to admit to myself that life had moved on for the better.

I ran through the night, leaving London behind and entering the quiet of the Kentish countryside. Running through the night is a privilege. There is such a deep sense of peace and solitude as a serenity replaces the hustle and bustle of modern life.

This serenity was replaced by the hard, dark hours just before the dawn. In all endurance events it is when people are most likely to throw in the towel. The novelty of the night has lost its lustre, the body needs rest and the night is at its coldest. If you can hold on for this crucial 90 minutes the sunrise will see a dramatic change in your body's reactions. The dawning light allows the world to take shape again and energy and optimism returns. I felt in good shape and with dawn the finish seemed a possibility. Optimism is a great thing but it can mask reality. I still had another ten hours running ahead of me. By the afternoon, I was really beginning to feel the distance and the interminable tarmac beneath my feet.

Finally, I reached a road junction that I knew well. It marks the beginning of the final road into Dover. It's a couple of miles long, winding into the town and finally takes me to the seafront. Waiting for me were the race directors and a couple of friends who were ready to look after me and check that I was okay for the next stage.

It was a relief to stop running and arrive intact, but my mind was already projecting on to the next stage of the task. I had noticed that the event organisers had been looking concerned and had been deep in discussions. I thought I knew what they were going to tell me. Sure enough Eddie, event founder, put his arm around my shoulder and told me that the weather forecast had been in a state of change and it now looked like there would be force 5 winds and above the following day. I was given the choice of waiting out for another weather window and thereby failing to complete my swim start within 48 hours of the run, or I could start the whole process again in a couple of weeks.

We took some time out and headed to our rooms for a rest and so that I could get some sleep in case the situation changed. Instead of getting my head down I answered texts from friends and well-wishers and even read a book. Finally, I fell asleep.

I don't know what time it was, but someone was rapping on my door. It was Dan, my race director; 'The weather has eased, you're going. Get your stuff together, eat as much breakfast as you can. We want you at the marina by 11.'

I walked out of the hotel to begin the hardest physical and mental task of my entire life. I was taken to Shakespeare Beach to attempt to swim the Channel.

The Channel part 3

All is lost.

I am done. I am distraught. The left side of my body is in agony and I am swimming with only one side in working order. I will never finish now. I know one thing, though; one crucial piece of information. This will pass. At some point my ordeal will end and I have chosen not to call an end to it myself. I have accepted failure but not defeat. I have made a decision that I will wait for my crew and Mike Oram, the pilot, to call the swim. I will not give up until they tell me to do so. I can keep going another minute, another hour, even if it is futile. The white light in my consciousness burns brighter still.

In the depths of this resigned stasis things begin to happen quickly. I am aware that Dan, who is also my designated support swimmer has jumped in to join me. To my addled brain that can only mean one miserable thing; he wants me to push hard so that we can beat another tide, otherwise it's another six hours swimming. I can't do this anymore and I can't speed up. I hurt and I ache and I can't face another tide.

Then Gallivant is gone. It is not on my left hand side where it has bobbed for 17 hours. As I realise that I am alone the miracle happens. The most remarkable thing that has ever happened to me. My right hand touches sand. Then my left. I stop swimming wondering what I have hit in the pitch black. I put my feet down. There is sand beneath my feet. The sand of France. I carry on swimming, but now my strokes are uneven because I am sobbing. Sobbing with relief, sobbing with joy, sobbing with jubilation. I have swum the English Channel. And contained in that simple sentence are the images to cherish for a lifetime. I replay those moments every single day of my life. Nothing can take them away from me. Writing this paragraph makes me become tearful as I remember 5.24 am, September 16th 2014. I hope that if you are reading this with a particular goal in mind, that you have a moment like my 5.24 am.

Finale

With the Channel complete, nothing would stop me finishing the Arch to Arc. I swam back to the boat, and was hauled on deck where I was given much needed tea and handed a chart of my swim. It had taken 17 hours and 25 minutes and with the push and pull of the tide I had covered a distance of 35 miles. As I sat on the boat deck there was a beautiful sunrise and Gallivant was bathed in the early morning sunlight. I was full of childish excitement. At Calais I was told to get some rest, but after a couple of hours of my excited chattering the team decided the only way to tire me out was to put me on the bike and get me to Paris.

We left Calais in the warm afternoon and I cycled along the coast to Boulogne before heading inland to Paris. The route took me past Wissant Beach where, on some unmarked spot, I had floundered ashore a few hours earlier. The team let me stop to look out and I spent a few minutes letting the enormity of the swim sink in. I cycled into the night and into the silent countryside of rural France. The night was clear and the stars were laser bright and infinite. I remember looking up and marveling at these precious moments. The relief of what had been such a huge undertaking now receding made me feel light and happy. This adventure would be finished.

I rode into Paris at the end of the rush hour on the morning of 17th September and arrived at the Arc de Triomphe to find a welcoming committee of friends, family and work colleagues, who had all sneaked over to Paris to surprise me and cheer me at the finish. It was all very emotional and I was incredibly proud to have arrived at the end of this challenge. I was too exhausted and emotional to believe that this was in any way profound and life changing. Those minutes at the Arc de Triomphe were just minutes like any other. They were all part of the process of change my life had been undergoing.

I prefer not to think in terms of defining "moments". If we do that, we could choose, on occasions, to define ourselves by the worst moments of our life. Instead, I like to appreciate the second chance I have been given. I've had some really tough moments since I got sober, but overall it has been an attempt to squeeze the most out of life. In return for putting down the bottle I have tried to inject adventure and enthusiasm into my everyday life, so that when I look back at it in its entirety and not measured in moments, I can feel that the trajectory of experience is a positive one. That is enough for me. I could try and bottle the feeling of euphoria I got from finishing the Arch to Arc, but instead I want to keep the cork out of the bottle and let it fill with other adventures and experiences that will help make this small, insignificant life just that little bit better. We all get a second chance. Every morning we are given a choice to reset or change if we need to. Take the chance, say "yes" to life and live! Live beyond your wildest imaginings.

Website: **paulsarch2arc.blogspot.com; aspire.org.uk**

Instagram: **@paulparrish65**

Twitter: **@paulparrish2**

Chapter 2

The Yes Train

by Caroline Twigg

'What do you mean you have to work?!'

'I know, I know it's rubbish … but it's a new job and it's a VIP event I'm overseeing. I can't do anything about it'.

I stared at my husband. It was about 9pm and he'd just walked in and was loosening his tie uncomfortably. He looked slightly gutted but kind of steely too... this wasn't going to be a conversation I could turn around.

'But we've lived here a month now. We came together - took ourselves off from our little life in Europe to here in the middle of Delhi, to be together. To adventure. To explore. Together. But you've just been working non-stop. It can't happen for the third weekend in a row!'

'I know, my love, I know. It's just it's really bad timing. It will get better. After this visit... I think I could be back by ten on Friday. And maybe have Saturday evening off. It's partly the time difference – London is working when it's evening here so we have to tune in then...'.

'Not on a Saturday they're not! Yann, I'm lonely! It's rubbish! Everything is hard – you think I do nothing all day but you have NO idea how hard it is to get across town in forty degree heat in a language I don't understand and rickshaws I think I'm going to fall out of. To go to places I don't know how they operate and try and sort out our house. To buy food and source clean water and get the internet connected and a phone line and fill out forms and get a bank account even though no one trusts me because I haven't got a job and I'm a woman... Can you even guess how hard it was to buy a light bulb?!'

I was on a roll now. Four weeks of pent up frustration, over-tiredness and over-heating had bubbled to the surface and was spewing out of me like a volcano.

'You sit in your AC office and tell me it's not that hot – well it is! Like when I'm stood in a market and they're ringing a chicken's neck in front of me and everything smells like warm blood and wee and then you hear the stupid mosquitos whining as they spear their way into you somewhere between the streams of sweat and you worry they're dengue mosquitos because your boss' wife, she had dengue, did you know that? All her hair fell out for two years and she was in bed for months! Did you know that?! They've drained the pond because of her, and we've got stagnant water on our balcony because that stupid pipe keeps leaking – breeding ground for dengue mosquitos that is! And all I want to do is buy some milk and light bulbs!'

I was nearly in tears now. Yann was staring at me. Neither of us knew where this was going.

'We've booked to get the train to Rishikesh, my man. Do you remember? Our first weekend away – into the mountains! MOUNTAINS! Fresh and clean and cold. And mountainous! No cars. No people. Mountains! The source of the Ganges! MOTHER GANGES!'

'I know. I know we had... we've got time, we'll have to go another weekend, when work has calmed down. It WILL calm down. I know it will. But I can't do anything about it for the next few weeks'.

He looked unshakable. He pushed each shoe off with the opposite toe and padded to the kitchen in his socks. I slumped onto the sofa. As he poured a cold beer, I looked around me. At the empty flat that was missing all our worldly possessions because they were somewhere on a container ship outside Mumbai harbour. At the horrible furniture. At the marble floors that were helpfully cooling but made it feel like we were living inside a tomb. At the phone line with no phone in and the internet box that wasn't connected. The potential to link to my familiar world severed before leaving the flat. At the one photo I'd carried in hand luggage of our wedding day – all our friends and family beaming out at us from a lush green English lawn. At the mosquito-mesh-covered windows that half sheltered us from the hot dusty chaos outside. I heard a stray dog howl and a car horn blared angrily through the evening. And I knew I couldn't spend another weekend and several long lonesome evenings here on my own again. I sighed and rubbed my eyes.

'It's ok, my man, I get it. It's a shocker and they shouldn't make you work so late when they know you've just arrived and I'm here on my own, but I get it.'

He looked at me half skeptical and half relieved.

'I do get it, honestly, I'm just tired. But I can't stay here on my own again... I think I'll just head to Rishikesh anyway.'

'On your own?' His eyebrows were raised and the beer stopped halfway to his mouth.

'Why not? I've travelled on my own before in all sorts of places. We've got a ticket booked. I'll find an ashram to stay in – Rishikesh is the home of ashrams isn't it? I'll do some yoga and drink lassis and read and breathe in the mountain air. I'll be fine'.

'Oh, the wife. I'm not sure... we don't really know India yet at all and it's a pretty remote place. Is it safe to go just you? The trains are supposed to be mad... and you'd be on your own... I don't think you should... I...'

'I'm doing it, my man. You said we don't really know India yet...
maybe true because you've not really left the office, but I'm starting
to get it... I'm going. I'll go crazy if not.'

The tables had turned – he realised I had made up my mind.

'Are you sure?'

'Yes. Yes, I'm sure' And I held my hands in prayer in front of my
heart, bowed my head slowly and said 'Ooooommmmmmmmmmm'
until I heard him chuckle.

'The wife, you're a wally – are you definitely sure? Don't do it just
because you're cross or to prove something'.

I looked at him. He was right. Why did I want to go? Was it for the
right reasons? Would it maybe be a bit rubbish but then I'd just
come home and say 'it was a bit rubbish but all part of the
adventure'? Would it most likely make me happy? Was it worth a
shot?

We looked at each other and I said it in small voice.

'Yes'.

He raised his eyebrows.

'YES, I'm going! Woo hoo!'

* * *

I leaned my top half out the stationary train window at Old Delhi
station, the window sill pushing into my ribcage and the top of my
head pressed against the top, and I watched the craziness swirl
around the platform. Smart but sweaty train guards busy answering

questions as passengers checked their names on the paper lists sellotaped to the carriage doors. I'd been amazed and relieved to find mine – clutching my scrappy paper ticket I'd gone to the right carriage and my name was there, printed officially in the list and decreeing I would be allowed a seat as the train departed. I'd climbed in and found my seat with its ornate brass number screwed into the headrest.

I watched the bustle outside the train. Porters in blood-red baggy trousers and loose tops were weaving in and out of crowds with huge checked bags somehow balanced on their heads. All along the platform, generations of families sat in colourful clusters – dads staring up at departure boards. Mums repeatedly scooping small children back to the blanket they'd set up as the Family Main Base. Grans sat silently waiting to be told what to do. Children in squirming heaps. Pots of food were passed round. Crisps eaten. Chai drank. Shoves and shouts and hair plaiting.

And all around, men in orange. Men of all ages carrying a small bag if carrying anything at all, smudged bindis between their eyes and coloured paint on their faces, worn sandals on their feet. Each draped in a scrappy saffron-orange robe. Jostling into the robed back in front of them as they pressed forward onto my train. There was orange as far as I could see along the endless platform – bobbing shaved heads poking out of the swirling orange sea.

I swallowed slowly. This was a pilgrimage weekend. I hadn't realised. I'd read about these weekends but hadn't looked up dates. They didn't happen that often and it hadn't crossed my mind it might be now. I suddenly felt quite small. And very non-Indian.

Pilgrims, all men, go up to Rishikesh all the time, to bathe in the waters and hike to the source of the Ganges bringing back small pots of the precious water to take home. But on a few weekends there are mass gatherings. Some people walk for days to reach Haridwar at the bottom of the mountain, worn sandals pounding the dry roads and orange robes swishing around in the dusty heat.

Others take the train to Haridwar and hike the 20km mountain road into Rishikesh. For most people who do it it's once or twice in a lifetime. Three or four generations of men travelling together as a rite of passage. Or groups of young men. Serious in intent and devout, but giddy from the sudden adventure and freedom from daily life.

I sat back in the hot seat and watched through the dirty glass. I was wearing a dark red kurta with a faint gold flower pattern dotted across it, goldy-beige leggings, and a matching dark red scarf draped backwards over my shoulders. I wore flip-flops, gripped a small rucksack on my lap, and had loose change in a pocket and most of my money tucked into my bra. The outfit made me feel adventurous and free, and was doing well to keep me cool. It was an Indian outfit. Did it make me look like I lived here and knew what was what, not to be messed with? Or was it the wrong type of outfit and made me look naïve and foreign and trying too hard? I'd felt empowered and excited when I left our flat that morning. Now I felt unsure and very alone.

And I heard a loud whistle and the train started off slowly. Along the platform people were still getting on and off the train. Passengers walking alongside the open train door holding the railing then stepping easily on to the high steps as if in sync with the train's rhythm. Boys with baskets of crisps and tissue packets and kettles of hot chai effortlessly stepping down in the gaps, onto the platform and over to another train to sell their wares. The train picked up speed and I smiled slowly. I was on my way.

I was in the first class carriage. The lady next to me was Indian but had been living in Ohio for twenty years. She seemed petrified that people were going to steal her luggage and that she'd get sick from the train breakfast. She explained she'd only been back once since she moved to the USA, and had now returned for a family funeral – she was plump and sweaty and seemed totally unhappy to be there. I took a deep breath and bit my bottom lip. The carriage door opened and a waft of sweet curry engulfed the air as the guard plonked a tray in front of each person. A small thermos of tea, some biscuits, a tinfoil-wrapped chapatti to dunk in a hot greasy curry, and a pot of warm runny yoghurt. My neighbour poked the foil with her painted nail and pushed the tray away.

I deliberated, then squeezed some antiseptic wash on my hands and unwrapped the steaming fresh chapatti. As I nibbled and dunked, I watched as we started leaving the crowded chaos of Delhi.

Outside seemed to be endless, parched dry countryside. Field after field unfolding in front of me as I peered through the grimy windows. Water buffalos ambled slowly into dusty village entrances or pulled carts along unmade-up tracks. Hundreds of red chilies lay drying on hessian sacking in the sun; storks perched in shallow creeks, and children and stray dogs chased the train carriages as they rumbled past, laughing and barking and waving and falling over. The stink from stagnant pools of water littered with sewage and rubbish and being picked through by birds and dogs made its way into the train carriage and I leaned forward to breath in the steam from my curry instead. Outside one village I saw a man having a dump on the railway tracks alongside ours. Squatting unceremoniously with his long white shirt gathered in his hands he watched blankly as our train passed. The plump Indian/American next to me wiped her hands with antiseptic gel and took out her magazine.

The 230km journey was 6 hours long. We stopped occasionally and some people left, but mostly others got on. More passengers and a collection of wallahs selling snacks and newspapers, shooting through the carriages bellowing about their goods and hopping down onto the platform as the train left and picked up speed again. Some stayed on to the next stop and then did the return journey at some point later in the day. I mostly watched out the window, and read and dozed, the heat and gentle rocking lulling me into a sleepy daze, one hand draped over my shoulder bag. At one point I went to the loo, choosing 'India style' over 'Western style' and finding a hole in the floor of compartment straight onto the platform. As I weed I watched the railway track speed past underneath me and gripped the window ledge even more tightly.

Finally we reached Haridwar, the Hindi characters nearly decipherable to me on the arrivals board. But mostly I could tell we were there because the orange-robed throngs swarmed off the train and into the station. I let myself be pulled along among them, blinking into the early afternoon sun as they siphoned off to the right to walk the final 20km into the hills and up to Rishikesh.

Without realising, I was in front of the taxi stands and what seemed like twenty men started shouting at me: 'Where you go Ma'am? This way Ma'am! Best taxi here Ma'am! Follow me, follow me …'. I backed up into the station lobby to loiter behind a pillar watching what needed to be done. Down the platform I saw what had to be a German couple coming: matching khaki trousers, 30 litre rucksacks with carabiners on each side for their water bottles, efficiently navigating via a map inside their Lonely Planet. I bee-lined to them just as the taxi drivers had bee-lined for me. In my A level German I introduced myself, beamed, and assured them they would love to have me join them on their bus trip to Rishikesh. They could see I wasn't a threat, and, when they found out I lived in Delhi, thought I might be an asset and may know how to get to the bus stop, so let me tag along.

An hour and a half later we still hadn't found the bus we needed. Haridwar main bus station had about twenty buses hurtling in every ten minutes. We drank fresh coconut water and were given endless assurance that ours was coming, until were eventually told it had been cancelled because of that weekend's five-thousand strong pilgrimage. Not only that but the road we needed was shut higher up because of the crowds. I stared up into the woody hills and wondered how we could reach Rishikesh without hiking the whole way. Maybe we should just do that I started thinking… embrace our inner pilgrim and join the masses…

But my German companions had found a taxi driver willing to try and take us as far as he could, so we clambered in and the car snaked up the mountain road alongside hundreds of pilgrims, many carrying glittering garlands on their shoulders or balancing wooden stretcher-type contraptions between several of them, flowers and statues stuck down at odd angles with sellotape.

We may as well have walked as were doing pedestrian pace among the pilgrims, and our driver eventually gave up and stopped the car. We prised open the door as orange robes pressed against the side of the car and I found myself pulled along among the crowd. Suddenly it felt claustrophobic and intimidating. Everyone else was a man. The German lady's hand found mine and she pulled me towards the edge of the road. We stood in a cluster watching the throng of people press forwards. I could tell there was a valley ahead because you could see the open blue sky through the trees. The Germans decided they needed to head uphill to get to their hostel, but mine was at the lower part of Rishikesh, so we said our byes and I watched them disappear into the crowds. I turned to the opposite direction and kept close to the edge of the road as we pulsed forward up the mountain road. I was trying to breathe deeply and kept my eyes focused ahead. I could sense the dark curious eyes taking me in. They seemed cold and unwelcoming in their blankness. I wasn't a threat but I was of interest. I pressed on. Suddenly the road turned a corner and in front was the vast blue sky, the tree-covered mountain-side opposite. The Ganges and Rishikesh.

The Ganges was immense, a huge pulsating river of swirling grey-white-blue water. The water was high at each bank, tumbling over itself at the edges as it urgently charged down the mountain, seemingly angrily hemmed in by steep, steep river banks. The holy town of Rishikesh clung to the sides of each bank. Temples and ashrams and cafes and walkways painted white and orange, split into two by the huge pounding river but re-joined with the thin, iron footbridge, Ram Jhula. 750 feet wide, it looked like part of an Indiana Jones set – although made of iron it seemed to be rickety and bowing under the weight of its pedestrians. Just a few people wide, it seemed too thin to be stretched across the river safely.

Monkeys swung from the struts and from foot-level at the bank to a hundred foot drop over the river just metres onto the bridge I realized it was my way over to the ashram. Lower down by the water, sunken jetties protruded out and small figures clutched flimsy handrails or ropes as they bathed in the holy water and tried not to be pulled downstream. The mountain sides in each direction were covered with dark green trees and birds and monkeys screeched all around. The air was clear and fresh, and there was a low hum as prayers were chanted and the pilgrims sung quietly as they walked. It was both peaceful and buzzing.

And everywhere you could see, were throngs and throngs of saffron robes. I felt very alone again, being swirled along in the midst of such a pulsing crowd. 99% of the pilgrims were men, every one dressed in orange like some huge throng of Dutch holy men who'd got on the wrong bus and ended up in the Himalayan foothills instead of the Ajax Stadium. For most this was a once-in-a-lifetime journey – many had never left their remote villages elsewhere in India before. The ones passing me as I stood to get my bearings were as bewildered as me to find themselves at the end of their week-long walk and come face-to-face with an overly freckly red-faced blonde girl trying to look as if she knew exactly why she was there. Which, by then, she didn't.

I followed my directions – 'down to the river, over Ram Jhula, right until you reach a big tower and on your left' – and found the Parvand Niketan Ashram. I side-stepped out the throng of chanting orange villagers into a calm courtyard. Small lawns housed blue statues of Hindi goddesses, frozen in a sunlit dance as they posed gracefully above the hushed worshippers moving between them. The pilgrims' chanting was a distant hum, and I heard my own sigh. I realized I'd been holding my breath for a lot of the journey.

I found a sort of reception desk, paid my £7 for 24 hours of food, room and 6am yoga classes, and was pointed in the direction of my room. En route I was adopted by an energetic Italian who told me where the yoga took place, how I could drink from the water fountains and not to go to the mountains as the crowds this week were too strong. 'Ganga Arti prayers by the river at 6, dinner at 7. Ciou bella!' and he was off.

My room was small and hot and clean. I lay on the bed and stared at the bare ceiling feeling a million miles from Delhi. I wondered what Yann was up to in his air conditioned office in the smartest part of town. Realising it was only an hour until Ganga Aarti, I stretched and yawned and dozed restlessly until 6. I wound my way back to the river and was ushered to sit just a foot from the brown water surrounded by chanting and clapping pilgrims.

Crowds were sat on the twenty or so steps right down to the water's edge. Shoulder to shoulder with folded up legs and knees close to their chests. Women in a rainbow of coloured saris and floaty tops, jasmine flowers woven among long plaits, dark and shiny from coconut oil. Men in loose white shirts or kurta tops, lots with neat moustaches, some with small children on their laps. Mostly the crowd was Indian with a few westerners dotted among them.

In the centre a red and gold blanket was draped over the steps and microphones stood in front of five seated holy men. In the centre of this make shift stage was the chief sadhu. Long wild hair framed his thin wrinkled face and an untamed beard seemed to engulf the bottom of his whole face. He wore faded dark orange robes and sat cross-legged with his eyes shut, hands clasped together as if in prayer in front of his chest. His hands, body and head swayed loosely with the deep long mantras he was chanting into the microphone in front of him. He was flanked by younger monks, teenage boys with sharp haircuts and cleaner, crisper robes in a lighter orange. They also had closed eyes, but their hands were quietly beating small hand drums held in their laps. Patterned drapes came over their left shoulders into their laps.

These five sat square on the steps facing the river, but at each level below them was another two monks facing each other. These mostly had shaved heads and were each tending a tower of small dishes of burning oil. Like something you'd find in Aladdin's cave, they shone magically, casting flickers and shadows all around them. Smoke streaked into the air above them and every so often a monk swirled his in the air around his head. The chants were becoming more intense – faster and almost urgent. The crowds swayed and I saw there were about ten of the youngest of the monks threading themselves through everyone selling folded palm leaves full of petals and small incense-dowsed threads. I pressed some rupees into a hand and clutched my offering.

I watched others: it seemed I should say a prayer and set my palm boat gently down into the water to bob downstream as an offering to the mighty Mother Ganges. Among the twenty leaf-and-flower boats elegantly spinning in the waters, mine hit an eddy after about ten seconds, up-ended and the fire went out with a hiss. The petals disappeared into the waves and the upside-down palm leaf headed unceremoniously out into the darkness. A few sympathetic glances from my neighbours were matched by triumphant looks from two fellow westerners who'd managed to send theirs off more successfully and hadn't dunked the end of their scarf in the water in the process.

I sat back with my dripping scarf and peaceful head and breathed deeply. A crescendo seemed to have been reached in the prayers, and the chanting was now low, rhythmic and very hypnotic. The crowds were quiet and calm. The daylight was fading quickly and twinkling lights sparkled into life on the opposite river bank. A huge statue of seated Lord Shiva presided over us, increasingly silhouetted against the clear sky. This was another world.

As the prayers died down fully and the apprentices stopped their rhythmic drumming, I headed to dinner in an airy room with small rush mats on the floor. I sat on a mat, underneath a sign saying 'prasad is a gift, please worship in silence'. Hot and plain but tasty daal, rice and veggies were spooned onto our metal plates. After dinner I wandered by the Ganges but it was almost pitch black and the deep waters felt scarily strong and close, so I headed to bed, buying a mango en route home to eat with my penknife as I leant over my sink and dripped mango juice down my chin. Then out like a light.

* * *

6am the next morning meant yoga in an upstairs hall, windows open to the morning breeze and the silence of the mountains... until a gang of monkeys began jumping on the corrugated iron roof just below our window. One somehow managed to use the roof like a trampoline and bounced its way onto the windowsill. It stared curiously inside, chattered something and seemed to laugh out loud, then looked as if it was preparing to lunge in and join us in the sun salutation. Our nimble-limbed yoga teacher bounced up to shut the window and it sat crestfallen for a while, watching us wistfully through the glass until it rejoined its troop to bounce on the iron roof again. Extra hard bouncing I think – it was pretty loud and sort of spoilt the karma.

After yoga was yoghurt, fruit and chapatti eaten cross-legged on the floor, then I wandered to a café overlooking the river and read. Sipping a lassi from a cold metal cup, I watched pants-only men jump in the Ganges, pushing themselves as far into the swirling river as they dared then grabbing each other and the handrails to get back to land. They looked ecstatic, which it seemed totally deserved after the effort to get there.

I missed Yann. This was such an experience. I sighed – it would be better to share it. But then I'm not sure he would have done the yoga, and he'd have hated sitting cross-legged to eat. I wasn't convinced he'd be happy to while away a few hours in the café actually – he'd want to be hiking. And I wonder what he'd have thought of the Ganga Aarti. A family came into the café and ate a whole meal without taking their gazes off me, including the year old baby with dark kohl eye liner round its eyes and an older brother who somehow plugged his mobile into the lightbulb to charge.

Rishikesh is famed for ayurvedic massage, and I found an ashram along the river which smelt of herbs and spices and had a couple of zen-looking westerners sat in deckchairs out the front. As two ladies simultaneously massaged me, the rhythmic chanting from the street outside lulled me into a sort of trance. I lay on my back covered in a thin cotton sheet with a pot of hot oil swinging slowly from side to side over my forehead and dripping oil down my face and through my hair. It felt like someone was gently stroking my temples with warm soft fingers, and I think I fell asleep. Before I left, I was sat cross-legged in a steam box with my head poking out the top like an oily boiled egg stuck in a square egg cup. I wasn't released until the lady was satisfied my legs had gone numb and my face couldn't go any redder. I was given sickly sweet boiling chai – made from home-picked mountain herbs with unspecified qualities – then stumbled to my room for a shower and promptly fell asleep again until that evening's Ganga Arti prayer session.

The rest of the day was spent by the river and in a café – watching, sitting, reading, writing, mulling, wondering, absorbing. And as the afternoon drew on, I headed back over the Lakshman Jhula bridge and made my way to a bus stop for Haridwar. From there the train, and a rickshaw home. As each hour of the journey went by, I felt as if I was passing through different atmospheres towards the planet I knew as home. This had been such a perfect first trip into 'real India' for me. And being on my own meant I could be totally absorbed by it, consumed by my own experiences as they plucked me up, swirled me around, and let me dance to my own tune. This would have been so different without the thinking time, the indulgent hours to daydream uninterrupted, to stop and stare and things I had noticed myself. Without the time in brief conversations with a myriad of other people, conversations that don't happen if you mosey on with a travelling companion by your side.

Yann opened the door in shorts and t-shirt with a beer in hand. He beamed, but wrinkled his nose as I took off my dusty, grubby, incense-infused scarf. He kissed me on the cheek and smiled questioningly.

'Yey you're back! How was it? You smell weird. Work has gone ok... will be glad when it's over but anyway. So I was thinking, we should book train tickets for the weekend after I finish – we could go back but together this time, I promise! I want to go to Rishikesh, or we go to another prayery place. What do you think? You're not too gutted I couldn't come are you?'.

I put my bag down and looked at him.

And the word that came to mind, unusually, wasn't yes. It would have been so different if we'd gone together. Not better, not worse probably, but different.

'You know what, my man ... that's a 'no'. Yes I'd like to go off adventuring with you, but no I'm not gutted at all. It was just perfect on my own. Namaste'.

Chapter 3

Learning to Live Again

By Kirstie Edwards

A wake up call

My lightbulb moment kind of crept up on me. Nothing particularly spectacular had been happening; it was an ordinary mundane day, filled with chores, life admin and the multitude of endless small tasks that take over your life as a chronically ill single mum.

I guess that was the point- I had been treading water for so long, I was so very tired. Tired of my life; tired of fighting for my health, tired of caring for my kids alone, tired of struggling to find my sense of self-worth...

Something had to change, and it was a chance Facebook post that caught my eye and did just that. I cast aside my anxiety and fears over the what ifs and potential risks.

I simply said "Yes".

The stage is set

My life up to this point, at the ripe old age of 38, had been a full and complex one; to tell my full story would fill an entire book in itself. As a young teenager I found myself constantly sick and in out of hospital with swollen joints and severe pain. After many months of tests, invasive procedures and some incredible specialist care (thanks NHS), I was diagnosed with a rare form of Rheumatoid arthritis. This wasn't your old lady wear and tear arthritis, but my own immune system attacking my body and causing wide spread inflammation, not only in a multitude of joints but my major organs also.

At 14 years old I was told to give up my dream of being on stage as a dancer. A career I had trained for and been my single passion for my entire short life.

Over.

Gone.

Forever.

I missed around 40% of my schooling over those formative teenage years but used the time in hospital and bed bound to throw myself into academia. Something that would ultimately save me from the pain and grief I felt at losing, for the first-time, my sense of identity. I was Kirstie the amazing dancer. I was born to dance and be on stage. Then, in the blink of an eye it was gone.

Looking back, I must have been only 15 years old when I said my first major 'Yes'. Yes, to a new version of myself- the super geek, the studious young woman that wouldn't let this diagnosis define her. I threw myself into my books and over the next few years achieved high grades at 12 GCSEs 3.5 A-levels, a BA Honours Degree, a Postgraduate Degree and Post Graduate Certificate in Education specialising in teaching adults. I was over half way to completing my Master's in Education, while lecturing degree students when disaster struck once again. My health took another serious dive and just like that, this new version of myself I had created was also forever lost.

I medically retired at 33 years old.

Changing direction forever more

Alongside this journey with my health I met and fell in love with two significant men, each of whom gave me two wonderful children.

At 20 years old, days into my final year of University, I discovered that I was pregnant with what would grow to be my son. I fought like a mother lion for his life. With the support of my parents I went onto finish my degree, have my eldest daughter 21 months later and leave their father for the final time soon after.

I don't want to dwell on this tale too much as it deserves a more detailed empowering message than I have the words to write here, but I had another significant Yes point in the year of 2001 when I decided to fly solo with my babies and forge a new life for us all.

A new life begins

Suddenly there I was, a working single mum of two at 23 years old. I had trained on the job as a chef in the year previously, as this allowed me to care for my children during the day and work while they slept.

We lived in a small hotel room for a few months after I became single, while we got ourselves back on our feet and my new life began in earnest.

Two years later I met the man who would go on to become my husband and it was at this point that I began my Post Graduate education. I always worked with the support of my specialist medical team and lots of pharmaceuticals. I always had been very driven to do more, to be more than just a set of symptoms and diagnosis. I went on to have two more daughters whilst studying and working full time. How I managed it I still don't know, but I did.

Life was good. It was tough and challenging, but good.

Then I got sick.

My immune system over reacts- it sounds weird, but an immune system that works too hard causes significant damage to your body, it doesn't heal it as it should. After years of medication and contracting swine flu in 2010 my kidneys started to struggle; I got sicker and sicker. I had to come off a lot of the medication that I took to keep me functioning so my body could heal, but this left me agony and with even more limited mobility. Eventually it was decided by my GP and specialist team that enough was enough- I needed to stop work and make it my fulltime job to manage my health.

There is a lot of misconception about people that are off work long term sick; it certainly isn't a holiday and I certainly wouldn't have chosen to give up my deeply rewarding, challenging and stimulating job as a university lecturer, particularly when I had fought so hard to reinvent myself as an academic at the ripe old age of 15.

I had already lost one version of my life, I now had the second version stolen from me and I was just 33.

Who was I now?

Kirstie the mum? Kirstie the sick woman? Kirstie who used to be, used to be, used to be?

Four years later I still struggled daily to be as well as I could and felt very lost. My marriage had broken down; both of us were unhappy, depressed and living a half-life- I was brave enough to acknowledge that out loud and we went our separate ways in the summer of 2015.

I ended up flying solo again. Now a mother of four children I was running a home and managing my health care independently. Doing it all myself.

But I began to feel alive.

Gradually the life blood seeped back into me. I had taken forays into journaling and began to write about my health with the intension of breeding a little compassion for those that are invisibly ill like me. To look at me, on the days I don't need to use my walking stick, I look normal.

Just your average nearly 40-year-old woman.

Average.

It's a strange word isn't it? I had never felt special and yet the circumstances that kept befalling me were certainly extraordinary. I find it baffling that some people float through life with very minimal drama or significant life events. Despite my best efforts, trauma seemed to stalk me in the shadows, no matter how hard I tried to escape it.

At 37 I had an opportunity. There was no one to tell me what to do or who to be anymore. I could decide what was right for me, what I was capable of and what I wanted to do. Problem was; I didn't have a clue what that was.

I began blogging about just that, being lost and confused and overwhelmed by the challenges of my life. I started picking up more and more readers. I tried to write about things that I cared and was passionate about, my day to day experiences and hopes, fears and dreams. I had a terrible experience with an ignorant woman and decided, for some unknown reason, to take a picture of myself crying after the event. I'm still unsure what made me do that, I just remember feeling like I wanted people to understand how hurtful and damaging ignorant attitudes are towards people like me.

This particular woman decided that it was appropriate to shame me outside my daughter's school, for using my blue badge. She had decided I didn't look sick enough to need to park in the perfectly safe and legal space I had parked in. This woman then took matters one step further and blocked my driver's door with a cone, whilst swearing at me in front of my two young children. I said nothing, just mumbled an apology and drove around the corner, before promptly breaking down.

I'm brave but generally polite as a person, so I rarely stand up for myself. I posted the picture on social media quoting 'this is how you make a person feel when you tell them that there is f*** all wrong with them'. I got asked about my experience and was encouraged to write about it, so I did. The article went viral and was picked up by several online outlets. My Twitter feed went crazy, at which point I was approached to begin writing as a contributor at themighty.com, an online magazine supporting people with a variety of medical issues.

I said yes and thus began my voluntary, unpaid career as a writer.

I finally had a new identity.

Learning to live

I was still sick all the time of course and battling to be as well and healthy as I possibly could be. I had started working with a new specialist physiotherapist the year previously. The old advice for somebody like me was rest, rest, rest- do not participate in any physical activity. However, after a lot of research, a group of rheumatologists got together and discovered that in fact continuing to strengthen and move your body as much as possible between flare ups was much better advice. Apparently, it hugely benefitted patients in terms of strength and support around their joints when in flare up and helped to protect their joints when not. Supervised exercise increased mobility and allowed the joints to naturally disperse (if done sensibly and with medical support) excess fluid from around the joints, helping me personally to reduce my permanent medication.

I took to the gym with my physiotherapist and lost 50lb. I started to swim regularly, then one day my good friend asked me to be brave and join her in the sea. I was scared that my joints would seize up and I wouldn't cope, so she accompanied me every time I went for the first few months.

I said 'Yes', and it changed my life.

I began getting my water confidence up. I realise every day, that I am lucky to live by the sea in a beautiful town, in Cornwall. I never thought that I, with all my health problems would be able to swim in the sea. Yet there I was, head tingling with the cold, body numb and aching. Man did I feel alive.

I was Alive.

For the first time in a very long time I felt like I was beginning to live again, instead of simply surviving.

As my confidence grew I began to appreciate the benefits other than the obvious ones to my physical health, of being in and on the water- the blue mind. This concept encompasses the idea that being out in, on or near water daily brings astounding benefits to mental health. I felt calmer, more relaxed and centred when in the sea. Even when I was in too much pain to get my wetsuit on and get in, I would still drive and roll down the window, fill my lungs with salty air and my mind with wisps of blue.

This was just the beginning.

At breakfast I had skimmed Facebook and noticed this same friend had tagged me in a local event- 'Half price paddle board hire this morning for mums of local school kids'.' You want to go?' she'd said.

I'd hesitated a moment.

What if I fell and hurt myself? What if my heart cramped? What if my joints seized up and I got swept out to sea? What if, what if, what if?

There is a name for this- it's called catastrophising. A mental health term associated with anxiety, I've learnt from my therapist. Fearing the worst. Always running the scenarios to their most horrific possible ending. It's pretty common, particularly for people that manage serious health problems on a daily basis.

I took a deep breath.

She would be with me. I would be wearing a PFD. I would be near to an experienced instructor.

I said 'Yes.'

Finding the love of my life

We went out for the first time in 1-2 foot waves and I spent more time in the water than on the board, but I was hooked. My body and mind buzzed with adrenaline. Within 10 minutes I was standing up and padding about, grinning from ear to ear.

SUP is a low impact sport and I found my joints coped perfectly with it. Sure, I was exhausted and ached later and the next day and maybe, in honesty, for the next few days, but it was worth it.

The benefits of that hour-long experience would have been worth a whole week stuck in bed to me; it still is. I have never felt so peaceful and comfortable with who I was or where I was in that moment.

SUP, or indeed many sports, force you to be very much focused on the present. This daily practice of mindfulness had been introduced to me without me knowing its name and its practices had been dramatically aided by my foray into the world of paddle-boarding.

Rule number one, you must be grounded and present in the moment. You must actively engage with where you are and what your body is doing to safely participate in any water sport, an essential facet of the mindfulness practice.

I was hooked.

Thus, began my love affair with all things SUP. I found local club WeSup paddleboard centre and despite my anxiety telling me that I am too old, too sick and too uncool to be accepted into this crowd of young, beautiful, fit, people, I ignored Burt (the anxious part of my mind that tells me I'm Rubbish. He's Australian and pretty irritating) and threw myself into club life. I embraced the diverse and wonderful people I met and the experiences that we shared.

I decided for the first time in my life that I would be brutally honest about my story and about my journey. I wanted these people to accept me as I was, not a version of myself that I had constructed. I wanted to be accepted as the real me. Sick. Lost. A guilt-ridden mama. A woman still searching for acceptance of herself from herself.

I laid it all bare as and when it came up. For the first time when I was asked what do you do for a living? I told the people I met honestly: 'I'm sick. Too sick to work full time, but I write about that. I care for myself and my children and I'm still searching for my purpose."

I began writing my own redemptive narrative. The new story of me.

Time passed, my confidence grew, and I began to have faith in my ability to be good at something physical, for the first time since all those years ago when I was 'Kirstie the dancer'. It took a long time to believe and have faith that this also wasn't going to be taken away from me.

Of course, I go through many phases when I am too ill to participate, and I look longingly out of the window at the water wishing I had a body different to mine. But I quickly shake myself out of that self-pity. The reality is that I can do much more than I ever thought possible. Yes, I pay a price in pain, but I'll take that. It's worth it.

Over the next year I became much more confident in my ability thanks to the mentoring and support of our SUP family. I felt supported and challenged. My mind was the only blockade that I had now, not my body. I have even rescued one or two other people on the water and written about it!

In particular, I was thrilled to safely complete the rescue of my, at the time, new boyfriend Sean in a traumatic sea kayak experience. The poor man proudly let me share that experience publicly and thus my SUP writing was born.

Who thought disabled, useless me could save someone's life?

No way, not me.

But YES, I did.

A big adventure

So, I became stronger and more confident, but I still had a mental blockade for some reason and a real lack of confidence in my own ability. I could paddle by now, for miles and had experienced the thrill of increasing the challenge by using more and more advanced boards, but the one thing I desperately wanted to do remained- a true SUP wilderness adventure.

I would watch my SUP squad pack up and load their boards, paddling off into the distance for a wild camp and remain at the shore envious but confident that I had made the right decision to stay behind once again. I can't cope with that. What about my medication? How would I keep myself warm and dry? What if my body resists and I need medical help and I'm out in the wilderness inaccessible by road? What if? what if? what if? (there is a pattern emerging here right?)

So, I kept saying 'No'.

Over and over. 'No, I can't. It's not safe.' 'No, I can't. I'm too ill.'

No. No. No.

Then one day my boyfriend Sean told me 'Go!'. "For God's sake Kirstie, what's the worst thing that is going to happen? If you get ill they get a boat and get you. Talk to the trip leader and see what he says. Tell him your fears and see if we can come up with a plan to make this happen for you. I'll have the kids. Do it. Pick up the phone and ask the question. How will you ever know if you don't try? You can spend the rest of your life living in fear of what might happen, or you can try and find out for yourself. Either way you learn: you grow. You'll live."

I sat a while in my bed crying and thinking on his words. He hadn't meant to be cross with me, but I felt ashamed.

Had I become a shadow? Where was that brave woman that I knew lived inside me? What had I done with her? Was my obsession with keeping my self safe and well, justification enough to stop me from truly living? Would I look back one day and regret that I never tried?

I picked up the phone to the club and laid it all bare.

"Look mate," said the trip leader, "you're more capable than you think. You are stronger than anyone I know. I have absolute faith that you've got this. What's the worst that's going to happen? We will tow you back if need be or call a life boat. Either way you'll be safe, I promise."

I let out a huge breath that I didn't realise I had been tightly holding.

'YES.'

I put the phone down and breathlessly called Sean back- "Are you sure you've got this with the kids? I can't get back easily?"

"Yes," he said.

"Are you sure I can do this?" I asked.

"I believe in you" he said.

So, I packed my bags.

Unlike your average individual going wild camping, I can't just chuck a couple of essentials in a bag. I take lots of medication. I have a special diet, I can't sleep on a hard floor. I feel extremely cold and need lots of aids to help me live as fully as possible. Frankly my kit bag bulged with medicine and waterproof layers and things like shewees (as I can't squat), grabbers and camp stools.

Everyone else turned up with a small bag and sleeping bag. Man I had enough kit for a week away! But I couldn't leave one thing behind- Fortunately, my SUP squad dispersed the load between our vehicles, no questions asked.

Once we arrived at our launch point and began loading up the boards, I did get a few quizzical looks from members of the group that I hadn't met before- I suspect they assumed I had simply packed like a girl. It turned out I was the only female in our group of 12 going. To be fair I would probably have assumed the same had another female turned up with similar volumes of kit. Just goes to show we all make assumptions and that you never really know the whole story. I would love to have slung a small back pack on and just gone. Part of my anxiety about going, was that I wouldn't really feel free and able to embrace the wild. I felt like having to taken so many items was like an anchor holding me back.

I had two options – don't go or get over myself and suck it up.

I obviously chose the latter.

Once the board was loaded I began to have a real wobble. My friend Faye had come to see us off and drive one of the vans back. I started to panic when I realised she wasn't coming, as she was one of the few people who knew and understood the concerns I had. She gave me a pep talk like a boss.' What are you worried about most?' She asked.

I stopped for a second. 'My biggest fear is falling with all my kit on the board." I said. I knew that once we arrived it would soon be dark- it was a Cornish spring day and the temperature drops quite quickly once darkness falls. "How will I get warm and dry if I go in? Will the cold seize my body up and leave me needing an immediate evac from the site?"

"Kirstie," she said, "You are one of the strongest paddlers I know, I know you can do this. You are not going to fall in. If you do the boys will get you up and sort you out. You'll have some fire and dry clothes- you'll be fine. Worst case scenario, if I have to, I will drive round and trek to get you."

She had a quiet word with a couple of the crew including our guide and leader who came and gave me a hug told me: 'Mate you are going to be fine, trust me, but more importantly trust yourself. You know you've got this so don't let your head win." (Burt raising his bloody head again, bloody bastard)

I took a deep breath. 'Ok. I'm going to be fine. I've got this,' I repeated over and over as we pushed off from the shore.

They were right. I am a strong paddler and can keep up with most of the men. We had a tough paddle into the wind to cross a wide section of the river at the mouth where it joined the ocean. Talk about a tough start. The bitter wind blew my long blonde hair back from my face and I shivered as I struggled to get my body moving. I had tensed up and was wound so tight with stress, I struggled to find my rhythm. The sky felt oppressive and moody, heavy with fine droplets of water, considering all the while whether to drop its load on our heads. The water was surprisingly flat, but covered in the tell-tale jagged ripples of strong wind skimming across the surface straight towards us. The spray that hit my hand with each stroke, felt like tiny icy pins penetrating my skin. I gritted my teeth and tried real hard not to panic, but instead to find sheer determination to keep going from within myself somewhere. "I will make it across. I will make it across" I repeated, my own mantra rhythmically spoken, in perfect time with each plunge of the paddle into the clear cold water below.

I tried to relax and focus on the next check point a white boat, a wooden boat, a buoy, I took shelter behind a small sail boat and held on to catch my breath after 20 minutes paddling feeling like I was going nowhere. I looked back and was surprised how much ground I had covered. So, I gritted my teeth and turned up river.

I'm not going to lie and make out this was the perfect night for SUP. This was not a relaxing, scenic evening paddle. This was a gritty, tough, if you stop putting in 100% effort you are losing ground, kind of paddle.

It was hard, but I persisted along the river edge, moving upstream, accompanied by various sidekicks. We tried to shelter from the wind by hugging the far shore line, dodging gnarly tree roots and hidden tow ropes attached to small craft as we went.

Finally, we reached the mouth of a small inlet and turned into it. Like magic the water stilled, as the oppressive sky cleared and the high trees surrounding the inlet gave us shelter from the wind. I was in paradise. I stopped to look up and around. In the distance down to the right I could see the hidden quay we were aiming for – only accessible by sea. We silently glided down the inlet like a flotilla of swans, towards the setting sun, calm and serene at last.

This was why I had come.

A lonely bass blew bubbles as she broke the surface; Cormorants dove under the surface and popped up playing with their dinner, inquisitive as to who and what we were. I kept my eyes peeled for seals but on this occasion saw none. I slowed my pace and for the first time let my surroundings absorb me and take over my senses. I felt calm and at peace. Suddenly all the stress of the journey and everything that had led to that exact point in my life seemed insignificant. I was here, now and life was perfect.

This was exactly where I was supposed to be.

I had naturally led the pack as everyone instinctively paddled to my speed. I'm sure they were subconsciously making sure that I was ok, so I slowed down and turned back to look over my crew. My SUP squad. My face broke into the biggest grin and I don't mind admitting I had a small tear. Damn it I'd done it, I was here about to camp out, away from everything and everyone with this small team of awesome individuals.

I'd said "Yes" and, my God, in that moment I felt like the strongest most brave and intrepid explorer that ever roamed the land or sea.

I know that may sound utterly ridiculous in the context of the other incredible stories you will read in this book. Epic adventurers travelling across thousands of miles in unknown cultures. Big, exciting adventures. But it's all relative right? I never thought I would get the chance to do something like this. It simply wasn't on my radar as something that I could ever achieve. Between the children and my health, I had given up hope of adventures and ever being able to participate like this.

When I joined the Yes Tribe it was partly, I confess, to watch enviously as others explored the world from my bed. At least I still felt connected and this was my tribe after all. These were my people. Wild. Free. Brave. Adventurous. It's just the small matter of my body not quite keeping up with my mind that was the problem.

So, I went. I saw. I conquered.

I pitched a small tent in between my friends- 7 tents squashed on a tiny quay only accessible by sea.

Someone made a fire in the centre as I struggled out of my wetsuit and into my many, many layers of clothes. It ended up that I was the only female explorer on this occasion and the boys were brilliant. They didn't molly coddle me but treated me as one of the tribe. We ate together, laughed together and had fun sat around the fire sharing stories and whiskey until we were weary.

I made some incredible new friends that night.

There is something about sitting in the dark, far from civilisation that makes people turn off that mental block button that makes them play it safe. I learnt things about my tribe I never would have without that journey. Hopes and fears, dreams, losses, failures... We debated next steps in our careers and relationships and mused over where we wanted to go with our lives. We compared wounds and marveled at how we had each ended up here in this exact moment. Our paths were so very diverse, our stories would fill ten books to the brim. A motley crew of such different backgrounds and careers- I don't think we ever would have been in the same intimate space together were it not for the shared love of adventure and SUP. And of course, simply saying 'Yes' when asked 'Who has 24 hours and fancies an adventure?'

I barely slept. Pain did get me in the night, like a silent panther creeping up on me in the darkness. My body hurt from top to toe and I admit I had a small moment in the velvety blackness, when I wondered if I had made the right decision or if I was in fact mad to ever attempt this. I could barely move from side to side without crying but had to wait 2 more hours for more pain meds. I wanted my bed, support pillows and physical help to get into a better, more comfortable position. There was a definite moment that night when I made a choice to, as my man calls it, 'suck it up'. So, instead of crying, I settled onto my back and stared into the darkness, alone but comforted by to gentle snores of the guys around me. I laid there a while, telling myself it was all ok, absolutely determined to remain positive and strong. I was warm at least- I listened to the gentle lap of the water just by my head. A pair owls called each other in the night. I marveled at the song birds announcing to each other that another beautiful day on planet earth was dawning. I gave up on sleep at 6 am and heaved my sore body upright, necked my pills and waited for relief to come. Once the pain had subsided, I hauled my body out of the tent.

I knew it would take me much longer to get packed down and ready than the lads- I must always allow extra time to account for pain and my limited mobility particularly as the day starts.

I had recently bought myself a Shewee at the insistence of my occupational therapist. What a genius idea. The thing I most feared was how to pee. As a disabled woman I can't squat and of course being so far from home didn't want to risk wet trousers- I would recommend any woman purchasing these wonder devices but if you have a weak lower body this is a game changer! I peed like a man, then sat on a log watching the world come to life as our camp began to stir.

Making peace with myself

After the wind of the previous day, the morning greeted us clear and calm and we soon were packed and loaded. I did allow the guys to help me a little that morning- I'm so stubborn and independent but sometimes it's just what needs to happen to get the job done. By 8 am our boards were reloaded, and the camp looked as it had when we arrived, clean and welcoming, ready for its next adventurers to happen upon it.

We paddled off silently into the pink morning, each of us sleepy and full of wonder at the beauty that surrounded us. It was so still and serene If I believed in something bigger than us, I would say, that morning He painted the world perfectly. I felt like I had been rewarded for my resilience and bravery with this perfect, blissful morning.

Again, I guess it sounds ridiculous- Some of you must be thinking: "Jeez, it's just camping for one night!" But this is something I didn't ever think I would be allowed to do or physically achieve, paddle boarding itself let alone going off into the wild with a bunch of guys for 24 hours. I never ever believed that would be possible for someone like me.

I have never felt more alive or blessed than I did in that next hour.

We glided silently, watching the light change across the water and the early morning visitors to the estuary catching their breakfast diving elegantly, ripples echoing across the surface creating the only slight sound.

Around half way back, gentle chatter broke out as we all began to welcome the new day and engage our minds back into the real world. Some had to head for work, some to the gym or for a big breakfast. I was heading home back to where I left my heart, with my man and children. I took my soul with me that night and boy was it returning full and nurtured.

As we hit the shore, a slight melancholy settled over the group. We decanted our things from board to van and silently strapped the boards to the roofs. We cast our gaze back over the still silent morning and looked at each other small smiles beginning to break out.

I for one returned changed. I felt braver and stronger than the woman that had left less than 24 hours previously. I knew that the next days would be hell on earth pain wise and I was right. I could barely move for almost a week without crying, but I knew that those moments had nurtured my spirit more than I could ever have hoped. I felt full of life and virile despite my broken body. I would do it all again in a heartbeat.

From that point on and to this very day, everything changed. Now all I ever have to do when pain and darkness try to take me, is close my eyes and remember that night- then I am truly free.

Thank you, from the bottom of my heart, Yes Tribe, for inspiring me to be brave.

Are you, dear reader, ready to do the same? It might just change your life.

Website: **www.kirstieedwardswrites.com**

Chapter 4

Rite of Passage

by Paul Betney

I've always loved the sea and tall ships. Both have always seemed to me to be living things with a dignity and a majesty that has inspired me for as long as I can remember. When the opportunity came to sail across the Atlantic I knew that I would say Yes.

It was a big Yes though. While I had my fair share of experience, there was another factor that I had to consider before I could embark on such a long and testing journey:

Parkinson's Disease.

I've had Parkinson's for about 26 years now. Very briefly put, it's a group of cells in the brain that are dying off prematurely. The loss of those cells reduces the brain's ability to create Dopamine and it's the lack of Dopamine that produces the symptoms that, combined, we call Parkinson's.

There are over 40 symptoms associated with the disease. Personally, my symptoms include tremor, fatigue, anxiety, depression, balance issues, memory issues, cognitive issues, disturbed sleep patterns and vivid dreams that I really should turn into films. The list goes on... It started when I was about 24 and by my early 30s I couldn't pick up a glass of water and drink without spilling most of it.

That situation was turned around dramatically in 2007 when I got a new consultant and new medication that calmed down the symptoms considerably. The medication is not a cure, it is only mitigating the symptoms for now. Parkinson's is both chronic and degenerative, so sooner or later the drugs will lose their efficacy and I'll have to look at other options. Even now with the medication, at times of heightened emotions, the tremor will still come back. But while the meds last, it's a window of opportunity that I have no intention of missing.

My 26 years so far with Parkinson's have been an emotional and complex journey, but I've never taken having the disease personally. I don't see it as a sentient being that's out to get me. I see it simply as a biological cock-up.

I don't think that God and the Universe sat down at a board meeting and when they got to the "B's" on the list said, 'Right, this Betney fella, we need to stitch him up right proper!' (Why God would be a cockney, I don't know…). It's one of those things. It happens and I don't intend to waste time wondering why it happened to me.

Since 2007 I'd had experience sailing on couple of square riggers and I'd taken part in the Tall Ships Races, but the transatlantic would be by far my longest and most challenging voyage to date. I knew how hard keeping to a watch system could be and the fatigue and other symptoms of PD had to be seriously considered. I was also joining the ship as a watch leader, so people would be relying on me to keep things running smoothly and safely.

To keep things really interesting, we would also be making the passage in winter. The ship, the TS Pelican of London (or "Peli" as she's affectionately known) had been on her way to the Antarctic, but that destination had been cancelled when she was mid Atlantic. She had diverted to the Caribbean and spent the first half of the winter in Barbados. Now she was in St Lucia, but it was important that she was back in the UK soon, so regardless of the weather, the trip was set for February through March.

The flight out to St Lucia was the first challenge. It was exhausting, not least because of my inability to control my tremor. I'm not afraid of flying. What I struggle with is having to stay seated for prolonged periods of time in situations where my personal space is dramatically reduced. It produces anxiety which triggers the tremor and the two will happily feed off each other in a nasty downward spiral.

By the time we touched down, I was shattered. So, I did the only sensible thing. I headed straight for the pub. When I arrived, most of the crew were already propping up the bar. There was some catching up to be done and beer to be drunk. I wanted to put the whole flight experience behind me.

Sitting at the bar, I could see the ship at anchor out in Rodney Bay. With the setting sun behind her, she was a majestic sight. The air was warm, the beer cold. We were in the Caribbean and life was good!

As can occasionally happen in these situations, one beer led to another and it ended up in the small wee hours with just myself and one crewmate left standing. So, we called a water taxi and headed out into the bay. When Peli finally emerged from the dark, the pilot ladder was up and the ship was asleep.

The Captain of the water taxi asked me how we were going to get aboard, to which I replied, "Somali pirate style I think." He put the nose of his boat to Peli's hull and we made a jump for the rail. As I was clambering up the side of the ship, I heard him click his outboard into reverse. I looked down just in time to see his bows slipping away below me. Fortunately, I found my footing and with one last heave I fell over the rail onto the deck. I was finally on board!

As it turned out, putting the flight behind me wasn't going to be that easy. The hangover was cruel in all its forms; the alcohol, the emotions, the physical and mental distress of the journey, all combined to make for a couple of really bad Parkinson's days. For most of the next day the shaking was very evident and a self-perpetuating spiral of embarrassment and shaking was not helping me to recover.

I had friends on board and was quickly getting to know the people I'd never met before, but I was still deeply self-conscious. I picked up that my friends were explaining things in the background, which meant that I didn't have to go through 'that' conversation a dozen times, which was really good of them. But, I began to realise that it was important that I talked about it too, not for anybody else's benefit, but for my own. It was really important that I was taking ownership of this situation and taking part in those conversations. As soon as I did, I felt a lot better.

I still had doubts though. The worst was a fear that living with Parkinson's had ingrained deeply in me over the years. It was a simple fear: was I going to be up to this or would I just be making a fool of myself? There was really only one way to find out. A day and a half after I'd arrived, we lifted the anchor and slipped out of the bay headed for Bermuda.

There were three watches, each named after a mast: Fore, Main and Mizzen. I ran Fore Watch and for the run up to Bermuda, I only had four people with me, Becca, Kerry, David and Ben, so there was certainly plenty to keep us busy. Fortunately, they were a lovely bunch. We all worked really well together.

The shaking was still bad though, in part because I was having trouble adjusting to the watch system.

There are various watch systems which dictate the amount of time spent on and off watch. On the passage to Bermuda we were doing something that I had never come across before; we were doing three hours on and six off. The time on watch went by very quickly, but the six hours off wasn't giving me enough time to rest. By the time I'd eaten and done all the other business of the ship I was getting very little sleep.

One of the things I've always loved about the great square rigged tall ships is climbing the masts and working out on the yards. High above the deck it's a view and a feeling that few will ever experience. It's like flying in a dream. The ever-changing face of the ocean unfolds it's shifting patterns of light and shade beneath you as high wave crests roll down into deep troughs. It has always filled me with awe.

I prefer to be up there alone or only with people who know me well. If the tremor kicks in it can make the unsuspecting nervous and that's never good when working at height, especially when you're all standing on the same foot rope.

Shortly after we left St Lucia, I climbed the mast, but found myself unable to go out onto the yard, because of the tremor. I sat in the crosstrees for a long time, trying to soak up this feeling that I love so much and talking with the ship's Bosun, Jezz. I was hoping that maybe I was just having a bad day, so the next day I climbed again, but it was the same story. I began to wonder if I would even go out there alone and a growing sense of mourning began to creep over me that my time climbing the mast at sea might be coming to an end.

Although I felt bad about not going aloft, I was growing in confidence with running operations from the deck. I knew I was doing well because I was being given more responsibility all the time. I was a bit reticent at first but encouraged by the permanent crew, I started taking charge of major sail changes and it felt great! I also finally figured out that, unused to the three on six off watch system, I had been under medicating myself, which was a huge relief. Finally, at long last, the tremor started to calm down. Looking back now, taking the right level of medication certainly played a key role in that, but I think that my growing appreciation of being valued as a member of the crew, of making a significant contribution, really enabled me to relax. I started to lay those fears of being inadequate aside and I believe that being appreciated and respected was vitally important to breaking that self-perpetuating anxiety/shaking spiral.

As we headed up into the Atlantic, the weather turned. We had four days of force 7's, 8's and 9's, and heels of up to 55 degrees with the wind driving merciless rain and huge swells. It was our first test, but no one got sick and everyone performed well. It was a very promising start. Shortly after the weather broke, we crossed into the Bermuda Triangle. I'm not sure what I thought I was expecting, maybe I thought the water would change colour. But it looked just like the rest of the ocean. We crossed without seeing a single alien spaceship, no tear in the fabric of the time and space and made Bermuda without incident.

Once alongside we spent a few days exploring this beautiful island paradise and chilling out. Due to a family emergency our original Captain, Mike, had to fly home, but our new Captain, Chris, arrived quickly, preceded by a fearsome reputation! He had been at sea all his life, captained tall ships across the globe and was known for pressing ships and crews hard. He sounded awesome!

The members of my watch had also changed and I was down to three people now, four including myself. The new Fore Watch consisted of Becca, Siobhan and Dan and if I thought the original Fore watch were good, these guys turned out to be legends! We didn't know it, but we were about to go through a baptism of fire that would bind us together as friends forever. As we pointed our bows into the North Atlantic and left Bermuda in our wake, the sunshine seemed to dim and the sky darkened. We were on our way and there was no turning back.

The bad weather came soon and it came hard. Between Bermuda and our next landfall in the Azores the wind rarely dropped below 50kts. On the Beaufort scale that's a Force 11, which is a "Violent Storm". The run up to Bermuda had given us a taste of what to expect, but the Atlantic was relentless. When you're living on an angle of 50 degrees and constantly being thrown around, everything becomes hard work. Making a cup of coffee is hard work, to the extent that you think twice or even three times about if it's really worth it. Getting dressed, washing, eating, doing the dishes, standing, sitting, going to bed, getting up, even sleeping, all becomes an immense effort. Then the fatigue starts to set in and the close proximity to other people can become an issue.

I don't know how long we'd been out there for, but it was early in that main crossing when I felt a meltdown coming on. The weather had been bad for days. Captain Chris had put us back onto four-on, eight-off watches and had declared that Sunday's would be a day off. That was great news for me, but my body was still adjusting and so was my medication. I was exhausted and I could feel myself heading towards an outburst that I didn't want to have and that nobody around me should have to put up with. All of the doubts, fears and anxieties I had about the trip seemed to be on the verge of erupting. I needed the one thing that it is most hard to find on a ship; I needed some space and some time to myself. So, when the jibs needed stowing on the bowsprit I jumped at the chance.

The bowsprit is a place many people love. With the safety netting slung beneath it, on sunny days it's a great place to sleep in the sunshine or to watch dolphins play beneath you and from the far end it's a perfect place to take photos of the ships bows cutting though the water. But this was not a sunny day. Today the ship was pitching heavily on steep waves. I told my watch that I would do the job by myself, clipped onto the safety line and stepped out over the bows onto the footrope under the boom. As I worked my way up the bowsprit I looked down. As we topped the waves the surface of the ocean seemed to be 50 or more feet away and as we hit the trough I felt the ocean press on my legs as the water came up to my knees. I didn't care though, because I was alone. I had space, I could think. As I lashed the sail to the jackstay I remember thinking, 'What the hell am I doing out here! This is madness!'

As I felt the water on my legs again and the coarse material of the sail in my hands, I knew the answer. I had always known the answer, I guess I'd just needed to ask the question.

I was there because I love it. I was there because there was nowhere else that I would rather be. I had chosen to be here and that was the first time that I consciously thought, 'I choose to give myself to this situation.' I wasn't surrendering to forces beyond my control, I was making a conscious decision to take responsibility for my circumstances and choosing how I would face the situation. I was taking control.

Pulling myself back along the bowsprit I couldn't wipe the smile from my face. I was *a lot* happier. I realised how much pressure I had been putting myself under. Although it would be some time before I made the connection, it saved the trip for me and would change the way I viewed my life, and especially Parkinson's role in it, forever. I was present, I was here. I may not be able to climb, but I could still contribute a lot.

I love helming and I like to think of myself as a competent helmsman. In the conditions which we were facing that belief had been put to the test and those skills had been sharpened. Sometimes, when I was on the helm, I would be struck by a sudden realisation of what I was doing. I was helming a tall ship, under sail, through a storm in the Atlantic Ocean and I would be filled with euphoria. Peli's helm is a hydraulic system and there is no kick back from the waves on the rudder up through the wheel, but the connection to the water and the ship filled me every time. Even though I knew the wheel would not turn if I took my hands off it I always liked to keep a hand in place, to keep my fingers in contact with the smooth wood and so that in the appalling weather the ship would know that I had not left her.

Shortly after the bowsprit moment I had a truly beautiful day. It began with a sunrise of orange, red and gold fire. It was like no other I had ever seen. It made me feel humble, privileged and in the cold Atlantic, it warmed my soul. Then Mick, the first officer asked me if I was up for a climb. He knew the problems that I had been having, but the work had to be done and couldn't wait. Fortunately, the timing was perfect. After all of my doubts over climbing and my ability to perform aloft with Parkinson's, right there and then I felt in exactly the right place to go for it. I knew that today I would be fine. I headed up the shrouds to the course yard. The course yard is the lowest yard, but also the longest and the sail that hangs from it is one of the largest on the ship. I had to prep it for setting and as I untied the gaskets and looped them back onto the jack stay, I took a moment to enjoy the fact that I was working aloft, leaning over a yard with nothing else but a footrope between me and the ocean, sailing into a glorious day.

I was cooking inside my wet weather gear by the time I had finished, but I didn't care, I was so happy. If I hadn't worked aloft in some capacity, I know that I would always have secretly, deep down, felt like a passenger. Now I actually felt like I was earning my anchor.

It is amazing what you can get used to, how your body and mind can adjust to make the most difficult of circumstances the norm. One of the main things that keeps you going is your shipmates and the laughter. As hard as mealtimes became, they were always fun and brought us together. Peter, our cook, and Lynn his partner and assistant in the galley, kept us amazingly well fed. The crew were always trying to find innovative ways of supporting their plates or bowls against the heel of the ship under sail. But, inevitably food flew through the air and sometimes I ended up wearing more than I ate. I caught plates regularly, was covered in cake and semolina, had pineapple in my boot and slid down a bench whilst putting jam on a piece of toast. Trying to get mugs of tea and coffee from the galley to the helm while they were still hot and before they tasted of salt became a good game. There were plenty of spillages and I joked that Parkinson's must be catching.

Routine maintenance tasks helped too. The somewhat ironically named "Happy Hour" when the ship is cleaned wasn't always popular, but with the right music and a lot of banter, it became a highlight!

You can never settle completely though. When Jezz started adding extra lines to brace the course yard and extra lines to strengthen the sheets on the topsails, I knew that something big was expected on the weather front.

We had been on the midnight watch. It was about 3am when the line squall hit.

The helm on Peli is exposed to the elements. so we knew what had happened as soon as it hit us. In already poor conditions, the night came suddenly and violently alive. The wind speed went through the roof and the wind direction veered by about 50 degrees. My brain registered the danger, but my body had no chance to catch up before the wind caught the spanker sail on the wrong side and it crash jibed. The boom that secures the bottom of the sail is as thick as a man's thigh, but it snapped like a twig directly above our heads. Even over the howling wind, it sounded like a shotgun going off next to my ear. In the darkness and driving rain I could just make out one end of the splintered boom swinging around wildly, still attached to the clew of the flogging sail.

I immediately took over the helm and told my watch to get clear and to wake the Captain. I tried to keep control while staying as low as I could, all the time waiting for a huge piece of wood to come flying out of the darkness and smash me into oblivion.

In the darkness I caught sight of Becca, Siobhan and Dan, crouched down low making their way back toward the helm. Jezz was with them, Yazz, the Bosun's Mate, and the Captain was there too. I'd like to say that I didn't panic, but that doesn't sound right. I simply felt numb and that left no room for anything else. I knew these people and I knew that they would sort it out. My job was to look after the helm. While they worked, the line squall continued to rage around us. Everyone was a hero that night and I am so proud to know each and every one of them and to call them all my friends. By the time the line squall had blown through and order had been restored I had been on the helm for an hour and I was exhausted. I realised that I was over steering and asked to be relieved. Miraculously, there were no serious casualties. Everyone was, physically at least, untouched. After the Captain had debriefed us in the mess, I went to my bunk and didn't even have the energy to undress. I lay down and the next thing I remembered was being woken for my next watch.

After losing the spanker boom, the rest of the crew decided to re-christen Fore Watch as the Wrecking Crew. Our reputation as destroyers of the ship was secured. The thing that seems odd to me now is that such a dramatic event seemed to have such little effect on me. I guess that to realise something about yourself you have to be able to think, but my brain had gone straight to auto pilot. The one thing that I did notice though, was that at a time when I would have expected them to be at their worst, my Parkinson's symptoms were nowhere to be seen.

It wasn't too long after that that we arrived in the Azores, a beautiful chain of volcanic islands. It was a gorgeous sunny day and the view from our berth was breath taking. It felt great to be alive having completed the main passage in such challenging conditions and we were all looking forward to some rest, a few beers and a couple of days exploring the island.

While most of the crew went ashore, I was happy to stay on board for the first day and help Jezz with the repairs. Jezz is a good friend and I'd seen surprisingly little of him on the voyage so far, so it was good to catch up while the ship was quiet. After a rewarding day, Jezz and I headed into the town and found some excellent steaks, had a couple of beers and met up with everyone a few hours later. Feeling very merry and very happy I returned to the ship for a couple of hours sleep before I had to be up for an hour of harbour watch.

When I came up on deck, it was very obvious that the weather had picked up dramatically. The ship was moving in a see-sawing motion against the quayside and the Captain was on deck. He told me to wake him if 'another' mooring line snapped and that if that happened, we'd be heading to anchor. About 5 minutes after he had retired for the night we lost another line and by the time I had roused him and got back on deck, another one had gone. In all, we lost four mooring lines.

All hands were called and we left the quayside to head out to the small anchorage just outside the mouth of the harbour. Once the anchor was down, I grabbed a couple of hours sleep only to wake to the news that the anchor had dragged in the night. At that point we were holding station using the engine. We couldn't go back alongside and a commercial gas tanker was due to take our spot in the anchorage. We had no choice other than to say a premature farewell to Horta and head out into a force 10.

It was not the news anybody wanted to hear. In all, we had spent 16 hours in Horta. The next stop would be Falmouth and that seemed like a lifetime away. Through it all though, that love for what I was doing, that choice to be there, kept me going. It also kept the worst effects of Parkinson's at bay, because I wasn't fighting it anymore. Slowly but surely, just like the weather, I was accepting it as a reality and that was giving me control over how I handled it.

The weather continued to test both the crew and the ship. For the majority of the Azores to Falmouth leg we saw mostly Force 9, strong/severe gales. The rain fell so hard it would sting my face when it hit. We would wrap up against the cold, but when we had to brace the yards or ware ship we would sweat with the physical effort. Fatigue became more and more of a factor. Sails tore, halliards were lost, the course brace broke, the list of damage grew. We knew we were getting close to the UK when the temperature began to drop, the rain drops became bigger and the squalls and gales started to bring in sleet and hail.

When we finally came into Falmouth harbour it hardly seemed real. There was no space on the quayside, so we had to tie up to a buoy in the harbour, but no one cared. We had crossed an ocean! We had

24 hours ashore to rest and relax before we set off on the final short leg, an easy run along the coast to Weymouth.

We left Falmouth the next day hungover and full of steak. We were on the engine, the sea was flat and calm with only the lightest of breezes. Someone joked that it was "too quiet", that the English Channel was mustering its forces for one last counter attack. As it turned out, they were right.

We knew that the forecast was for strong easterly winds, but when they came, they hit with much greater severity than had been forecast. We were now faced with trying to punch through massive swells and vicious winds. When we reached Portland Bill, the combination of its fierce tides and the strong winds meant that no matter how hard we tried, we couldn't push through. So close to home, after so many trials and so much effort we were faced with an impenetrable wall. To add to our troubles, we were running out of fuel.

The decision was made to wait in the lee of the Bill and hope for a weather window. When Captain Chris made the announcement that we could be stuck here for days it was very hard to take. More delays, more watches, more wet, more cold, more fatigue. It was Horta all over again.

More than a few people had to take themselves out of that crew meeting, including myself. I'm sure my Parkinson's tremor would have kicked in, but I was just too tired. Out on the well deck I stood looking at the long beach just a few hundred yards away. I knew that here was nothing else for it. This was how it was. I had to choose my attitude. I wasn't going to give in. Not now, not so close to the end.

Fortunately for everyone, the weather window came much sooner than expected. The wind was expected to drop at midnight when the tide would be slack, so if we timed it right we should be able to sneak around that long finger of land and finally make our home port. We spent the evening crawling up and down the length of the

Bill. Helming was difficult with the water moving so slowly over the rudder and strong gusts catching the rigging, but when midnight came we were perfectly positioned and we slipped around the narrow promontory without a hitch. In celebration of the moment we exchanged exhausted smiles, handed over our watch and very gratefully went to bed.

One last wake up call. We dock in 20 minutes!

We raced onto deck to help bring her alongside and emerged into an early morning fog. After everything we had been through, we expected nothing less. The fog soon burned off though and we slipped into a still slumbering Weymouth. By now there wasn't enough water to flush the toilets and the generators had been shut down to save fuel. Worst of all, we had run out of milk for the tea.

As we came alongside, we were greeted by a small party of Peli's shore-based office staff and sailors and ships officers who hadn't been able to make the trip. They had come to welcome us home and to throw us some newly purchased mooring lines. After a loud cheer, many hugs and some tears we stepped ashore.

We were home.

It would take a long time to understand all the ways in which that trip changed me. One thing I realised quickly though, was that I liked being challenged and I wanted more of that in my life. I was also no longer afraid of making a fool of myself, whether that was fuelled by Parkinson's or anything else. Perhaps most importantly, I had learned to take that step back and, just like on the bowsprit, to give myself to life's difficult situations. That doesn't mean giving in to something because I'm 'stuck with it'. It means making a conscious decision for my own well-being to set aside fear and resentment and to bring love to it. It means taking ownership and control.

That is the power of Yes.

Website: **paulbetney.com**

Instagram: **@Paulbetney**

Facebook: **Paul Betney**

Chapter 5

A Journey into Aid Work

by Emma

Under the scorching blaze of the midday heat in a country in Africa we sweat and struggle; me, my team, and the 500 prisoners sitting before us barely covered by the branches of the one and only tree. We are surrounded by high walls adorned with the names and messages of all who have resided within them. The cerulean blue sky is obstructed by the rusty barbed wire and security posts. On one side freedom; the other deprivation and comradeship. There is a small static river of white and green water next to the platform we stand on, dangerous yet glistening in the sunlight.

'One hundred and ninety-two centimetres'.

The Dinka are tall! My neck aches from craning to look up at them. I move up and down from my tip toes to a bench to be able to read all of their height and weight measurements.

We're managing a food programme and we need to regularly measure each and every detainee to see which ones are acutely malnourished.

It's a big event, a source of learning and entertainment so the prisoners surround us trying to see every aspect of what we are doing. It is also a chance to be kind and helpful so the measurements are echoed among them like a Mexican wave. So much is happening second by second, the sound of chains clunking, sweat glistening over the scars adorning their foreheads and, oh, the smells! The heavy stench of urine and sweat do not easily lift in the static air.

Some people present obvious ailments in need of treatment. One man has the left side of his face so swollen from a nose and ear infection that his eye is bulging. I remember all of those people, the ones with treatable illnesses that escalate to something horrifying. Once a man arrived clutching his stomach with a big white snake of a tapeworm shoved into a plastic bottle. I hope there will be none of those today.

Remaining focused on the task is important. I try to pronounce the names of the prisoners which results in a chorus of laughter and cheer. Laughter in a prison? YES! It's so joyful, I can't take it!

Some of them remember us from last time and recall the moment of meeting. We pretend to remember but in truth this is often impossible because we travel to different places of detention in different parts of the country every other week. The hundreds here become thousands overall. The communities different but problems mostly the same. Everyday a waiting game. A passing of time for that one important meal.

It's hard to breathe, there is no air. Lethargy takes a hold from fluid loss and the battle to cool. Maybe the humidity will bring the furious and exciting rain. Will it hold off until we can complete our task? There is no moment to stop what we are doing; to slow things down or create space feels impossible in the crowds and commotion. Whatever happens… I cannot need the toilet. There's nowhere to go for that. I'm taking part in a precarious balancing game to drink enough but not too much.

There is almost a fight for my empty water bottle. It's the most useful item in existence.

My hands are dirty. The hand sanitizer only groups the dirt into tiny lumps. I peel my t shirt away gingerly from my stomach but the feeling of air against my skin that I long for won't arrive. My pounding head turns up the volume with the small window of stillness and attention.

Looking around and the team seem alright. The elation of completion means a chance to sit down and begin to process. As we leave the prison a marathon begins of long handshakes and each one a disgusting sweat exchange but critical reminder that we are all one. Even though we speak different languages, the handshake remains the same and everyone is worthy of such an exchange and acknowledgement.

I sit on the small bed in the guest room and feel tremendous gratitude for my freedom. I crave hugging my family and telling them how much I love them. I want to squeeze my Labrador and put kisses all over her head. They are so far away and the list of barriers endless: a car journey, a remote airstrip, a teeny tiny plane which may or may not arrive, a large tent of an airport in the capital city where moving between sections is a fight for survival. Too many people push and shove and are squished in like sardines on the London underground - only with more heat and longer waiting times.

I think about the concept of freedom and my experiences of it. Even as we leave the prison after a day of work, we are not free. Moving on foot outside is mostly forbidden. Hallucinations begin... cold morning frost in the UK. Being able to skip, hop and fly through the park. Why did I only run around it before I came here? Things will be different next time I visit that park and each time thereafter. I count down the days until I leave for my break. My Shawshank Redemption moment.

The country I am working in is the world's newest country and a chronic humanitarian crisis. It has also, most recently, been declared as the most dangerous country in the world to be a humanitarian aid worker. This issue of personal safety is like white noise. Every problem you could possibly imagine is happening. Millions have fled their homes due to war and lost loved ones and their livelihoods in the process. Severe food insecurity means there are regular warnings of famine. Healthcare services are almost non-existent. Rape and gender based violence are rife and thousands of children are estimated to have been recruited by armed actors.

My path to this mission is a story of struggle. It is a story of 'Yes' and a testament to the concept that it is the journey that makes us.

This is my journey:

Creating core values

↓

Being Inspired

↓

Committing to my Dream

↓

Taking opportunities

↓

Living the Dream (and the cost involved)

Creating my core values

I was 21 and had just finished university. The experience of university had been so impactful that I did not know how to move on from it and felt in a state of personal crisis. The first in my family to get a degree created pressure to find a great job immediately.

I'd worked alongside my degree and had enough money for a trip so I decided to volunteer in South Africa. My announcement to my family was met with disapproval. My mother was absolutely convinced I might die on the trip or contract HIV and was trying to persuade me not to go as if it were a life and death matter.

I went anyway.

My first time alone in an airport felt terrifying. How would I transfer between airports? Would my Nokia brick phone work on arrival? Did they have payphones? I was travelling to the Valley of a Thousand Hills with no idea of whether I would be able to find it. I had to face the potential death I'd been lectured about and discover all of these things for myself.

Whilst volunteering abroad often has a lot of fairly negative connotations, I believe there to be lots of benefits depending on the type of work and length of time and the way in which it is arranged. I have no idea whether I had any positive impact on anyone in South Africa but the projects I was a part of had a positive impact on me and stole my heart.

I was very struck by the notion of chance. The latitude and longitude of our birth place determining life outcomes was something to grapple with continuously while getting to know each person and their challenges.

My volunteer work was comprised of a variety of activities. Everything from cheering up patients with AIDS, bringing them food, massaging their feet, reading to them and organising fun outings for orphaned and vulnerable children.

On my final day, the events that occurred irrevocably changed my life forever.

I woke up with all my bags packed ready to attend a clinic under a big tree to help a local organisation who were working with sexually abused children. When we arrived, the expert local staff ran activities with the children whilst we, as volunteers, sat with the women under the tree. We gave them food and hygiene items and talked with them, comforted them and even sang with them.

Whilst I was under the tree with the women someone handed me a baby. Seeing and holding that baby was like a knife in my heart. She was docile, eyes glazed over and not fully present. She had not had her nappy changed in what must have been several days.

I had never before seen a baby like that. Both of her parents had passed and a grandmother was caring for her but as she was a very elderly lady she seemed to be struggling.

Everything around me, all the noise and singing and chaos felt suddenly quiet in that moment. Time stood still. Seconds felt like hours. One of the women working for the organisation said that she did not expect the baby to live much longer. Immediately I wondered why this baby had been passed to me? I was not qualified to look after her in her hour of need.

I proceeded to wash the baby in the back of a car with minimal resources. She was too small, too delicate and shivering from the cold water. I wrapped her up in clean fabric. Eventually she started to wriggle and her eyes met mine, properly. She had the most beautiful eyes. Where had they been? What had she been through and what would happen for her now? Her vulnerability overwhelmed and consumed me.

The grandmother looked happy and emotional when we passed the baby back to her fresh and clean. I was choked and had to borrow someone's sunglasses because I didn't want them to see me crying when we were trying to create positivity for them. It was a tumultuous moment, wanting to help so much but only being able to do a small gesture of support. My heart was deeply invested in their situation and wellbeing and yet I would have to tear away from it to leave the country within hours.

Moments later there was a leaving ceremony under a tree and the women sang to me. It was all a bit too much. My heart felt heavy and my eyes were sore.

It was there that I made a promise to myself that I was going to live differently. I wanted my life to be about service and contribution. I vowed never to take anything or any people in my life for granted again.

There is a quotation by R Wesley which sums up the commitment I made to myself in that moment:

Do all the good you can,

By all the means you can,

In all the ways you can,

In all the places you can,

At all the times you can,

To all the people you can,

As long as ever you can.

These, I discovered, are my core values.

Being inspired

When I returned from South Africa I adhered to these core values right, left and centre in a multitude of ways. Wherever there appeared to be an opportunity to do some kindness for someone I took that opportunity with an open heart.

I started by sending dozens of toweled reusable nappies to the organisation I volunteered with in a shipment and I fundraised tirelessly. At that point, I knew I had very little skills to offer anyone but in truth I don't think you need to be a life-saving front line emergency worker to contribute. Everyone everywhere needs a bit of help sometimes and you can do a lot just through having energy, being personable and giving time to people.

I started thinking about how it doesn't even really matter what job you do. People are queueing up for all kinds of jobs. Everyone is replaceable in their jobs so perhaps what matters most is how we spend our time outside of work, the things we do which otherwise would never happen. It is the things we create which would otherwise never exist. If everyone volunteered in their communities even just a few hours a week in addition to their paid work, this could be globally transformational.

With this in mind, I had an idea to go into the voluntary sector.

Committing to my dream

I contacted charities in London and eventually created volunteering opportunities. Letter stuffing turned into internships and before I knew it I was running fundraising auctions, delivering food to the homeless and working on school linkages in Ethiopia.

I volunteered full time for a little over a year and was not fortunate to have a free roof over my head. I worked to earn money in every spare hour possible outside of my voluntary work and undertook long journeys between voluntary and paid work. I slept in a different location most nights (friend's houses, sofas, their parents' houses) and lived out of a small suitcase. I put money in jars, paid for my friend's dinners and towards their household bills.

Everything felt really tiring and I dropped 2 dress sizes. It was difficult to maintain hope of finding a job. I had a few moments of getting stuck on train platforms for hours in the rain, going to bed very hungry or going from one thing to the next on no sleep. There were a few teary moments over the year.

The people at each volunteer organisation didn't know how life was. The struggle was private in that I didn't share it. And yet it was not private at all as I had no bedroom to sit and be alone in or any time to myself.

My parents were unhappy that I did not go straight into something more straightforward with the magical degree. Going home at the weekends was pressured and uncomfortable. It felt like I'd made a crazy decision.

Eventually I started to get job interviews but attending them was difficult. Firstly, there was the suitcase to explain, the lack of nice clothing and then there was the 'having to act normal' component. All I wanted to do was start yelling examples of everything I was trying to do simultaneously. What bigger sign of desperation and commitment could possibly exist?!

But instead I talked about the specific tasks in the voluntary jobs and tried to appear a normal, balanced individual suitable for hire.

I eventually landed my first job with an international organisation focused on providing medical care in emergencies. I was sat in my old banger of a car when I received the call about the job offer. I screamed my lungs out continuously for almost the entire length of the M3. It wasn't safe to be driving that day!

I stopped at every service station to repeatedly check the call log to make sure that it was real. How could it be real? They didn't mind the suitcase? They didn't mind my bad clothes? They didn't see my frustration and exhaustion? I thought they must have been really good people. Or I'd just managed to pull off the con of my life.

It took several days to return to calmness and be able to sleep properly.

With gratitude, I did everything under the sun in my first job and continued to survive on very little money.

I managed to find a box room for cheap rent. It was underground with no window or furniture. I remember the first time I got to sit on my own in it. The quietness was incredible. I didn't have to wait for other people to go to bed first. I had proper bedding. No one would wake me up in the night. No more having to get dressed in a bathroom.

The room was so small I would practice my yoga with half of my body under the bed. There was no TV or phone signal so every evening was made up of a swim at my local council pool (cheapest membership activity) and reading a book. I really appreciated all of it.

I knew I wanted to go back overseas and see the world, to understand it more. My boss did not seem to be helpful in making that happen so with what little money I could save over a period of time, I flew myself to Kenya. In addition to a fun backpacking trip with a friend I was able to visit the projects of the organisation and declare my overseas work ambition to anyone who would listen.

Shortly after my return there was a Cholera outbreak in Zimbabwe

– around 98,000 cases. The Emergency Response Coordinator offered me a short deployment opportunity on the basis of departure within about 48 hours. This was not a 48 hour decision… it was an immediate YES and 1 hour of packing.

Reluctantly my boss agreed and released me. I worked harder than ever on this deployment and it led to a proper contract in Zimbabwe with real work responsibilities. I don't think I had ever been so excited about anything before and was motivated to work night and day.

Going to the airport was exciting and special. I smiled my head off and this time no one dared to lecture me about my potential death. The work was expansive. I organised hygiene promotion road shows that toured the country and managed community health interventions. By the time I left the mission there were only 3 Cholera cases. It is still hard to believe… 98,000 to 3 in only a year!

It was here I started to become interested in Public Health and Nutrition. I saw how simple health and nutrition community based interventions could reduce deaths from preventable causes and this motivated me to try and carve out a career in this direction.

There was one school with a golden reputation which at the time was ranked the number one postgraduate institution in the world by the Times. The London School of Hygiene and Tropical Medicine.

LSHTM was at the time taking about one in seven applicants so naturally I didn't think I would make it in. In fact, I went through 3 whole years of applying.

The rejections were down to not having enough field experience so I kept pushing to do more work overseas. I went to the 2010 Haiti Earthquake response and all over East Africa region for the food insecurity crisis in 2011. I finally found a job where I was working alongside a graduate from LSHTM who was pregnant and couldn't travel. I took on some of her work and she wrote me a stellar reference. Throughout these years of applying I had saved almost every penny I earned in order to eventually be able to pay for the course.

On receipt of the acceptance letter I was astonished and re-read it continuously. Whilst I should have been jumping for joy, the elation was partly squashed by fear. My Dad came to meet me for a coffee. I expressed my concern about my ability to pass and the fact that this was my entire savings. The risk felt suddenly very high and saying 'Yes' felt like a difficult decision.

My Dad blew the steam from his coffee cup. We sat in silence for a moment contemplating the challenging choice I had ahead of me. Eventually he looked me in the eye and gently said 'Would you be able to live with yourself if you didn't try? Would it be better to try and fail or live with that regret?'

From the wisdom in his voice, I knew that the decision was clear. I had to say 'YES'.

It was difficult to fully commit to saying 'yes' because those savings were more than money. They represented sacrifices of all kinds: nights out, holidays, fun! The course fees were £9,000 and then there were the London living costs...

Fear can be quite a controlling emotion. In my case it resulted in extreme discipline. I spent a year studying very hard in every spare hour in preparation. I watched over 800 maths and science videos on Khan Academy, had private Maths tutoring and studied biochemistry frantically annotating every book in sight. I went through GCSE and A Level syllabuses and then onto undergraduate degree level.

When the time came to begin the course, I knew the money wouldn't quite be enough so I sold almost everything I owned on eBay. I managed to find cheap accommodation with an elderly couple and two other girls from Iran and Romania.

I also managed to earn additional money by tutoring and helping a lady with her Open University course assignments. During the year, aside from my rent, I made a commitment to trying to live on £1 a day (although in reality it was about £1.50 and there was the odd splurge on a canteen lunch when desperate).

I walked everywhere in London and to make life fun I kept a food blog showing how to eat well on a budget where I analysed the nutrient content of the portions I was cooking and ranked meals on taste, cost efficiency and nutrient content. Each meal I cooked was costed at around 30p.

I even made sandwiches and froze them to last longer. Those were given rankings too and were mostly terrible, some even inedible. I would know the exact moment they would be defrosted enough in my bag to eat.

Through a great deal of research, I knew exactly which supermarkets would put reduced food out and when they would do it. I wore the same clothes all year (4 jumpers, a gilet and 2 pairs of jeans). If it was cold, I would double the jumpers over each other under the gilet and continue walking.

Nights out were a rare occasion. I didn't fit in with the people on my course even though I really liked them. I felt poor, secondary, silly in the same clothes with my frozen sandwich bags.

On reflection, I think it is good to go through a time in life of being poor. In my initial eBay selling I had kept back my beloved camera but there was a point where half way through the year I had to sell that too and it was upsetting. When I next was able to buy a camera, I appreciated it so much and probably took better photos as a result. Nothing worth having comes easy as they say.

The course itself was terrifying. Giving your soul was required just to obtain a basic pass. The fear of the money I had spent made me push myself to my absolute limits. I would have nightmares about failure and bankruptcy and returning home.

When I received the exam results it was one of the most terrifying and greatest moments of my life.

I'd passed!

Speaking was impossible. It felt like the kind of happiness impossible to recover from. I was sky high, over the moon and jumping for joy. It was like summiting a mountain without adequate resources and taking a deep cold breath in disbelief. The breath flowed through my body making me forget everything else in the world. Money troubles, risks of finding future work, difficult living, all of it was insignificant. I definitely spent more than £1 that day. I knew no one in the world would ever be able to relate to my relief and euphoria because again most of that struggle was private.

Taking opportunities

Post Masters I was immediately offered a Health and Nutrition Manager role on the Syria response team. It was during the beginning phase of the crisis in 2013. Without caring about the terms, the answer was 'YES'.

I spent over a year managing cross-border emergency health and nutrition projects in areas that fell under IS control. It was challenging in many different ways but I began to thrive and I finally felt the sense of contribution I had been striving to be able to make. The money, the sacrifice was beginning to go directly into the planet.

Many difficult things happened on the Syria response. IS were flying in through numerous countries and were crossing the Turkish border. They quickly became the controlling entity and we had to find ways to continue working regardless.

One day they came to our clinics and went through all of our things and shut them down. They took four of our Syrian staff and transported them to their main headquarters for the area. The staff were held there for four months. We shut down our operation. It was the one time in my life I really prayed. I'd lie awake every night praying for hours and hours and eventually fall asleep praying. One of the staff even had a baby born that he couldn't meet. The injustice was heart wrenching. I prayed not only for their release and for their families but that the place they were held would not be hit by any of the airstrikes. I had a job offer from another organisation in Syria but I could not say yes when everything around me reminded me of them.

With that I headed for the Ebola Response in both Liberia and Sierra Leone. I worked in Ebola Treatment Centres (ETC) for several months which encompassed everything from training local staff to red zone monitoring activities, to visiting survivors in the community. The ETCs were 24/7 operations with hundreds of staff involved. Everything was high risk and had consequences. I remember some of the patients vividly, their joyous happy shower recovery dancing as they passed through the final ceremonious washing to re-join the real world.

And I remember the dead being taken to the morgue.

I remember the young boy who survived and went home emaciated. I took therapeutic food to him every week. He turned up to the survivor clinic weeks later wearing his best suit. He walked in quietly and proudly and weighed in at normal weight. I was so happy and proud of what we had done collectively. I was proud to know him and witness how he had fought against all odds for survival. It filled my heart with hope. We were beating Ebola, slowly but surely crushing it.

The staff in Syria were released while I was working on this response. Tears of joy and relief!

At the end of my Ebola contract I received a medal from the Queen.

This was unexpected and it dropped through the front door letter box as I was doing yoga on my parent's kitchen floor. I gave the medal to my mother.

From this point forward I began to say 'yes' more to unknowns comfortably having had so much practice. Whatever it was that could happen, I would handle it.

Subsequent to the Ebola outbreak I deployed to Yemen as a first responder after the March 2015 Houthi takeover. I remember arriving at the airport the first time on an UNHAS flight, there was not a soul in sight. Blown up aircraft looked like burnt and blackened carcasses along the runway.

Inside the airport broken glass crunched under our feet and feral cats darted for the corners. There was no people in sight.

Very few of us could get visas so I worked with 3 expatriates and many national staff to help re-establish programmes that had been previously suspended because of the conflict. We worked tirelessly in confined conditions because of the security situation. The Saudi coalition were constantly hitting the city of Sana'a with airstrikes and we were frequently evacuated to Djibouti and Jordan. The mountain near our compound was a target and the force shattered our windows. In addition to the Saudi coalition there were many other factions such as Al Qaeda and IS who were operational in different areas. Our office in Taiz was destroyed by a rocket but fortunately no staff were present. One of the most difficult things to see was the fear of the Yemeni staff. They had lived through so much more than us.

Visually seeing the direct output of the work was helpful for mentally processing personal risk, making decisions and keeping up spirit. Getting essential surgical supplies into areas with large numbers of trauma cases that were deemed completely inaccessible felt like something worth staying up all hours to work on to the point where it wasn't a choice. I wore body armour in the car and an Abaya to Hospital and field sites which seemed strange after previously putting on scrubs and a PPE Ebola suit. The contrast of the emergency responses was as refreshing as taking a break. New challenges, new culture and new ways to adapt and look at the world.

I jumped between jobs that excited me always saying 'yes' with confidence. It wasn't anything to do with confidence in the opportunity but confidence and positivity within. It got to the point where there was too much work opportunity and constant deployment requests.

Throughout this decade, I frequently pulled myself back to my moment with the baby underneath the tree. I maintained links with the people and projects I volunteered on in South Africa by becoming a Trustee of an organisation that supported them. Ten years later during a break I went back for a visit. It was incredible to see the children all grown up and very grounding to be where it all started.

Living the Dream (and the cost involved)

Travel became normality. Jobs were interesting. People entered and left. Friendships continued via Skype.

A progressive shift happened within me as I changed location so regularly. Saying goodbye to immersive experiences to join new ones began to grate my soul. It felt fickle to continuously begin again. In trying to live deliberately and say 'yes' to one way of life, some doors and opportunities opened up but with that others had closed down.

Things I had accidentally said no to:

- Freedom

- Long term in person friendships
- A community
- A serious relationship
- A home
- Hobbies and interests outside of work
- My own country

I decided to go home for a period to re-start some of those things that were missing.

At first this was difficult. Drawing on the fish out of water concept, it was like going from being a trout in a fast-flowing river to being dropped into a goldfish bowl. It took a huge amount of patience and perseverance to re-integrate.

It was lonely at first. Most of my old friends had experienced a different but equally exciting life progression and only really wanted catch ups. I appreciated those catch ups and then managed to find new friends with things in common who wanted to create shared life experience.

I even managed to buy a property with the money I had saved whilst working away. From £1 a day living to property ownership felt almost unbelievable.

I set out to get to know my country again by hiking, scrambling, climbing and road-tripping every weekend. I started to see all that I had missed whilst I'd been living in the bubble that I had created by working overseas.

After more than 10 years in the aid industry I started to crave the opportunity for change.

It was towards the end of that year that I was offered the prison job.

Saying 'yes' to leaving what I had begun to create was really difficult. I feared it would ruin my newly balanced mind set completely. But there were multiple reasons for saying 'yes'... to once again contribute and be challenged but also to save some money that might go towards facilitating a change in contribution.

Since taking on my role working in prisons, I have never missed home so much, but I have such overwhelming gratitude now for my home, friends, my grey and rainy country and all of its rugged beauty. The years of sacrificing facilitated intense appreciation, a feeling of aliveness. In the heat of the day in prison when sitting with detainees or taking a breather at the side I often feel a strong sense of peace in my heart. I will be returning home at the right moment to hug my family, friends and dog that little bit longer and harder and tell them how much I love and miss them.

My core values remain exactly the same and require constant effort to put into practice daily but the motivation is as strong as the day in South Africa. I hope to find new ways to realise them by continuing to say 'yes'.

We only get one chance at this life. Whether things work out better or worse for saying 'yes' more, we become better people because of the positivity. Taking the hard road and pushing, or taking a risk or exploring something new or different are ways to develop faith in ourselves. To develop faith in the unknown. To break routine. To facilitate an open mind.

I am so grateful for the expansion that saying 'yes' more has brought me.

As Rumi says:

> *The wound is the place where the light enters you.*

Chapter 6

Wee Ged - A Slow Travel Girl

by Ged McFaul

We arrived in Cardiff train station like a pair of tortoises with giant backpacks on. Our lives, our homes and our clothes for 300 miles and the next 3 weeks were on our backs. We were very much aware of the privilege of choice that we had - we could select what to carry and what to leave behind. Everything else would be there when we returned home. The refugees who were fleeing war in Syria at the time did not have such choice - often they had nothing or had to leave precious items behind with no chance of ever going back for them.

If we had a £1 for every time someone said 'you know it would be quicker to take the train to London' when we told them what we were doing we would've raised a fortune for charity! Still, it made us smile and feel proud of the challenge we had set ourselves.

We had probably walked for about an hour and were on the outskirts of Cardiff when we came to a huge roundabout with traffic coming and going from the A48M motorway. As I stepped onto the grass area at the corner something caught my eye - two massive horses. Each had a chain dangling from their neck but it wasn't long before we realised that these chains were not tethered to the ground...

And the horses were now coming towards us.

Fast!

We had a choice - the horses or the speeding vehicles navigating the roundabout. Within seconds we chose the traffic, dodged the lorries and found ourselves in the middle island.

Phew!

All we had to do was get ourselves back off the island and onto the road on the other side. Easier said than done now that we had time to think about the danger we were facing, but we made it. We documented our safe arrival to the other side on video and this captured my adrenaline perfectly - I nearly jumped out of my skin when a car ran over a crisp packet and it popped like a balloon!

On our planning calls I had reassured Erin that we had no poisonous snakes or spiders and no bears to worry about. What I hadn't known about was the wild horses that would chase us into busy traffic. In fact, there were numerous wild horses all around that area. Eventually our nerves got the better of us and we called a friend who came and 'rescued' us in his car. We slept well that night and had our saviour's advice on a better, horse free route ringing in our ears.

Erin lives in the USA and had visited the UK only once before our walk. We had long Skype chats in the weeks and months leading up to the walk making plans, discussing ideas and generally getting more and more excited. However, some of our cultural differences and assumptions remained in each of our heads and only came to light once we started walking.

Once we left the city streets and housing estates we were soon out in the countryside roads with no pavements. I didn't even notice this and automatically went to walk on the right hand side facing the oncoming traffic. Erin was uncomfortable with this idea, particularly when there was a right hand bend where she couldn't see the car coming in advance. She stopped me and asked if we should cross over and walk on the other side - on the tiny slope of grass between the hedgerow and the road.

I explained that walking into the traffic is an accepted rule in the UK and that facing into the traffic meant we could either see the oncoming traffic or know that they saw us. It also gave us the chance to stop and/or move to the right until they passed.

Having been in the USA a few times, I know where Erin's concerns were coming from. American drivers would probably gesticulate and shout obscenities (at best) or run us off the road altogether because 'we shouldn't be there'!

It took me a while to convince a very reluctant Erin to trust that my plan was reasonably safe and off we went again.

Erin, from Chicago, and I, a wee Glaswegian, first met on a sailing trip from Miami to the Cayman Islands (as you do!). We had both said YES! to Exploring Mindset - a retreat to challenge and develop our life adventures. This is the brainchild of Dave Cornthwaite and Emily Penn and it was set on a 72' yacht called Sea Dragon. 9 days at sea will bond most crew, but ours was made thanks to the high seas and big winds almost as soon as we left Miami harbour - the fish were well fed that afternoon!

I had gone aboard with just one goal and that was to go up the mast. I have sailed probably over 2500 nautical miles - in Scotland's West Coast, a circumnavigation of Ireland, in Croatia and in Canada - but I had never been to the top of the mast. I highly recommend that if you are going to go over 90ft into the air on a fabric 'nappy' held together with rope for the first time in your life, do it on anchor off the coast of an uninhabited tropical island about 70 miles South of Key West, Florida!

I spent a brilliant hour or so hanging on a rope in the sky. Close your eyes and imagine a tropical, Caribbean island - I was there! It was virtually silent with only faint sounds of laughter coming from the guys on deck. I had a birds eye view of the incredible sandstone Jefferson Fort walls rising majestically from the coastline in the shape of a 50 pence piece, the white sandy beaches, the turquoise sea and the greenery of parkland that makes up the centre of the Fort. The curve of the horizon was more prominent than I've ever seen in my life. I really felt like I was on top of the world.

While I was up there, the others rigged up a massive rope swing and had a whale of a time taking turns swinging from the boat and dropping into the sea maybe 70 or 80ft away. The squeals of delight and the competition among the lads for the most ridiculous water entry added to my entertainment from the sky.

When I came back down I was buzzing with delight and chatted to Erin about how much fun I'd had. As our skipper was hoisting me up the mast, Erin had been telling me how brave I was - she has vertigo and couldn't contemplate doing this. On my return though she went on to describe how disappointed she was not to go on the rope swing either. She wished she had.

Me? It never once occurred to me to do that - not because of any height fear or the drop from the swing to the water but the idea of having to swim those 70 odd feet back to the boat. Not a chance!

In theory, I could swim, but I usually 'forget' to breathe. Or, more accurately, I hold my breath in fear and of course this sets me off in panic mode. What is a non-swimmer doing with a love of sailing? Well, the plan is to stay in the boat and not fall in the water! And besides, my lifejacket would keep me afloat in an emergency.

Neither of us could relate to the others' fears - Erin loves swimming and I had just spent a happy hour 90ft in the air!

The next half hour or so drew us into an 'I will if you will' game of dare/double dare! If Erin could jump off the boat I was happy to follow her in - provided she then helped me get back aboard in one piece. A great big 'YES' from us both.

Erin's first jump, from the gate at midship didn't take long and we all cheered wildly. She smiled with glee.

I went straight in at her back and submerged into the warmth of the sea. I re-surfaced and immediately took a gulp - of salty water!

Poor Erin had to get straight to work to calm me down from my state of complete panic. She talked me into slowing my arm flapping, turning onto my back and realising that I could float, albeit with legs kicking like mad beneath. She gladly stayed by my side and encouraged me to stay positive until I was back on board... Not before I almost drowned my buddy by grabbing her around the neck in a last minute scare!

We were both delighted with our achievements and we'd pushed each other's boundaries. Erin jumped from the bowsprit (think "my heart will go on" in Titanic) and the following day I circumnavigated Sea Dragon and smashed my previous 'furthest I've ever swum in my life' record which now stands at about 150 feet. There is a rather well edited video of this achievement - you could even be fooled into thinking I swam all the way without help or panic!

Having bonded over our fears and challenged each other to success, Erin and I decided that we wanted to go on an adventure together since we had a common 'at our own pace' attitude. The Slow Travel Girls were born!

Meanwhile, whilst walking through a housing estate near Newport, Gemma was unloading shopping from her car and became our first ever kind stranger. The first of many we were yet to meet.

We stopped briefly to confirm our directions, and once we knew where to go, Gemma went in to her house to get a donation for us. Later that day she made another donation online and told all her family and friends about us. They continue to support us to this day.

We also had our first encounter with a bull that day! Since neither of us were confident about ignoring or dealing with him, we diverted our route around rather than through the field. A bit like our kind strangers, this is an experience and diversion decision we would encounter again and again before we got to London.

The rain was relentless for a few days between leaving Wales and heading up towards Gloucester. Thankfully there were plenty of lovely wee country pubs en route and it would've been rude of us not to pop in and say hello to the locals and to dry out a wee bit.

I still think it's hilarious knowing that the two characters that we chatted to in the Cross Hands Pub in Alveston had no idea that I was practically naked beneath my jacket and waterproof trousers - all of my wet clothes were drying on the radiators around us!

Mind you, our drookit (Scottish for drenched) appearance in the Huntsman Inn later that afternoon clear won us some more kind strangers. We dumped our bags in front of the fab roaring log fire and giggled at our own predicament. We ordered tea and cake even before we sat down and handed our Slow Travel Girls cards to the couple smiling at us from the sofa nearby. As we took off our wet layers (only the outer layers this time) they giggled and we realised that they were already checking out or Facebook page. We had a fun hour chatting with them and the bar owners before getting ready to head back out to the rain. It was only then that we discovered that the lovely smiling couple had already settled our bill for us!

Frampton on Severn has the longest village green in England and I would say that we probably had our longest lunch break of the whole trip in the Ley Bistro at the south side of the village. The manager and her husband honeymooned on the Cayman Islands - our final destination on our sailing trip! We chatted and shared stories with them and would happily have stayed longer but finally headed off when we felt that our feet were suitably rested.

Our route took us along the Gloucester and Sharpness Canal towards the city of Gloucester. Regardless of our lovely, extended lunch break, this was one of our longest days of walking - around

18 or 19 miles. Our feet and legs were, to put it mildly, in bits. Although walking along a canal is prettier than in towns, it's much harder to judge how far we had to go until our destination. Our minds were as tired as our bodies and we were almost staggering with pain.

It was about 7pm and although still light, there had been few people on the path for a while. I spotted a middle aged man standing on the path just ahead, facing towards the water but with a big hedge in front of him. He turned to face us but it was as if he was staring right through us...

My instincts felt uneasy. I was walking a few feet in front of Erin but I was too scared to say anything to her or even turn around. Instead I found a second and third gear in my broken legs and suddenly I was marching like I was in a speed-walking race. Erin kept up with me in silence until we passed the man.

I'm half deaf so Erin and I had a system whereby she would shout, 'Bike back!' to let me know to move to the left if a cyclist was approaching from behind. Our system worked a treat.

Until now.

This time, when Erin called for me to move out of the way of an oncoming bike I automatically assumed that she had screamed. I yelled, jumped and swung around to see what had happened... and promptly knocked a teenager off his bike into the bushes towards the water!

I don't know who got the biggest fright.

Thankfully the bushes saved him from a swim in the canal and he was back on his bike as quickly as he fell off. He left with my apologies ringing in his ear.

It transpired that we were actually only a mile from the outskirts of Gloucester and, with the help of another kind stranger, we got a lift to the city centre where we found rooms for the night.

I should probably explain what a Slow Travel Girl is.

Well, I have always been a Slow Travel Girl - I nearly didn't come last ONCE in a school race. That was over 40 years ago. I can still remember how delighted and excited I felt when I realised that I had <u>almost</u> caught up with Gina Morton in front of me.

I am youngest of 9 siblings and then, as if my parents didn't have enough work on their hands, I came along with a hole in my heart. Surgery at 18 months and again aged 7 put me right and my Dad had me believe that I had a bionic heart. He used to sneak me chocolate whenever I was in intensive care. I loved this but I'm not sure he was so popular among the nurses. In the heat of the ward the chocolate would melt all over me, the tubes and the machines attached to me. They probably thought my stitches has burst open.

I can only imagine how difficult that period was for my parents and family while I just took it in my stride. As if to prove it, on the first day that I returned to school after 8 weeks from that second open heart surgery, there was a maths test - and only one of us got 25 out of 25!

I am in no doubt that this was a big factor on the bullying that I encountered from then on and throughout my primary and secondary school years. I cannot deny that being called 'the ugly monster' affected me and to a certain extent always will. However, I can now look back and understand the logic behind it - this girl who was seemingly off school a lot (lucky her!) and yet the teachers talked about and prayed for her constantly. Then, when she comes back to school she's in the top 2 or 3 in just about every test or exam. 'It's just not fair'.

My stubborn, pragmatic personality along with my bionic heart enables me to travel slowly and that's why I am a Slow Travel Girl.

On the day we found the source of the Thames - which was as dry as a stone, we found ourselves in the home of a friend, Ben, and his Dad, Simon, who both met us for lunch. They ended up "kindnapping" us (thanks to Anna McNuff for that ace word!) and drove us 30 miles, fed, watered and thoroughly entertained us. The next morning they returned us to the spot where we met them the day before.

Simon was particularly amused by our Scottish/American combination and took great delight in asking us to pronounce words like Gloucester, Worcestershire! We hadn't met him before but both he and Ben continued to provide us with advice and information throughout our journey ahead.

It was early evening and we still had a few miles to get to Newbridge. Following the Thames Path often involved going through fields and this made walking more difficult for my wee legs. The long grass forced me to lift my feet higher for every step and then the uneven ground rutted by livestock and moles meant my body was often thrown side to side on every footstep. With the addition of my heavy rucksack, this day was one that I was really looking forward to finishing.

We must've walked about 4 or 5 miles like this when we realised that we were sharing a huge plot with about 20 cows and a rather horny bull. (Erin's camera zoom confirms this latter observation!) They were at the far end of the field, I'm guessing about 100 metres away from us. Erin was keen that we turn around and retrace our steps. Already tired of the terrain, the last thing I wanted to do was re-walk those 5 miles before we found a proper path or road.

I spotted a gate opposite us that would mean we were still going forward and around the bull but this would involve crossing the field and hoping he didn't see us. We became rooted to the spot in our stalemate of refusing to go the way that the other was suggesting. Eventually, after what seemed like forever but was probably less than 5 minutes, we compromised and began walking around the edge of the field near the hedges (we were prepared to jump in if necessary) to *my* gate and off we went.

The bull and his harem spotted us and were beginning to come and investigate their visitors. We moved as quickly as we could, in silent fear.

Suddenly I found my face in the mud. Long grass tickling my ears. I had no idea why I was down here but Erin was frantic.

'Get up! Get up! The bull is coming! Ged, quick!'

Truth was, I couldn't move. Not because I had been knocked out, nor had I hurt myself in the soft mud and grass, but because I was completely pinned to the ground by my stupidly heavy rucksack!

I raised my hand for Erin to help me up and, without looking to see where the cattle were, we ran back to the gate we had entered the field from and retraced our steps.

It's at times like these that you are reminded of why you are putting yourself through such trials and challenges. We raised over £3000 to split between our two chosen charities. Erin's was for StoryCorps which records interviews and stories from around the world and maintains the single largest collection of human voices at the Library of Congress in the USA.

My reason for walking follows a trip I made to Ukraine in 2008 to see the work of Hope and Homes for Children. It was just a 4 day trip, but it has left an indelible mark on me and a pledge to support them for as long as I'm able.

Hope and Homes for Children work in Eastern Europe and Africa. In Ukraine the primary aim is to work in partnership with local and national government to influence the reform process of the state system of care. This includes the closure of large institutions for orphans and children deprived of parental care and the setup of community based alternatives including foster families and adoption. They also established Mother and Baby Units

(MBUs) to help prevent the abandonment of children often by young mothers who desperately want to keep their babies but need extra support to enable them to do so.

Our first visit was to a foster family and it was like walking into my own family cine films from the 1970s - all the kids lined up on the couch excitedly waiting for the visitors to arrive. It wasn't long before Rostyslav, aged 5 (and one of the cutest little boys in the world), stood up to recite 2 poems. His sisters soon followed with a few songs.

The Sypakiny family have fostered 23 children since 1990. We were shown around the house and there were photos everywhere of all the children brought up here. We will no doubt be on the visitors' gallery soon.

The parents talked often and proudly about all of their children but the most striking story for me was the one about the three youngest siblings aged 7, 6 and 4. They were found wandering in the woods. Stanislav, 4, then commented that his new mother was old but that this is still better than his real mother.

The following day it felt to me like we were going back another 50 years.

The real reasons for our visit fell fully into focus for me within minutes of arriving at the Boyarka baby home which was not yet being supported by HHC. The white coats worn by staff and the masks we were given was bad enough, but hearing that the 'beautiful children' are more likely to be adopted than the 'un-beautiful children' hit my already sensitive nerves. The latter are those with disabilities and my tears fell silently.

The staff believe that they have the children's best interests at heart but their work is a legacy that is 70 years old. In the last 20 years HHC have certainly transformed significant elements of the childcare system and, having seen the outcomes, I feel compelled to support them with this valuable work. I will hold on to my memories of the mother and baby unit, foster families and supported families that leave me in no doubt about the positive outcomes that HHC can achieve.

Neither of us had wild camped in the UK before this trip. We camped 6 times in the end, mainly because we kept getting kind-napped or when we had particularly tough days we felt we deserved a good sleep and rest in a B&B. On the first night we camped, Erin insisted that our tents touched and I was appointed "wild animal chaser". By the third time, Erin couldn't pitch far enough away - she chose the animals over my snoring!

Before reaching Oxford, we stayed two nights with a friend, Andrew, and his two magnificent sons. This gave us the opportunity to have our first and only "day off" - though we still walked 5 miles around the historic and beautiful University town.

About an hour after Andrew dropped us off to head towards Abingdon and beyond I received a text message – 'Hi, we are looking forward to having you girls stay with us tonight. Just phone when you get closer and we will collect you, Di.'

Erin and I then spent the next while trying to work out who on earth Di was and how she got my number. Eventually Andrew text to explain - he had put out a call on his own Facebook page to tell his friends that we were heading south and would appreciate a place to stay for the night. Di saw this, thought it sounded like fun and text her husband at his work to say that two girls from the internet were coming to stay!

Di's husband, Dan, collected two almost broken girls sat on the kerb and the three of us, I'm sure, puzzled and entertained the queue of his local fish and chip shop as we excitedly shared stories of our journey.

A brilliant evening ensued and would you believe that Di and Dan were thanking *us* for coming to stay? We are still in touch with them today and Erin visited them recently. I am looking forward to welcoming them to Scotland soon.

I had no idea what to expect before we set out on this journey except sore legs but this adventure certainly proved how lovely strangers can be - some even becoming life-long friends.

We set out on the final stretch from Hammersmith to our finish line at Tower Bridge, slowly, very slowly. Erin's feet were almost entirely covered in blisters and I had developed a nasty shin splint just a couple of days before. Anyone watching our laboured staggering and regular stopping might have thought we had spent the last 21 days drinking and dancing late into the night.

Despite our pains, we were really excited to get so close to the finish line and to see our friends who were coming to walk with us on our last day.

Gradually several friends joined our walking train. Each of our cheerleaders coached and chivvied us along from the moment they joined us. Little did we know that part of the reason for their 'keep going, you are nearly there' was because they'd secretly been coordinating with Andrew, who had travelled down from Oxford with his two boys to surprise us at Parliament Square. I often thought they were being rather rude when they kept making phone calls as I chatted.

Another lovely surprise came in the shape of Ben who was a stranger only a week before when we met him on the Thames Path. He had specifically come to London that day to see us across the finish line at Tower Bridge. What a delight!

We really enjoyed everyone's company and chat on that final day. However, looking back, I realise that it was rather an unfamiliar experience. We had become very used to mainly having only one person to talk to. Someone who knew how the other person felt. Someone who understood when a rest was needed and instinctively knew when it was time to move along.

In fact, I can't really remember much of what we saw that day because we spent it so differently - in a good way. I think there is a good chance that Erin and I will set out to walk the final stretch of our Slow Travel Girls walk again, to somehow recreate it as it might have been with only the two of us.

I think we'll leave the backpacks, blisters and shin splints behind though!

In the meantime, we have recently walked our second Slow Travel Girls challenge - 300 miles between all 7 of Scotland's cities. Whilst you try to name them, no google cheating please, I will start to write that story for you to read another time!

You can see our many photos and videos from our trip on Facebook and Instagram @SlowTravelGirls and on our website **www.slowtravelgirls.com**.

Chapter 7

Life of a Reindeer Herder

by Adam Cunningham-White

This is the Arctic.

It's -43°C at two o'clock in the afternoon on December 29th. The snowstorm that had engulfed the mountains is subsiding. One eyelid is now completely frozen shut. I exhale deeply. The vapour in my breath glistens as it leaves my mouth. My toes, while once affixed to the ends of my feet, are now debating whether it's in their interest to drop off in an attempt to save their host. It's been 17 days since the sun deserted this place for pastures new.

Eight thousand reindeer now stand, defeated, densely packed in a pen. The once constant hum of seven snowmobile engines begins to dissipate into the icy wind as they shut down. Three Sami herders yawn in unison. The reindeer restlessly pace, grunting and carving 3-foot deep channels in the freshly laid snow. A small cloud of steam follows behind each animal. A calf stops in front of me. We lock our stares before the faint groan from the mother abruptly ends the confrontation. I glance skywards, to a scene more attributed to a dream, the famous green and purple waltz of the Aurora Borealis. This is the Arctic.

The last slurp of coffee slurped. The last chunk of chewing tobacco chewed.

The oldest Sami, at the ripe old age of 74, stands there, hands behind his back, clenched tightly, conserving energy and evaluating each and every reindeer that passes. Suddenly, with the energy of a small child, he casts a frosty lasso into the direction of a group of reindeer as they sprint past. The rope, while stiff from the cold, sinks perfectly over a set of antlers. A 4-year old female has been snared and promptly falls down into the snow. Through the fresh batch of 'snus' tobacco, nestled between his gums and lips, he calls to me for help. I grab her antlers as she thrashes around, trying desperately to calm her. A tug of war ensues, though a sense of apprehension brings her to a nervous halt. I stand over her, staring into her deep, dark eyes; she returns the gesture. I watch frivolously, already knowing the next stage of this pre-determined drama. I breathe in. *THUD*. I breathe out. Her legs collapse under her weight. Her eyes suddenly shallow and lifeless. Her legs twitch, under the impression that there is still weight to bear. She felt nothing.

The Sami herders stand at ease around the fallen, like a wartime hero. A knife stands to attention, perpendicular to her neck and pointing to the on-going Aurora above. The old man, stands over the kill, characteristic of the wolves he shares this frostbitten land with. He looks to me and says: *'Dat leat min eallin ja mii leat daid'.*

~ They are our lives, and we theirs ~

* * *

Years ago, when I was a mere awestruck young teenager, I distinctly remember an evening episode of my life where I, along with my family, went out for dinner at some mildly upbeat restaurant in the mildly downbeat town of Calais, France. We were on our way home from a short road trip from inside Europe. Although we barely scratched the surface, having only been to Dunkirk and back, this still felt like a road trip at the time.

To cut this long, rather uneventful story down, and to spare you the insignificant details on the few 'sights' that Calais does its best to offer, I'll share the one detail of this journey I do clearly remember. The incomprehensible (to me) noise that my mum made when addressing the waiter in French. For it to be greeted with surprise, and even a reply, from the French waiter was equally astonishing.

I do not recall my mum being able to speak French prior to this meal, but afterwards I made it a goal of mine to one day attain the level of being *bilingual;* the first level of being a polyglot. It turns out that my mum had lived in France for 6 months with a family that spoke no English whatsoever when she was 18. One either learns quickly or has only themselves to talk to.

Years later, I had just finished my yearly university exams, when two friends and I decided to have a long and fruitful summer trip to India during our time off. A route that took us from Chennai to Delhi. This trip ended up with a month-long jaunt to the Andaman and Nicobar Islands while completing my Scuba Diving Instructor Exams. These islands are situated below Myanmar but owned by India. Returned to British ownership in 1945 from the Japanese, they then served as a late gift from the departing British in 1947 to the newly independent India.

Throughout my time in Asia, and especially while in India, I met a barrage of people from all over the world. From Israeli apache helicopter conscripts having just finished their service, to middle-aged and late-aged Europeans and Americans. These silver travellers tended to be worn out from the stresses of office-life, instead deciding to *find themselves* before their pension drawing age. A choice I whole-heartedly support.

Being able to converse with such people, learning about their lives, their cultures and traditions, is one of my favourite things while travelling. Also, be warned, that conversations with travellers were always generally steered back to the most common and pressing concern. Namely, where the last place was that the local cuisine had a detrimental effect on their GI system. Normally it's trotted out as an ice-breaker.

But it's not until you are with a group of like-minded travellers that you realise just how boring it can be to sit around a grotty table down a side street while everyone else converses in their mother tongue and you're stuck in *'I only need to speak English'* land. And thus, the story of my mum all those years ago was regurgitated and reignited.

The bilingual dream was back on. The first real 'YES' of my story. Although talk of reefs, sun, sand and sea is normally enough to persuade me to buy a plane ticket, years of 'nomading' around the tropics in search of scuba diving locations suddenly had me longing for a change of pace. A considerably colder change of pace.

I was going to learn a language. For real this time. Not just saying it because mum can do it. Oh, and also in Sweden.

What languages do they speak in Sweden? Correct. Swedish. (Well actually, more than just Swedish, but that comes later.)

I had learnt the odd word in Swedish from an old friend of mine while working together in London and felt, 'Well, I may as well continue'. Plus, it's cold there, something I wanted.

Little did I know that becoming rather good at another language is actually, in fact, more difficult than just learning 'how are you?' and 'how much does this cost?'. Oh, and also a number of useful (useless) swear words. The only problem was that I was about to begin the second year of my degree. How could I be exploring somewhere and learning a language while studying?

It was time to find a place to live.

Workaway.info is a website dedicated to helping people that need help with farming, building, looking after kids etc. It is effectively an au pair website. As an au pair through this site, you make a profile to 'sell yourself', and to do your best to convince the hosts that you are the one that would be best suited to their needs and the work in question. I was in *advanced* talks with at least 4 families within 2 weeks of setting up the profile. I have no idea if this meant that I had an appealing profile, or whether these certain families just needed urgent help, but it was a good return on investment nonetheless.

At Delhi Airport, lingering like a bad smell for 7 hours while awaiting my delayed flight, I rattled off a few emails to the relevant families. This was primarily because I was after a few extra details on what work they were wanting me to do. But secondly, and perhaps more importantly, I wanted some *facetime* with which to put faces to names; Skype is a traveler's best comrade.

The first to reply failed to mention anything about the *work* they had in mind for me. Alas, they simply mentioned that they were a Sami family, and that they lived in Jokkmokk; a Swedish village in the Arctic. Nevertheless, a Skype conversation was planned and penned in my diary for when I was back on British shores. And had recovered from jet-lag.

Most people have heard of Stockholm and Gothenburg. Perhaps even Malmo or Lund, but Jokkmokk? Safe to say that even with my self-proclaimed good knowledge of all things geographical, Jokkmokk was not on any list that I could claim to know anything about.

In addition, the Sami people? All I really knew about them was that they were one of the few remaining indigenous peoples of Europe, living in the Northern reaches of Scandinavia.

One evening, a few days after I had made the journey back from Delhi to the land of the shining white cliffs of Dover, I was *mid-chat* on Skype with the aforementioned Sami family in Jokkmokk; the other 3 families, to save the details, were all down in Southern Sweden. The appealing nature of living above the Arctic circle made this family my preferred choice. After all, I was after temperatures that begin with a minus sign.

During the conversation, they made clear that although they were more than happy to speak Swedish with me, the main language spoken in the house was Northern Sami. This shot of information was not enough to act as a deterrent, the answer was still 'yes'.

As it happens, the family's choice of speaking purely Sami inside the house was a result of not only because they were inherently Sami, but also due to the oppression towards the Sami people over the past many years by various Swedish governments. The number of Sami language speakers saw a huge decline and thus, many Sami now feel it a duty to teach their children. The tide has since changed and the oppressive laws forbidding the use of written or spoken Sami have disappeared. There has since been a reassuring resurgence of the number of people that speak it.

I will learn one of the Sami languages one day. They really are beautiful. One language at a time though, and for now, it was the Swedish language that was first up.

The conversation continued, and the next volley of questions soon followed: 'We have a 10-month-old and a 3-year-old. This may mean that you're woken up many times during the night. We also eat primarily elk, reindeer, fish and potatoes. We hope you're not a vegetarian'.

Once again, I fired a volley back, exclaiming that neither of these things brought about an issue with me. The 'Yes' remained intact.

A broadside then arrived. 'We don't need any help in the house with the kids or cleaning or cooking, but would you still be interested in coming to us if your work was with my husband instead?'.

A short pause ensued. 'Of course. May I ask what your job is?'.

They looked at each other on the video screen, then back at me. I immediately braced myself. The husband then proclaimed, rather quietly, 'I'm one of the few reindeer herders that belongs to the Jåhkågasske Sami tribe. My 74-year-old father isn't getting younger, and we've decided that it would be good to get some help regarding the demanding nature of the work.'

Another pause ensued, this time purely on my part. I remember watching a documentary once, all about the reindeer people, the yoik music, and the northern lights and it all seemed so magical to me. Even though my knowledge on their lifestyle and culture was limited, the list of 4 families that I was in talks to co-habit with rapidly became truncated.

The onslaught of questions continued yet still. 'Would you proclaim that you're suited to a life outside?'

I thought back to my childhood in sunny Sussex: weekends with walking and camping along the South Downs. 'How hard can being outside be', I asked myself. After all, I love nature.

'What's your experience in working for 20+ hours in a labour-intensive setting'. I moved on from this question rather rapidly, doing my best to hide my reluctance to actually offer anything in terms of an answer to that one.

The other questions all resembled the same pretext. Questions unending about whether I'd take an issue with working consecutive days, with the days potentially running into weeks. Whether I had any special dietary requirements. Whether I have any predisposed condition where working in extreme temperatures and conditions presented any sort of worry or discomfort.

In my mind, it mattered little if the temperature was -10C or -45C. There was no difference to me. I was purely interested in that minus sign. As it turned out, the difference between these temperatures resembled eight layers of woolen clothing. Still, at the time, I was scarcely affected by this; the little minus sign being the critical lure.

Whilst most of this conservation was light-hearted and friendly, I do remember this chat ending with a few points about death, which did worry me. Hearing sentences such as: 'You could drive a snowmobile off a cliff in bad weather' and, 'Of course working with reindeer brings dangers such as receiving a horn through your eye or ear'.

'What's the chance of that?' I asked myself.

Exclaiming that the long hours, extreme conditions, and lack of sustenance weren't an issue seemed easy. But I will contend that I did suddenly doubt that this job was for me, when faced with the dangerous consequences that were brought about at the end of this chat.

Unfortunately, the bulk of the individual questions from this conclusive Skype conversation have been erased from memory, as have my *exact* answers to the questions themselves. Ultimately, they were extremely pleased and excited to see how pleased and excited I seemed.

I kept the concern of being injured bottled up. Naturally though, I'm sure they wouldn't have held this uneasiness against me at this point if I had brought this up with them.

I found out a year later that all of the aforementioned questions were in place to try and weed out the people that seemed nervous or worried about any of it. Not that they were lying, the issues behind the questions were very much real. Although wanting my help, they were merely trying to dissuade me as much as they could. Working in the Arctic, as a Sami, is not for the faint hearted.

My utter enthusiasm when answering these questions was enough and it landed me the position. It was left with me to decide whether I would go through with becoming an *English-Sami* reindeer herder.

As it turns out, this was one of the easiest questions I've ever had the pleasure of asking myself.

'Yes. Absolutely. Yes. When can I come?'

That evening I booked a flight to Stockholm and the subsequent night train to the Arctic, leaving two weeks later. Everything was starting to fall into place. My first 'un-orthodox' adventure was soon to be reality. I sorted out what I needed to take with me with which to continue my degree; books, pens and pads, and also what kind of clothing I would need. Coming from Southern England, where at worst we would be subject to a few nights of -5C in the depths of winter, I had no appreciation for the extreme conditions by which the Sami people live in.

I knew that it would be cold, perhaps even reach below -40C sometimes, but I had nothing to compare that to. I had no yardstick to tell me just how cold that was, or how much clothing I'd need, or when to wear it. Nor did I have anyone that I knew that could offer me any pointers on the matter. I would just have to learn how to survive as I went along.

Two weeks later, I woke up. It was early morning and it was 'leaving day'. My bags were packed. I've always prided myself on being as resourceful as possible when I travel and being able to be one of those irritating travelers that somehow packs next to nothing. But somehow, I had managed to pack my 120L scuba bag and my 70L backpack to their brims.

The journey to the Arctic town of Jokkmokk was rather uneventful, taking 27 hours in total; door to door. I arrived at a land covered in white, illuminated by street lamps and car lights; it was of course still dark at 11am. I had never seen anything like it. It was surreal.

Huge pine forests either side of the road draped in snow. The road itself was unrecognizable. It too had been completely engulfed. The drive from the station, to my *new* house took 45 minutes, with a good 44 of those staring out of the window in wonder.

I arrived at the house, mentally tired from both the journey and the sheer excitement of actually standing above the Arctic circle for the first time. I almost felt dizzy being that *high*. I was shown to my room, leaving my overweight bags there, before heading back into the kitchen area to sit with my new family. The anxiety that I had been feeling for the weeks prior just dissipated into the cold, crisp air outside. This was now *home*.

Fortunately, my *host* family spoke faultless English. The reindeer herder himself had previously studied engineering at University in Northern Sweden before deciding to take the *reins* from his father by carrying on with his ancestor's lineage. His wife also had perfect English. She, in fact, was studying for a teaching degree, with all course materials being almost entirely in English. The language barrier, at this point, had not reared its head.

On reflection, I was somewhat negligent during these first few weeks with regard to my previous goal of attaining the rank of bi-linguist. It's very easy, I found, to just do enough to *get by* and not push yourself. It was also very easy to just speak English, considering they were both so capable.

I was immediately thrown into the thick of it and off to the mountains I went. The work was intense. The weather was atrocious, or at least, so they said. I was of a different mind. I thought working in a snow-storm, wading through 3 foot of fresh snow, at -25C Celsius in the pitch-black of mid-afternoon was the experience I was looking for.

I came to agree with them later on, that these conditions, maybe aren't the most pleasant or the most desirable to work under for days on end.

Not only was the work intense and the weather *awful*, but I was told to drive a snowmobile with an attached GPS unit, and given a headset with which to talk to the other Sami's with; so as not to get lost. This might sound alright, apart from the fact that I couldn't drive a snowmobile, I had no idea where I was, didn't know a thing about tracking reindeer, and most importantly, bar my new family and some of the younger ones, none of the Sami's spoke English.

It wasn't long before the issues surrounding my lack of both Swedish and Sami, and the Sami's lack of English, made the language barrier a rather large gulf to swim across.

Every day was different. It could be -30C one day, and the next day it was +2C. To make things even more tricky, I couldn't just look at the thermometer to see how cold it is. One must check the wind, whether it snowed overnight, is currently snowing, or will snow soon, to name a few. All these things affected what gear I needed during that day of work.

Fortunately, my Sami family helped me tremendously during this time. After all, it is their livelihood. 'Minus 45C is just another day' - I recall one of the Sami's saying to me once, and that is the mentality towards the extreme weather that I now seem to have adopted. 'It's just another day'.

People often ask me, now that I'm back in England, 'what was it like to work in minus 45C?'. It will be always be a question that's difficult for me to answer. In fact, these days, I seem to not bother explaining my answer to any great detail anymore. I just say that it was precisely that. Minus 45C. Cold. Really cold. But you just get on with it. There's no time with which to adjust to it. This is the thing when one hasn't experienced extreme cold before, one has nothing to compare it to, and thus finds it hard to accept anything else apart from 'it is cold'.

Preparing for work was always easier when it was 20C and below. Any day that is warmer than that, and especially when warmer than -5C, meant that the snow will melt from your body heat, and your clothing will become wet. You need to make yourself as water tight as possible. Gore-Tex is your friend here, not wool. But don't wear too much that you look like an advert. The clothing must also breathe, because when working in temperatures below zero, you will heat up quickly when working. Excess body heat means sweat;

when you sweat in sub-zero degrees, the sweat will freeze in your armpits, and that is as uncomfortable as it sounds.

However, when it is inconceivably cold, reindeer fur and big woolly jumpers will keep your heart beating and that's all that matters.

Days where my beard froze itself shut were not uncommon. It's like having a sizeable stalactite hanging from your face.

I had a similar routine every morning before work. It was easy to get sorted. Look at the thermometer, check the forecast, and get a wind reading. Plan and dress accordingly. Simple.

One more tip - if you, dear reader, do ever take a trip to the Arctic, don't bother showering in the morning. The thin layer of oil that your body secretes overnight genuinely does help keep the heat in. Sounds gross but I found it to help. There's a reason that not one Sami that I ever met washes in the morning when they're working in the wilderness.

One of the many jobs I had during my first season was to head into the local forest and help the elderly Sami man, the one that I came to *replace*, on his daily ward-round. This meant driving half an hour to the part of the forest where we stashed the snowmobiles, filling up the snowmobiles, checking the fluid levels, packing our coffee and food and any other spare bits of equipment we may need (an axe, saw and spade were crucial) and then driving around the forest, tracking reindeer. We were making sure they're grazing in areas with good food conditions and no predators.

Not the most labour-intensive work, but the days are extremely long when you're with an elderly Sami reindeer herder, doing his utmost to teach you centuries-worth of indigenous knowledge, and you're struggling to grasp any of it.

I came to adore him. He literally treated me as his adopted son. But, it must be said, his proficiency of the English language was limited to the word 'cheers'.

I'm sure he knew I couldn't understand, but he carried on regardless. As grateful as I'm sure he was, considering that I was a willing student, I did feel rather ineffective.

Within two months of me being there, I decided that maybe I should stop merely following the only herder that could understand me, and actively really put 110% into being an asset to them. This meant, first and foremost, breaking the language barrier.

I had to choose; Swedish or Sami.

At this point, the Sami language was completely new to my Western brain. It has no connection to any Germanic or Latin language at all. I maintained my earlier ideals and reaffirmed to myself that learning Swedish would be the most beneficial during my stay. In any case, everyone there speaks Swedish, so it seemed to be the best middle-ground.

I started free language classes and told both the family and the other reindeer herders to only speak Swedish with me. If they wanted the most out of me, I'd need to be able to communicate with them.

A few months in and my Swedish had become noticeably better. I could understand a fair amount and could pigeon my way through the basics. I'm sure the grammar resembled roadkill but considering the circumstances, I was just happy to be at a point where I could start talking to others.

I came to appreciate that language is such an integral part of *identity*. It's of huge cultural importance to have one's own language. The Sami's are of no exception. Regretfully, I can't claim to speak Sami, but after applying myself and making a determined effort, it has made me realize just how much of their culture that I was missing out on when I couldn't converse.

Even in its most basic form, having the ability to communicate through language opens up so much more to any experience. Safe to say that me becoming so integrated into the Sami tribe weighed heavily on my communication proficiency, and how quickly I was then able to make myself useful.

Language is everything.

It was now the middle of winter. The days were at their bleakest. It'd been a long time since the mercury in the thermometers had been visible. I was standing in a large pen, surrounded by reindeer. This is an event known in Swedish as a 'skiljning', which duly translates to 'separation'. Good luck pronouncing it. I know you just tried.

This term describes the process by which the reindeer that have been rounded up from the mountains are brought down into the forests and channeled into a pen. They are then systematically *sorted* by their ear markings into their *families*. Sami herders from the neighboring communities will be invited to come to the pen and collect the reindeer that they own. The reindeer are manually taken, by their horns and dragged into trailers.

It's incredibly demanding work.

Each individual herder looks to take every reindeer that they own and transport them to an area of the forest that their ancestors used – each Sami herding family has an indigenous right to certain areas of land that has been used for generations past.

The more reindeer in the herd from the mountains, the longer it takes. Once started, these events don't end until every reindeer has been separated. You can't leave *unsorted* reindeer in the pen as they will die very rapidly from lack of food. Reindeer must constantly eat throughout the winter to survive.

The first skiljning that I ever went to was 150 kilometers away from the forest that we had to release the reindeer in to. It was -30C and snowing. We had roughly 450 reindeer, yet only three trailers that could take 24 each. I hadn't even yet been taught how to identify the reindeer from each other by studying the different ear markings. I felt incredibly out of my depth.

That skiljning went on for 3 days.

It was a sobering event, particularly after being so awe-struck and content when I first arrived. These separating events are frequent during November and December, with all the neighboring Sami communities rounding up their mountain areas and emptying them of reindeer.

One skiljning event that ended up being intensely eventful, reminded me why my *host* family were right to warn me of the dangers when working with reindeer during that deciding Skype conversation months earlier.

It was while a Sami man from a neighbouring tribe was loading one of his reindeer into his trailer when it happened.

Unsurprisingly, it was snowing. Not intensely, but enough for it to be known. The pen was perfectly circular, with a 2-meter-high wire fence covered with nylon sheeting; acting to obstruct the reindeer from seeing freedom. Pine trees were dotted around inside the pen. Merely leaning on the tree brought a thick shower of fresh snowfall down on your head.

A most unpleasant feeling it is to have an ice-cube rolled down your back. Imagine the feeling of instant regret when taking the weight off your feet against one of these pine trees and dislodging its rooftop cargo.

Not much speaking takes place inside the pens. It's a solemn affair. Only when a reindeer with unknown ear markings is discovered does a voiced inquest begin. When one is found, the poor reindeer becomes subject a sudden perverse number of fingers being shoved *in* its ears. The reindeer herders tirelessly attempting to work out who the owner may be and what then to do with it.

I was stood beside the Sami man in the pen when we both lunged forward in unison. Each of us grabbing a reindeer. One hand grasping the reindeers' antlers tightly, with the other hand carefully feeling inside the ears; determining the owner of the reindeer from the incisions they received as calves.

I identify *my* reindeer as belonging to my host family. He identifies *his* reindeer as being his wife's. We haul ourselves with reindeer in tow, through the snow, to the small wooden gate of the pen, and out towards the trailers.

This is the most precarious part. You become the only thing standing in the way of the reindeer from its freedom. If you let go, the reindeer is gone. Potentially losing the owner a lot of money. Imagine dropping £500 and watching it slip through a drain cover. Now imagine your friend dropping your £500 and watching it slip through a drain cover. There's a difference.

All of a sudden, *his* reindeer made a break for it, catching him entirely by surprise. It swung its huge antlers upwards in an effort to force the man to release his grip, but to no avail.

All of those Swedish lessons I had had come to no use at all as I watched the sharp point of the antler completely rip through the man's right ear. There were words used but I doubt they would make it onto the curriculum.

It happened strikingly fast. No one would have the reaction speed to swerve away from those antlers. I still had *my* reindeer in my grip, rendering me useless until I had loaded my cargo.

It's surprising just how much blood one has in one's ears. It's also surprising that after having his ear torn in two, he kept hold of a thrashing reindeer. The man was in his late sixties but was in no mood to let the reindeer escape to freedom. Two others rushed to his aid. Interestingly, they took the reindeer and loaded it into the trailer first before making sure he was okay. The Sami's are a tough people.

Marking the ears of the reindeer calves is typically performed during the summer months as to avert avoidable pain. In the depths of winter, the extreme cold makes this necessary process regrettably quite painful for the reindeer. In addition, it takes a lot longer for the bleeding to cease in sub-zero temperatures.

By sheer misfortune, the injured man had received his own *mark* from a reindeer. The irony.

To add to the irony, the splitting in half of his right ear made him look unmistakably like the reindeer owned by another well-known reindeer herder in *my* tribe. Many jokes about ownership and the slaughterhouse were made at his expense.

Finally, my Swedish lessons did come into use. I sat him down, washed his torn ear with fresh water, and organized another herder to take him to the hospital; a mere 2 hour's drive away. I even just about managed to reassure him that his nephew, who was helping him during the skiljning, wouldn't have to drag and load on his own. I would help.

There was a substantial bright-red stain on the perfectly white snow beneath where he sat. The usually rigid cartilaginous look of an ear was long lost. Despite not seeming in much pain, his ear looked disgusting. I held the two pieces of limp flesh together in a vague attempt to stem the bleeding.

He did his best to inform everyone that his ear just required some tape, before conceding that maybe he should pay a quick visit to the *sjukhus*; hospital in my native tongue.

He was a humorous and witty character. As I sat there with him, washing his ear and face clean, he kept cupping the grisly remains of his ear, telling me to speak up. He even still managed to remark, 'That's a nice new jacket, Adam.'

I replied that it wasn't new, and that I wear it almost every day in the forests.

He then returned with, 'Oh, well it looks new. When are you going to start working then?'

He made a full recovery.

It wasn't an overly horrific accident, and thankfully the defibrillator didn't need unboxing, but it was one that *painfully* reminded me that I am working with wild animals.

Three years is a long time to remain in any one country. Even more so when it was only meant to be a brief expedition to explore a new land.

During times past, the reindeer acted as a walking bank account, wardrobe and fridge. The meat provided money, the fur provided clothing and shoes, and the meat provided the calories to survive this unforgiving land. Any one of these being ample reason to prune the number within a herd by one.

I can't begin to imagine what would have gone through my mind if I was exposed to the sacrificing of a reindeer during my first few weeks. I lacked the awareness of the intimate relationship between the herders and their reindeer upon my arrival. I wouldn't have understood the reasoning behind it, nor understood why sometimes it is necessary.

Those lessons were strictly reserved for after I had earned their trust and respect.

When necessary to kill a reindeer, it is concluded with the calmness and dignity that would be expected. It's never a decision taken lightly. There are many motives behind deciding that a certain reindeer may be excused from the land of the living. I have now seen and assisted the process a number of times now. Every time leaving me feeling empty inside.

One of the Sami's that I was close to once mentioned to me that the only way he could get accustom to killing these beautiful animals was to turn away as soon as the knife slide into the spine. He would wait 15 seconds, with his eyes shut, before carrying on. I was with him on one occasion when we had to put down a young reindeer calf; a victim of a traffic accident. In reality, closing one's eyes doesn't help. One knows exactly what one has just done.

The truth is harsh, but it *is* life. It is *their* life. The reindeer that belong to them are afforded the best chance of survival. Predominantly due to the dedication of their owners.

The first time I was asked to assist in this ritual took me by surprise. I didn't immediately know what to say. I had been working non-stop for a week with a group of Sami's in the wilderness. I had been helping to herd reindeer across *my* tribe's mountainous terrain, when we finally reached our goal of containing the 8000 strong herd in a pen.

The elderly Sami man looked disinterested at first, as he called me over to where he stood. Maybe I was in denial of what was about to happen. Subconsciously, I think I knew. I took hold of the set of antlers belonging to a female reindeer that he had just snared.

I saw it all.

The man simultaneously spitting out his tobacco and taking hold of his knife from his belt. The grunting noise of the reindeer as I held her antlers, trying desperately to keep head between my knees and her gaze away from the knife.

The wind was bitter that day, and the temperature had been steadily falling for the past 24 hours. Yet all I could think about was coffee and reindeer meat.

And there I was. Stood over the lifeless corpse of the reindeer, the snow falling softly around, and the knife still embedded in the neck of the beast.

It's a strange feeling, to see and feel life in front of you and then to see and feel it disappear, almost instantly. I remember feeling literally cold and emotionally callous as soon I watched the blade nestle into the reindeer's neck this first time.

It was quick. The spinal cord immediately severed and rendered obsolete. Not a sound came from the reindeer. It was over in a slice.

I'd never proclaim to understand much Sami at all, but those words that were said to me as we stood around the lifeless reindeer, are etched into my mind. The Sami herders taught me a lot. But the most important thing in their eyes, was that *they are our lives, and we theirs'*.

~ Dat leat min eallin ja mii leat daid ~

* * *

The 3 years that I spent living as a Sami, were the best years of my life.

I originally travelled to Sweden, with the goal of learning *some* Swedish, to experience the cold, and learn about a new culture; while of course continuing my degree. I now speak Swedish, survived weeks in the most remote regions with temperatures down to -45 Celsius, and became completely adopted into a Sami tribe. I did go on to obtain an upper-second class degree in Biology through the Open University, and as of September 2018, will be starting my next 5-year journey at Aberdeen Medical School to become a doctor.

Never in my wildest dreams would I have said before leaving on this adventure that this trip would change me. I left for a few months, perhaps a winter season, but not 3 years. The Sami people, the climate, the lifestyle, the traditions, the culture, the nature, and even the reindeer themselves really made an impact on me as a person and taught me many valuable lessons.

I have never been more thankful that I said yes to this idea of mine. That's all it was. An idea. An idea that I had on a sweltering hot Indian day.

Never doubt yourself. Be weird. Be wonderful. Live life and love everyone.

Website: **nomadicadam.co.uk**

Instagram: **@nomadicadam_**

Facebook: **Nomadic Adam**

Chapter 8

Adventures on the Pan Am

by Janneke Holzner (and Konstantin Holzner)

"Oh my god Konstantin...." I screamed, gripping the steering wheel of our beloved fire truck in terror. "What the hell do I do?".

The back end was swinging out of control. Konstantin had no time to reply. The van began spinning violently on the ice rink of a road. Once. Twice. Three times. Round and round. There was nothing I could do but hold desperately onto the steering wheel.

The Beginning

Six years before, I'd dramatically bowed out of a job I hated (you know what they say about not burning bridges, well, erm, no-one gave me that memo). It was my first job out of university and I had innocently believed that this was it. This was my career. A year of slogging away for terrible pay and I'd had enough.

My poor friend Chris had to bare the brunt of a 'screw this' phone call one afternoon in May, where I dramatically declared, 'sod this, I'm coming cycling.' I had decided to say 'YES' to his Facebook event - a trip cycling from Munich to the Black Sea along the Danube. Poor Chris didn't really have much choice in the matter.

And so, in June 2011, a motley crew of six assembled in Munich. We were a hodgepodge of creaking bikes, inexperience and particularly naïve optimism. Not least because we weren't sure we could buy any food in Germany on a Sunday. Or that the six of us could fit in Chris's friend Konstantin's ridiculously small studio flat. We squashed in, hungry, and started to really get to know one another.

I'm not going to lie, Konstantin had made an impression. His mop of curls ticked a major (I'll admit, very shallow) box for me. Any potential father of my children must have curly hair to give the child the biggest possible chance of inheriting the *Lockenkopf* gene. He also had a Z in his surname, which meant it would score highly in a game of surname scrabble (not like Smith or Brown, yawn). So with completely rational interest peeked, we had a full three days to get to know each other before Konstantin had to return to Munich for exams.

We cycled along and I desperately tried to make a good impression. I even pretended to be interested in physics. He sounded so cool - he raced downhill mountain bikes. He was training to be a ski instructor. He was exotic (okay, this might be a stretch, I mean, he wasn't British).

I wanted him to think I was cool too. This was hard. Mainly because I'm not. But, here, on the bikes, I could pretend. I even sort of looked like I knew what I was doing. I had proper shiny yellow panniers and everything. I could pull of being cool.

That was until the log happened.

Konstantin shouted a warning as he jumped his bike gracefully over a massive log crossing the path. I had no time to react - I hit it square on, whacked on one set of brakes like a complete amateur, and went flying over my handlebars and landed fully on my head right at Konstantin's feet.

My lip ballooned to twice its normal size and blood was pouring out of my knee. I went full child and started to cry. I'm still not sure who was more traumatised by this experience - me, who was fairly used to my own clumsy mishaps, or Konstantin, who had a fully grown woman he had just met weeping at his feet. Suffice to say, there were mutual feelings of discomfort and embarrassment. A firm basis of a relationship. For that's what it became (some 9 months later).

We navigated the complications of a long distance relationship between Aberdeen and Munich by meeting 'in the middle' in a variety of awesome cities. And we soon got to know each other better. I introduced him to the concept of 'taking the mick' (a move I often now regret), excessive alcohol at family gatherings and the excitement of London rent prices. He introduced me to salt and pepper on bread (only German bread, natürlich), sausage salads (no greenery was harmed in the making of this salad) and very large glasses of beer. It was a mutual learning curve.

And amongst all this mingling of cultures, we discovered a shared adventure goal. We both wanted to travel the Pan American Highway. As the months grew into years, we continued to fantasise about this incredible journey - What car would we buy? How would we fund it? How long would it take?

But fantasy is one thing. Reality is another. And, unfortunately, no amount of talking got round that fact that it just never seemed to be the right time. Konstantin had started a three and half year long PhD in London and I was trying to build a career in the transport industry. We needed time and money to be able to pull together the logistics for such a trip, and we had neither. But, more than anything, we needed focus.

It was time to say 'YES'. This would no longer be an idea. This was a trip we were actually planning.

We agreed on a hypothetical leaving date - April 2017 (about 2 years away at this point) and we started telling people about it. This felt a bit odd at first - particularly when a random stranger came up to me at the first ever Yestival and said 'You're the one driving the Pan American Highway?'

I remember looking around to see what legitimate adventurer they could actually be talking to. 'What me? Oh yes, of course, me!'

Unfortunately, we were to learn the hard way that saying 'yes' in theory is only half the battle. Making our 'yes' a reality was tough, stressful and really hard work. But, it was also exhilarating, rewarding, and a whole lot of fun.

We had a pretty long to-do list. We needed to buy a left-hand-drive vehicle (unfortunately, some Central American countries don't allow right-hand-drive), convert it into a campervan, insure it, ship it over to Canada, and fly out to meet it. All within about 12 months and on top of a full-time job and the last stages of a PhD in physics. Simple right?

First hurdle was finding a van, which meant a trip to Germany. We kept trying to find enough time for this, but daily life kept getting in the way. Konstantin would suddenly have precious time in his lab or I would have a really busy time at work.

By October 2016, we still hadn't got the most important first step on our plan sorted. It was time for difficult decisions. We said no to the second Yestival and instead booked last minute flights to Germany. We had a week to buy a van, insure it and drive it the 1300 km back to the UK. Bish, bash, bosh.

In the lead up to this trip to Germany Konstantin was Chief Van Researcher. In fact, it was difficult to have a conversation about anything but van related stuff.

'Janneke, Janneke. Look at this cool campervan.' Konstantin would jostle me awake at midnight to show me a picture of yet another (admittedly very cool looking) van.

Walking down the street was difficult. Every van that passed launched a commentary from Konstantin about its merits and downsides, and always ended with a sigh and a faraway look of, 'Oh, I wonder what van we're going to get.' It wasn't that I didn't care, it's just Konstantin has one of two modes - utterly obsessed or not interested. And, well, I like vans, but just not THAT much.

As the van-purchasing trip rolled round it occurred to me that I hadn't actually really looked at any of the daily barrage of links to different vans Konstantin had been pinging me. So, the day before we flew out, I decided to do a little bit of my own research.

'Mercedes vans; under 11000 euros; 4wd' I typed into the main German auto site. I sifted through the white Mercedes Sprinters, and then, nestled in the results, I spotted it.

'Oh my God, Konstantin. I think I'm in love, we have to get this.' I sent him a link straightaway.

It was beautiful. A shiny red 1991 Austrian Mercedes fire engine.

Konstantin messaged back instantly – 'Very cool. But it's a lot bigger than you wanted, and I thought you wanted a VW, and you can't stand up in it.' My specifications for his search had basically been the complete opposite of this hunk of gleaming red.

'None of that matters if it's a fire truck,' I replied.

The next day we flew into Munich, picked up a hire car, and drove straight to the fire truck seller. There it was, sparkling in the October sun. I looked at Konstantin, trying to read his expression. Was he interested? We didn't want to give too much away and look too keen in front of the seller. But now I wasn't sure whether Konstantin was keen at all. And I was keen, my God I was keen. It was amazing.

I whispered to Konstantin, 'So, erm, what dya think?' Nervously hoping we were on the same page.

'It's awesome. I love it,' he whispered back.

We didn't want to completely rush into the decision, as the vehicle was completely different to any that Konstantin had spent his last six months researching. So, we went back to a friend's house in Munich and spent the evening researching in order to back up the decision we'd already made.

We were going to say 'YES' to the fire truck.

We rang back the seller, who thankfully hadn't had another opportunity to sell it between 3pm on a Saturday and 9am on the Sunday morning, and so, it was OURS! At least after we'd sorted some minor, rather stressful, bureaucracy - officially importing it to Germany from Austria, re-registering it, replacing the tyres and giving it a German safety exam.

But all the stress was worth it, and by the Thursday, we were sailing down the Autobahn (at a speedy 90 kph!) in our incredible new van. We were in love. Could it get better than this?

Yup. Turns out the siren still worked. And was pretty effective in clearing traffic.

Project Get Everything Together in a Very Short Amount of Time

The great thing about goals is they give you focus. The bad thing about goals is they can make everything a little bit more stressful.

Having only just bought the van in October, our April 2017 start date was starting to look a little bit ambitious with only the weekends to work on it. Konstantin was also moving into the final 6 months of his PhD and was confined for up to 15 hours a day in a cold, dark, depressing underground lab. As much as converting the van was a welcome break from the sometimes soul-destroying ins and outs of atomic and molecular physics, it was also another pressure. We decided to push our start date back three months to July. It never feels great to move the goalposts, but having taken some of the pressure off we could start to really enjoy the highs and lows of converting a van.

Because there were amazing highs, and some pretty dramatic lows. We learnt a lot about each other - we had very different working styles.

Konstantin is an ideas guy. He would sit for hours at a time thinking about all the endless possibilities and ways of approaching the conversion. This is great, but it also didn't get wood cut. I'm more of a do-er, urging us to get started and get things going, aware of the ticking clock to our start date. This is great, but it meant the wood often got cut in the wrong shapes.

We stumbled along, rejoicing at achieving the little hurdles. The insulation was in. The lights worked. My sister finished the amazing upholstery. We had a roof extension which turned out perfectly. However, it was a challenge, there were also a lot of very late, very cold nights (tip: don't convert a van in the middle of winter or at least buy very good gloves) and sometimes it just felt like we would never get it finished.

But by March, we actually had something that looked like a campervan. And so now, the wheels of bureaucracy meant we had to take a trip back to Germany in it before we left to get our paperwork in order. I'd love to say that this trip was an absolute breeze and we sorted everything straightaway and then gallivanted around Germany seeing the sites. But no, the fire truck wouldn't start at least 10 times, we couldn't get our gas installation tested because Germany uses different connectors, and we spent the whole week trying to get hold of some olives (not the tasty kind, the gas installation kind). But after a week of raised blood pressure, it was done. Our paperwork was in order. We were good to go.

Alas, if only it was that simple. With the van all legal and nearly finished, we started seriously looking into insurance for Canada and the USA. Something that seemed quite a simple piece of admin became a massive headache. For some reason, in March 2017, all the insurance companies in the USA decided to collectively stop insuring foreign vehicles - particularly if they were campervans and over 25 years old.

We rang and emailed countless companies, but were continually met with the same answer - no.

After everything - the long nights working on the van and the stress of getting everything legal - our whole trip was in jeopardy because of a piece of paperwork.

We considered our choices - travelling without insurance wasn't an option. And so, after years of fantasising about sitting by a campfire on a lake in Canada, exploring the majestic mountains of Alaska and driving down the Californian Coast, we were suddenly having to think about a new trip and a new plan without visiting these amazing countries. For weeks I couldn't listen to any California based music without crying. It might seem dramatic, but this was a trip we had put so much time and commitment into - my work knew I was leaving, we'd told countless people about our plans and now it felt so stupid (and incredibly frustrating) to be thwarted by bureaucracy.

July crept ever closer.

We started looking into options to ship the van to Mexico. It was possible, but would take time. Maybe we could go to Canada and the US in the meantime. Maybe we should just go and travel Europe. Maybe we should just jack it all in and buy some bicycles. Much simpler.

Ha, no, we chuckled at the thought. This trip was about a van. As much as we liked cycling, we didn't want to cycle the Pan America. We wanted a van so we could experience lots of different activities - hiking, surfing, canoeing, climbing, and, every so often, cycling.

'If we haven't found a solution by the 1st June, we enact plan B, whatever that might be,' I declared one May evening.

We had one final option. An insurance company said they might be able to insure us if we could prove our conversion was professionally done within the last 15 years. We weren't professionals (see countless pieces of mis-cut wood), but the person who put our roof extension in was – and we had the evidence of that. It seemed a bit far-fetched, but when you're all out of options, you'll try anything.

We sent off the application and waited. And waited. And waited. All of about 24 hours, but it felt like weeks.

'Yes, our insurance company is happy to insure you,' the broker replied. We rushed through the paperwork and by the 31st May we were insured and booked onto a ship leaving Liverpool in a few weeks' time. No need for Plan B - this time.

While sorting all this out, finishing PhDs, putting the last minute touches to the van, and trying desperately to visit all our friends and family before leaving, Konstantin and I felt we didn't have enough on our plate. So, we decided to get married as well.

We'd organised a big leaving party in my parents' garden for the 1st July, and it seemed sensible to just high-jack that and shove a wedding before it. We kept it all very quiet, inviting just our closest family and a few friends to the registry office and the meal. We then got back to my parents' house around 4pm, quickly changed into our party clothes and pretended nothing had happened. At 7pm, once most of the evening guests had arrived, we announced that they were all actually at a wedding. It was a great send off.

And so, with a PhD basically complete, one job quit, various hurdles overcome, and a van on its way from Liverpool to Halifax (the Halifax on the east coast of Canada), a couple of newly-weds took a flight from Gatwick to Canada on the 11th July 2017 to start the adventure (and honeymoon!) of a lifetime.

It all comes together

We stepped off the plane in Canada with a complete jumble of emotions. This was it. This was actually happening. We were excited, apprehensive and very impatient. We wanted our van, but it was still somewhere in the Atlantic. We busied ourselves with a few days in Newfoundland, watching whales, photographing beautiful gannets and listening to great folk music, and then headed to Halifax for more impatient toe tapping and refreshing of our emails to see whether the boat had arrived.

Eventually we had confirmation - our beloved fire truck was in the same country as us. All we now needed to do was navigate a fair bit of paperwork and Canadian customs, and we would be reunited. The paperwork was surprisingly easy, but customs is always nerve-wracking. They have so much power. We spent far too long obsessing over all the things that could go wrong - would they not release the vehicle? Impound it? We gave ourselves a whole morning to sort everything out.

'You got any alcohol in the van?' the customs lady barely looked up from her paperwork.

'No.'

'Any firearms?'

'No.'

Stamp. Stamp.

'You're good to go.'

It took about 5 minutes. All that worrying for nothing. Now all we had to do was swap some paperwork for the fire truck.

A jolly lady greeted us at the port collection office. 'The red one, no problem, just go and check it over. I've got something for you to sign, and then you're good to go.'

And that was it. We checked it for damage and found nothing. Papers signed and we were on our way. So simple, we couldn't believe it!

And so began our journey through stunning Canada. I'd be lying if we said it didn't take us a bit of time to find our feet. The months leading up to our departure had been so full of organising, activities and goodbyes, we'd hardly had time to ourselves. And here we were now, just me, Konstantin, an awesome fire truck and the whole of the Americas to explore. It didn't really feel real.

But we soon got into the flow of driving from beautiful place to beautiful place, finding gorgeous secluded spots next to lakes to camp. We hired canoes in Ontario and headed out into the back country. We saw our first bear in Manitoba. We played around on the dirt backroads through the endless fields of Saskatchewan. We spent weeks in the Canadian Rockies, sleeping in the shadow of the majestic mountains and going off exploring the countless hiking trails.

Suffice to say, the van was in its element. Not only did we love it, the Canadians loved it too. We would hardly have finished parking in a Walmart before we'd be surrounded by people excitedly asking about the van and taking photos. We just learnt very quickly to shut the curtains when getting changed, as you'd just see a nose and a set of eyes peering through the window while you had your pants down!

All those long nights, the seemingly never ending bureaucracy challenges, the stress and the organisation. They had all been worth it.

We headed further north into the very sparsely populated Yukon. The long roads stretched out for 100s of kilometres with nothing but bison, moose and the odd bear for company. The air got cooler and we began to wake to frost on our windows. We 'treated' ourselves to a spot in the Klondike Road Relay - a 160km running race from Alaska into the Yukon - Konstantin ended up with the 2 am slot, me the 9 am - our fire truck becoming our luxury support vehicle. We drove the unbelievable Dempster Highway, a dirt road that took us past the Arctic Circle to some of the most northern communities in the world. And after watching one of the last Dancehall shows of the season in the gold-rush town of Dawson City, we crossed over into Alaska.

By this point we were really getting into the swing of van-life. Yes, Alaska in October was cold, but after a while you get used to having to de-ice the inside of your windows and remove icicles from above the bed. The van was actually very cosy. We had our little heater and some good down sleeping bags and we were really enjoying snuggling up and reading a book and keeping our own, completely random schedule. Four days into Alaska, we had our first snow of the season and were bewitched by the gorgeous cover of white on the landscape. We drove past glaciers, woke up to grizzly bears eating salmon next to our van and stayed in remote woodland cabins. It was an incredibly special place. But, we reluctantly had to pull ourselves away. In the words of Jon Snow, winter was coming, and we wanted to get south and see British Columbia.

It all falls apart

On the way up to the Yukon and Alaska we had taken the famous

Alaska Highway. So after Alaska, on our way back down, we wanted to take the other option - the Stewart Cassier Highway. This is a very remote road through the far corners of British Columbia, also said to be a must see.

And, well, it was gloriously remote. We took a detour off onto a windy, steep road to a place called Telegraph Creek. As we drove out to this isolated community, the sun was shining and we were excited about how the van enabled us to take these cool little side trips. Even if, when we got there, the promised restaurant was shut for the season!

The day after our side trip to Telegraph Creek the weather had turned. Rain was pelting down and the dirt road from Telegraph Creek was washing away. We crept along, taking the corners carefully and making a journey that took us 1.5 hours the day before take nearly 3. We arrived back in Dease Lake with no issues and filled up the van for our next section. There was a beautiful lake about 100km south where we were going to camp.

While Konstantin went back into the petrol station shop, I slid over into the driver's seat. We tried to be pretty fair on dividing up the driving. And he'd just done a pretty epic drive. The rain was still pounding down, but we didn't think anything of it. We'd been driving in snow for weeks by this point, a little rain wouldn't hurt. We just hadn't really noticed that it was freezing solid as it hit the ground.

I drove out of town, taking a number of corners without any issue. But then, we hit a long straight stretch. I felt the back of the van start swinging, swooshing from side to side across the (thankfully) deserted road. I had no idea what was happening.

'Oh my god Konstantin...' I screamed, gripping the steering wheel of our beloved fire truck in terror. 'What the hell do I do?'.

Time stopped for just a second. There was a moment where the van seemed to right itself. And then, everything collapsed. We fell into a free-spin, violently skidding along the icy tarmac with our heads flying from side to side. We came hurtling off the road, careering down the snow covered ditch. Our front left wheel slammed the earth first, the impact tipping us dramatically on our side.

For a moment, everything was quiet, just the faint hum of the engine still purring in the background and the thumping of our hearts pierced the calm winters day. I looked over to Konstantin. He was, rather comically, suspended midair in the cab by his seatbelt.

'Are you alright?!' We both said in unison. The initial shock over, we surveyed our surroundings and ourselves. I looked around the cab - no blood. Incredibly, we were both fine. Shook up, but fine.

But, we weren't out of the woods yet. The smell of fuel filled the van - we needed to get out of the vehicle as soon as possible. This was easier said than done. My door wasn't an option (being rather well acquainted with the ditch) and the passenger door wasn't much simpler - opening it up rather than out meant gravity was fighting valiantly against our escape attempts. Konstantin contorted himself round in his seatbelt harness, summoned all his remaining energy, and eventually, pushed it open. We were able to clamber out and survey the damage. It did not look good.

A man drove by and gave me a lift to the towing place in the nearest town while Konstantin stayed with the truck. I enlisted the help of Charlie the tow truck man, and we made our way precariously to the scene of the crash, slipping and skidding on the road and nearly coming off the road twice.

'Man, it is a freaking ice rink out here. You guys are lucky you are walking away!' Charlie exclaimed, making me feel slightly better about the whole thing. He set up a traffic control and righted the van, allowing us to assess the damage a bit more closely.

'Damn,' Charlie said.

'Yup,' Konstantin agreed.

'What????' I interjected.

'It's bent. The unibody frame is bent. I can't fix that. Sorry guys. This is a write off,' Charlie apologised.

We checked into the only motel in Dease Lake. Once the pressure of trying to stay strong in front of Charlie had been lifted, the emotions came flooding out. I cried, and cried and cried. Konstantin hugged me.

'It's not your fault,' he comforted me. 'I don't think I would have done anything differently. And it could have been a lot worse.'

'I've ruined our trip,' I wailed. We were both okay, we knew that was the main thing. But the potential loss of our van was just heartbreaking. After so many months of work on it, so much stress getting to the start line, to have only travelled in it for 3 months was just sad.

'There's always a way,' Konstantin declared. 'The van is not dead yet.'

A Series of Unfortunate Events

'First things first. We need to see if we can get this frame unbent.' Konstantin got to work ringing up all the body work specialists in the area. 'The area' here being a very loose term. The nearest was 700km away. Wayne's place in Houston was able to help, but we needed to get the van there.

We'd contacted the insurance and they seemed relatively happy for us to make a few decisions about what we wanted to do with the van. 'Tow it 700km to Houston?' we asked.

'Fine, but we're not promising we'll pay for it.'

So we took a gulp of breath and paid $2000 Canadian for one of the most expensive car journeys of our lives. Wayne was brilliant, a week later - we had a (mostly) repaired van. Things were looking up. I posted a photo of our happy faces to Facebook. 'Back on the road!!!!!'

Now, I would love if I could just finish this story here. We drove off into the sunset and lived happily ever after. In fact, if you want that story, I would look away right now. Stop reading. Because, in the words of the great Lemony Snicket, the story that is to follow contains a series of very unfortunate events. For only a mere 10 minutes after posting our positive Facebook update, the NOISE started.

'What's that?' I asked Konstantin.

'Ermmmm. I don't know,' he replied.

It got louder. We pulled over. We couldn't see anything. We kept driving. The whurring and vibrating filled the van, the NOISE adding a dull beat under our music. This was not good.

We drove the 1000 km to Vancouver without too many issues (just a small near miss and a run in with the police, but those are tales for another time!), but we definitely needed to get it sorted. And quickly.

Maybe it was just a problem with the wheel balance? So we headed to Mr. Lube and got them to rebalance our wheels. In 30 minutes we were all sorted. We went to pay and the manager said:

'Nah, it's on the house. Not often we get to see such a cool old truck. You guys have a good trip... hope the noise is sorted.'

A lovely, positive experience, but alas the NOISE was still there, loud and clear.

Still, we knew the rim was a bit bent, so perhaps that was the source of the NOISE. We went to another tire place called Kal Tire and they swapped the wheel for the spare. We went to pay, and they said:

'Mate, our guys in the shop have had such fun with the siren, this one's on the house.'

Another, lovely positive experience. But, unfortunately, the NOISE persisted.

It looked like our best case scenario options were slipping away. Our plans for quickly sorting it out, and getting south to the Californian sunshine were looking less and less likely. The mechanics we were taking the van to were looking rather confused at our old Mercedes truck. It wasn't in their systems. They couldn't do anything. We started to get a little exasperated.

Enter Hans.

Hans is North America's number 1 Mercedes Unimog specialist. Admittedly, we were not a Unimog, but we were a Mercedes, and we hoped to appeal to his general love of German vehicles. We got back in our creaking van and ventured out into the countryside.

'Do you think that might be it?' I said, pointing to a drive that had about five imported (very hardcore looking) Mercedes Unimogs scattered around it. This looked like our guy.

We found Hans in a portakabin pouring over paperwork.

'Urm, hi. We have a NOISE we need to fix and were hoping you would help', we said (auf Deutsch, naturlich - unsurprisingly with a name like Hans, Hans was German).

Hans looked our little fire truck over, and Konstantin and him went off for a drive. We spent a couple of hours going back and forth, taking photos of part numbers, poking things, putting it up on a rack and checking the 4 wheel drive (also no longer working). I followed the German as best I could, but my GCSE level didn't go into advanced mechanics so I got a bit lost.

Eventually the conversation switched to English. 'Do you know what's going on?' Hans asked.

'Urm,' I replied. The little I had picked up had not been positive.

'Basically, your front axle has bent and there's something broken in the front differential,' Hans started to explain (...the switch to English didn't really help my understanding). But, finally we were getting somewhere.

'Can you fix it?' we asked eagerly.

'I'm not sure. I'll need to take it apart and we might need some more parts. It'll be at least a couple of weeks,' Hans replied. 'Bring it back next Monday and I'll get working on it.'

A couple of weeks. That was ages. But, if it meant we had a working, happy van, we'd take it. So, we explored Vancouver (in the rain) and then dropped off our beloved truck the following Monday. We weren't going to wait around feeling sorry for ourselves, so we packed up two rucksacks, got on a bus and headed to Vancouver Island for 10 days.

This was bliss. We checked into a beautiful resort (with a hot tub, a luxury our van was sadly missing!) and just relaxed. After all the drama of the crash and the resulting stress of trying to resurrect our truck, we needed some time to just forget about everything.

And, so far, things were looking positive. Hans rang halfway through our Vancouver Island break to say he'd found the issue and had ordered the part. It'd be another couple of weeks - but we'd be on our way.

As lovely as British Columbia is, in November in the rainy season it can start to be a bit oppressive. So another couple of weeks trying to entertain ourselves in torrential rain didn't really appeal. We looked into our options and found some flights to Hawaii in a Black Friday deal - it never was part of our plan to spend ten days on Maui, but it was just the tonic we needed. We sat on black sand beaches in the sunshine, climbed volcanoes, and ate incredibly yummy fresh tuna poke. It wasn't the worst waiting room for a sick van.

Alas, all good things come to an end, and we dragged ourselves away from Maui and the sunshine in mid-December, Konstantin reluctantly admitting he was not going to become a pro surfer with four hours of practice. Our van was going to be ready on Thursday, so we called upon the hospitality of our good friend Ruona who lived nearby to wait it out.

On Tuesday we spoke to Hans. 'Ja, it is all gut,' he explained. 'The parts arrived yesterday. The new radiator is in. You should be good to go on Thursday.'

This was exactly the news we wanted. For the first time in six weeks we could actually, properly, consider our next steps.

Things were looking up. Our insurance was going to pay us for the van. We'd been able to sort our new insurance for the US without much hassle. And we should be able to pick up our van on Thursday and get on our way. Just a second, I hear you cry, I thought you said this was a series of unfortunate events, this all sounds very positive. Yes, indeed. It was. Until we heard from Hans lunchtime on the Wednesday.

'I'm really sorry. There's a big problem,' Hans' email began. 'The new drive shaft is 5cm too short.'

We'd been waiting for this part for three weeks, and were getting pretty desperate to get back in the van. This was a rather major setback.

'It gets worse,' Konstantin continued. 'He is really struggling to find the actual part.'

Having crashed our van at the end of October, we were now nearly at Christmas. Hans assured us he was almost 100% sure he'd found the right part, but we'd have to take the risk on the delivery. If it was wrong, we'd be liable for the £1000, and still not have a working van. Happy Christmas!

But, he was pretty sure it was right, and he hoped that we would have everything ready and good to go before the 1st January. There was something quite poetic about this I liked - new year, working van, back on the road. We hired a car and decided to head South - we'd continue to stay positive and make use of our time by doing a tour of the US, hitting the Oregon Coast, San Francisco, and Los Angeles.

On Christmas Eve we found out that Hans hadn't actually ordered the (possibly right) part, as he had spent hours ringing up the voluntary Austrian fire service, the 4x4 company and Mercedes and had found us the 100%, absolutely sure, correct part. Frustratingly, someone about 25 years ago had mislabeled some of the major parts of our van - hence the part being 5cm too short and the struggles finding the correct one. So, this was positive, but, everybody who could send it to us from Germany was on holiday for Christmas. We'd maybe have the part by mid-January. Yet more delays.

This was becoming a very active lesson in staying positive and trying to make the most out of difficult situations. We extended our US tour to include Yosemite, Reno and Portland.

And then, finally.

'We can go pick it up,' I declared with nervous excitement to Konstantin.

After delay, after delay, after delay, the part had arrived, been installed, and the van was good to go. We jumped in the hire car and drove round to Hans' workshop. There it was. Our lovely red fire truck. With four wheels attached! We paid Hans and got on our way - we had a friend near Seattle who was cooking up some

Tortilla Soup and had some beers in the fridge. After so much waiting, this was it. We were off to re-start our trip.

We got about 30 km down the road.

'What's that?' I strained my ears to an odd crunching sound as we sped along the highway.

'I'm not sure,' replied Konstantin. 'It doesn't sound good.'

'Oh no.'

'What?'

'The NOISE is back!'

Lessons in Bounce-Back-Ability

After three months of trying desperately to resurrect the van, with setback after setback, but trying to maintain positivity, I had had enough. I burst into tears. We have a phrase in my family called 'bounce-back-ability'. The ability to bounce back from awful situations, try and look at the positives and make the best of things. This whole situation was testing my 'bounce-back-ability' to the extreme.

We turned around and went back to our friend Ruona's place to work out what we were going to do. Ruona opened her home again to us without question, giving us a massive hug and an equally massive - and much needed - glass of red wine.

We were back at square one. We had had 30 glorious kilometres of feeling like the trip was back on track. And then everything came crashing down. The part that we had waited for for three months had broken again. There was obviously something more fundamentally wrong. Even if we could get things fixed, it would be very expensive, take more time, and it would be unlikely that the van would pass a German Safety Exam when we took it back to Europe after the trip. We would probably just be delaying the inevitable - the van joining a van graveyard.

'I don't know if I can do this anymore.' As heartbreaking as it was, throwing more time, money and mental energy at the van didn't feel like the right decision.

'I agree,' confirmed Konstantin.

We reflected on our situation. We'd had three amazing months in the van and made some incredible memories. Crashing the van was awful, but we'd come out of it without a scratch. In the ongoing saga of trying to fix the van, we'd met amazing people, travelled to incredible places, and learnt that the trip was actually much more than just the fire truck.

'Let's buy bicycles,' I suggested. 'Sell the van. I think it's cursed.'

I barely had time to finish my sentence and Konstantin was researching touring bikes.

'I'll take that as a yes.'

'Yes. Definite yes,' replied Konstantin.

We launched ourselves into planning for this new chapter of our trip. We sent most of our belongings back to the UK and sold our van to our friend Alex in Seattle (a transaction that also contained a series of very unfortunate events - arrests, jobsworth border guards, failed imports, and a lot of effort, but we succeeded). With just two bags of stuff remaining, we got on a flight to San Diego.

It felt great to have focus again, to have the trip back in our control - not at the mercy of parts that didn't fit or someone else's schedule.

We arrived in San Diego on the Wednesday and by Saturday we both had bought touring bicycles, had picked up panniers and some other supplies and were ready to go.

We'd be lying if we said we weren't apprehensive about this change. We had both been cycle touring before - I mean, that's how we had first met. But we hadn't planned this trip around cycle touring. It wasn't really what we wanted to do originally.

And, well, I'm sat writing this in the port town of La Paz, at the end of the Baja peninsula, and I'm feeling pretty awesome about our change of transport (I've just asked Konstantin - he says he also feels awesome). It's been a month so far, and we've covered 1500km of incredible cactus lined roads, pedaling through barren deserts and along the beautiful coast. We've spent our evenings under the stars in an array of wild-camping spots. We've seen whales jumping and playing in the bays. We've swam in crystal clear water and got a LOT of sand in our tent. And, we've eaten tacos, burritos and enchiladas by the dozen (Reason 1 to love cycling: unlimited food).

Our life has simplified dramatically. Now our biggest worries are whether we have shrimp or fish in our tacos and how stupid our tan lines are getting. The biggest mechanical issue we've had so far is a puncture. Much easier, quicker and cheaper to fix than a NOISE!

But, it is different. Not bad different, just different. Where with the bicycles we are able to slow down and really take in the 'in between', we also can't as easily take the 50km detour to the really cool beach. On the bicycles we don't have to worry as much about 'stealth camping' - we just turn into the cactuses, walk a bit, and we're hidden. A bright red fire truck is a little less subtle. In the van, we could store food for at least a week, on the bicycles, maybe three days (and given the fact I carry the food, I do this reluctantly!).

But, the trip is back in our control. We may have lost our van, but we have gained some very good thighs. Sorry, I mean experiences. We've gained some very good experiences. We've learnt a huge amount about positivity, bouncing-back and resilience. And, we're incredibly excited to see what the next chapters will bring. For now, we're enjoying two wheels, so we're going to head over to the Mexico mainland and continue South. Maybe we'll get all the way to Ushuaia in Argentina (our original goal with the fire truck), but we're open minded about where the road will take us. So, go grab your yes. And if it doesn't completely turn out as planned, know that there are other equally amazing yes's out there.

Want to find out more about our adventures? You can! Follow us:

Website: **guidiary.com**

Facebook: **guidiary**

Twitter: **@guidiary**

Instagram: **@guidiary**

Chapter 9

Conquer Yourself

by Alessandra Boeri

'I don't know if I can keep going,' I said shivering as I tried to sit on a cold rock.

My hands were trembling from the below freezing cold weather, my vision was hazy, and I was close to collapsing from loss of energy and coordination. *What was I thinking climbing this mountain,* I thought. I was falling asleep on my feet. I wanted to scream in frustration but I was too weak to even talk. *Go away negative thoughts! You're almost there!* But just the thought of dragging my legs a couple more hours in this torturous state was horrifying. It wasn't just a constant physical battle, but a mental one. I had to constantly remind myself to stay strong but this was nothing like what I had trained for. I was now standing at 5,300m above sea level and altitude sickness had gotten the best of me.

I had planned to climb Mount Kilimanjaro for over a year and spent months training for it. I was running 5 to 10ks weekly, cycling and doing long hikes around England to bigger climbs in the French Pyrenees. Kilimanjaro is the world's tallest freestanding mountain, rising at 19,341 feet and is the highest point in Africa. I knew it would be tough but there was a greater challenge I'd have to overcome. One that I couldn't really train for - the altitude.

It becomes more of a mental challenge when you start to notice all the things that start to concern you. The constant migraines.

Watching team members slowly get ill. Sleep deprivation. Resisting having to use the loo in the middle of the night because you're too wrapped up in your sleeping bag. You don't even dare to step outside because you're too cold to move a muscle.

* * *

The journey began on August 22, 2017 after we spent the night in a hotel in Moshi in the Northern part of Tanzania to regain our energy from the long flights and long hours in the airport. There was 26 of us including our Action Challenge leader and doctor. We started off as strangers, and we came back as companions. It's incredible how much you connect with people when you're trekking for long hours.

After one last good shower of the week and breakfast, we made our way to Londorossi Gate by bus. The excitement started to kick as we gazed out the window and were surrounded by giraffes and zebras prancing free in the wild. The bus ride to the start of the trek suddenly felt like a wild safari adventure as we gazed out of the windows desperately scanning the hills for other animals.

Our excitement came to a quiet pause when we spotted it. At a distance, we could see Mount Kilimanjaro standing tall as King of the African mountains. We all stared at it in awe. We were speechless, intimidated by the presence of this massive, dormant volcano. The nerves started to kick in, and we were anxious to start trekking. There's no turning back. In just a few days, we would be up there.

Once we met our porters, had our bags weighed to ensure it was within the 15 kg limit, and had our bellies fed, we were finally off to start our trek via the Lemosho route.

Climbing Kilimanjaro means climbing through distinctive vegetation zones and four seasons in just a few days. Our trek started along the Montane Forest, surrounded by incredible flora and fauna. Beautiful moss covered green trees with distinct shapes wound around us. Walking into a fairytale of dangling branches and elegant violas flowering on the ground made our trek more beautiful as we walked higher through the lush rainforest. Along the way, we spotted some black and white Colobus monkeys traversing from tree to tree, some hiding through the dense thicket of branches.

After a 650m elevation gain, we successfully made it to the first camp, Mti Mkubwa and I was feeling good. We all started to bond over tent meals and stories. I was amazed at what the cooks prepared for us at such high altitude. From chips, to beef, and even a cake! I can barely even make a cake at sea level.

The whole crew was really polite and generous. The hard work they do on a daily basis: getting up even earlier than us to prepare breakfast and pack, from carrying a load of weight on their backs, keeping things clean, while keeping us motivated. Their efforts were deeply appreciated by us hikers. They were superheroes.

After dinner, it became routine to try to use the toilet before bed to avoid getting up in the middle of the night while it was freezing. By toilet, I mean, portable toilet inside the toilet tent. That was actually a luxury on the mountain. I had expected that I'd have to dig up my own hole. Baths consisted of wet wipes and one bowl of water to do some quick rinsing. The reality was it didn't matter how many times you rinsed. We were sleeping on a volcano on the dirt. You just had to embrace it, somehow.

And sleep? For me, trying to sleep every night on Kilimanjaro caused me anxiety. My first sleep at Mti Mkubwa was unsuccessful. I was up every hour of the night with an upset stomach. I was already feeling cold and we weren't even at the highest point. After only a couple hours, everything went quiet, and I could hear the monkeys coming down the trees and moving outside our tents. I couldn't help but make stories in my head thinking the monkeys were stealing our boots and I had to stay awake to keep an eye out while Sara slept. I really needed those boots to get to the top! But mostly, I was awake, worried that it was night one, and I already wasn't sleeping.

12,355 feet

On the morning of Day Two, we got called by one of the crew at about 5AM who offered us some tea and biscuits. 'Hello! Good morning!' they'd say cheerily outside our tent.

We had a full 10-12 hours of trekking ahead of us. Surprisingly, I managed to start the morning laughing with my tent mate, Sara, even after getting zero hours of sleep. We weren't even delirious on altitude, it was just natural bonding. The group thought we had come together as friends because we got along so well, but we had just met a day ago. We managed to keep each other in good spirits throughout the whole journey even when we were at our most miserable state. It makes such a difference having positive people around you.

As for the usual morning routine: we'd get our kit ready, repack our bags, have breakfast, refill our water bottles, and start our day's trek. I tried to ignore the uncomfortable feeling in my stomach and focus on my steps. 'Poly ,poly.', the Swahili for 'slowly, slowly', is one of the key secrets to acclimatizing on Kilimanjaro. The guides set the pace for us each day and I made sure to practice my breathing from day one. I never dared to walk a bit faster because I knew how much energy I needed to conserve for the next few days.

Day 2 was a long, exhausting day. It was about ten hours of trekking under the heat of the sun. I found myself feeling out of breath. Our Action Challenge guide Steve talked me through some breathing techniques and eased my fears and I managed to push through the long hours. We walked at a steady pace to allow our bodies to acclimatize as we crossed the Shira plateau. Getting through each day was always a relief. However, there was also a slight increase in anxiety as summit night approached.

'Poly, poly...' One foot in front of the other. The mountain guides kept us motivated as we walked, constantly reminding us to walk slowly.

On the morning of day 3, just before we departed for our trek, the whole crew of 92 men, sang the Kilimanjaro song and introduced themselves while dancing and singing in Swahili. 'Jambo, jambo bwana...'

I shed a tear because I was already feeling quite worried at that point, and hearing them sing really lifted my spirits. I have no idea what they were saying but it was inspiring, calming and just the motivation that we all needed. The people really make the experience a much better place.

13,000 feet

One of my favorite days was on Day 4, climbing the Barranco Wall. It was a very slow climb because of the amount of people scrambling but this allowed for more bonding as a group. We scrambled over the Barranco Wall using all 4 of our limbs. If you decide to do this, it's recommended not to use your trekking poles on this portion of the hike.

Once we reached the top, we were at about 4,000m (13,000 feet) with a stunning stop above the clouds where we took some photos and relaxed before we made our way to Karanga Camp. I took some time to myself sipping on some fruit juice. I had forgotten what day it was and I loved it. We were completely immersed in the moment, in the now, above the clouds in complete serenity. Mount Meru was standing tall across from us, just above the cloud line where the sunset glowed with shades of purples, blues, and hints of red. It was another life up here. This was the beauty of climbing without technology. No distractions. Being able to appreciate each other's company while really being present in the now.

The night sky was glistening with mesmerizing stars. My eyes danced across the dazzling infinity of the milky way and the glow of distant galaxies. As cold as I was, I must have stood there for about thirty minutes in awe of this glorious infinite sky. I would have slept outside the tent stargazing all night, feeling little in this immense universe but fascinated in this incredible environment. It was the most beautiful, magically packed sky I had ever seen. I was frozen, not because of the cold, but because of the moment.

15,300 feet

There were only two nights where I managed to get a few hours of sleep in the whole week. The rest, I'd be lying cold in the tent growing more nervous as I felt the altitude kicking in. I could hear the sound of people coughing in the surrounding tents. I was constantly blowing my nose, which was filled with dirt and blood. The tissue was always black. People were slowly getting ill (two had already turned back down) and we still had the biggest night to face - the summit.

Breathing at this elevation was becoming a challenge. Every exhalation was a race to inhale again. Sometimes I'd fall asleep and then immediately my body would jerk, gasping for air. I was suffering from on and off migraines during the treks. Migraines so strong, I could feel my head bursting. I was sleep deprived. It was becoming increasingly harder to stay positive with everything I was feeling. But I kept going.

On Day 5, we all, very slowly, made our way to Barafu Camp and ascended to about 4645m (15,287 feet). We could see the summit so clearly from here. It was getting a lot colder now, and I was wearing a lot more layers at this point. I was becoming quieter, conserving as much energy as I could. Breathing, heavily.

On this Lemosho route, we would "climb high, sleep low" which means you reach a maximum altitude and then return to a lower height to sleep. However, six days at high altitude doesn't allow for long-term adaptations, a process that can take weeks. But this was still the best acclimatization route. And I had made it this far. I had to keep walking.

Sara and I had managed to stay strong even though we started feeling slightly miserable. Once we reached Barafu Camp in the afternoon, I could tell something was wrong. Sara was really quiet, concerned. Just like me. I tried to keep her motivated, although I was struggling myself. We were getting emotional and worried about summit night.

I started to feel dizzy, and I was losing my appetite. *Please be hungry. Please be hungry.* I tried doing the "hamburger test." But it didn't work. The hamburger test was my strategy to see if I still had my appetite - I was craving a big juicy burger on most days of the trek. Barafu Camp this was the second time I had failed the hamburger test. The thought of it made me nauseous. I ran through all my favourite foods on my mind, but I failed to crave them all. *Oh no. A sign of altitude sickness*, I thought. *Loss of appetite*. I knew how much I needed to eat because summit night was only a handful of hours away.

Sara said she didn't feel hungry either. It was the first time I had seen her like that. I felt really worried for her and I wanted to take care of her and myself at the same time. We ended up sitting near the exit of the tent during lunch just in case we have to run out and throw up. I told her to eat even though I didn't feel like eating.

She said, 'We have to try. We have to eat. We need the energy.' She slowly started drinking the soup, and I did my best to follow. I probably wouldn't have if I didn't see her try, but we helped each other get through those little challenges.

Back in the tent, we prepared our summit bags - I removed everything from my bag that would add to the weight because in thin air, everything weighs a ton more. We got all our summit layers and snacks ready. I put my water bottles inside a sock, and turned them upside down as Steve, our guide told us that it would make it less likely to freeze on summit night.

I had found some chocolates I really liked in my "emergency food summit" bag - this I had saved, in case I'd lose my appetite. I gave one to Sara and told her it would make her feel better and we managed to get back to a better spirit and share some laughs.

Although, we were still emotional, it was now 5pm. This was a really early night for us to attempt to sleep before being awoken at 11:30pm to get ready to summit.

I remembered reading and learning about all the symptoms and consequences of altitude sickness before I left. Symptoms including: headache, difficulty breathing, nausea, dizziness, loss of appetite. I was worried I hadn't eaten hardly anything in the past few hours because of the nausea. I was checking through the symptoms that I was going through and knew I had to drink more water, get myself to eat more and stay strong to avoid the more serious type of altitude sickness, HACE.

High Altitude Cerebral Oedema is the swelling of the brain caused by a lack of oxygen. The person with HACE won't realize how ill they are and that they need help. The symptoms including: weakness, nausea, loss of coordination, feeling confused, hallucinations. The only way to treat it? Move down to a lower altitude immediately, take medication for brain swelling, bottled oxygen, if available.

But that's not all, there's also HAPE, High Altitude Pulmonary

Oedema which is a build up of fluid in the lungs. Some symptoms include a persistent cough that produces frothy sputum that may be tinged with blood, tiredness and extreme breathing difficulties.

After running all of these symptoms and illnesses through my mind I was too nervous to fall asleep. Thankfully, a couple times, I must have dozed off. I was at my most emotional state, thinking about my family but at the same time, proud of myself for making it this far.

In the dead of the night it was really quiet. I counted my blessings. All the people who supported me doing this crazy challenge and all the people who I met during the journey. I felt lucky to have a such a lovely tent mate, Sara. And lucky to have had such a good group of people by my side. I was in deep contemplation. I was reflecting on the journey and reminding myself why I did this. For me, it was about attempting an 'out of my comfort zone' challenge and doing it in Africa was always a dream of mine. I could feel my family thinking about me and sending me their strength. I missed them. I missed them so much.

Summit Night

We were now at over 15,000 feet. My heart was racing. Thumping, loudly. The time had come.

We were awoken just before midnight in the freezing weather. It was long before dawn and we'd have to reach the summit by torchlight. I put on the rest of my warm layers, my thickest mountaineering socks, along with three pairs of gloves, one inside the other and clicked on my head torch. It was time.

Slowly, very slowly, we started our ascent in the darkness. 'I'm okay, I'm okay, I got this,' I told myself. I did feel okay at first, but for only about thirty minutes.

I felt something strange happening to my body. I suddenly felt immensely fatigued. Every step up, the fatigue worsened. I kept thinking, *I should have gotten more sleep.* I was trying so hard to stay awake and focus on the steps in front of me, in the dark, but now my vision was becoming hazy. Everyone was so quiet. Occasionally, you'd hear a guide singing brief motivational words in Swahili. I wondered, how they did it in such a torturous condition. But they were experts. Heroes. And even those brief words, helped me.

After a couple of hours of dragging my legs, I felt drunk. Out of my mind. Delirious. The scene felt apocalyptic, like a horror movie. As if we were all chained up slowly dragging our bodies to the top. I could hear the sound of the wind howling and the sound of our boots swishing up the slippery bits of scree and gravelly sand. Sometimes, it was so slippery and steep that I'd fall onto the mountainside from loss of balance. I was too fatigued to even use my trekking poles to stop my fall and was slowly collapsing onto the scree slope. Every step was a painful reminder of how far I had come and how many steps we had ahead of us.

I tried not to look up because when I did, all I could see was a trail of torches in the long, dark, steep trail. Slowly blinking in a haze, I couldn't tell which ones were stars and which ones were torches. The mountain kept going, the headlamps glowing far in the distance. *Where was the summit? How much longer?* Climbing in the darkness was a real challenge. I couldn't see the top, nothing at all. And I was falling asleep on my feet.

'Focus..' I told myself. I didn't want to think negative thoughts but I was at my weakest and most miserable state. Immediately I brushed those thoughts away and tried mental tricks to try to stay awake. Every type of trick I could think of. Quick flashes went through my head. *Mom. Dad. Dani. Leo. Sun. Warmth. Bed. Bed. Bed.*

Oh no, I might puke now. I thought about stopping, it was the first time nausea had really hit me. I had to stop a few times but I didn't throw up. Nothing was working! It was hard not to become emotional. I was grunting in frustration. I was sadly going mad. At one point, I remember trying to take a few steps and actually falling asleep. I didn't realize that I was slowly dying, that I was suffering from severe altitude sickness.

I suddenly started thinking about every person and every moment that made me happy. I quickly imagined my mom hugging me, and my dad smiling at me, telling me that I could do this. I remembered that amazing steak my sister and her husband cooked for me in Canada, and that time my brother told me I was ready to climb Kilimanjaro after we trained in the Pyrenees. I saw all my friends waiting for me. They were cheering. When I shook my head, I was still walking in the dark, losing my balance, still climbing in this 45 degree incline with the speed slower than a turtle. When I looked up again, I saw a line of blurry torches walking in the dark, my head slowly falling - still confused.

Come on, sunlight! Where are you!? I was desperate for a hint of sunrise. I felt that if the sun started to shine, it would make this terrible, miserable, weak feeling go away and give me some hope.

As we climbed higher, I was weaker. The oxygen was so thin. There was barely enough air to breathe. I don't even know how I had dragged myself that far. I had now lost my coordination.

One of the guides saw me in the dark, struggling to walk alone and told me, 'You can't be sleepy, we're almost there.' He wrapped my arm in his and helped me to walk. He dragged me slowly, step by step. I couldn't even use my trekking poles to balance myself anymore.

'I'm...so...tired.-.I don't know if... I can... I need to stop and take a nap. Please, let me sleep.' I felt frustrated. I wondered if I should have taken altitude sickness medication, eaten more, slept more. But I knew that wondering about the past wouldn't have changed anything now.

My head was spinning in fatigue. I could no longer feel my brain with my body. Now, there were two men dragging me to the top. They knew how close I was. They struggled to carry me because I could barely even walk anymore and I was falling all over the place. I didn't even know if I was on the edge of a cliff or close to a fall. It was pure darkness. I needed to sit down, my hands were shivering strongly from the cold. My water was slightly frozen. I remember someone trying to give me some juice but I could barely even open my own mouth. They were trying to change my gloves and keep me warm.

I sat there on a rock, shivering, begging for a nap. I remember seeing some faces in the dark from my group saying, 'Come on Ale, you got this!' I vaguely remembered who they were while in a haze but then I saw their faces.

He was determined with a face set hard. She was crying silent tears glistening in the torchlight. They turned and trudged on very weak and very slowly. I wanted to tell her 'Keep going! You got this!' but I couldn't talk anymore. I was so proud of them all.

My eyes were now spinning in fatigue. Steve found me and looked really concerned. He said we needed to wait for the doctor, who was in the back of the queue, to have a look at me.

When she got there and measured my oxygen level, it was at about 42%. I was dying.

Normal oxygen saturation at sea level is above 95%, usually close to 100%. The doctor told me that, at the elevation we were in, something in the high 70-80 percentile would have been acceptable. I was severely lacking in oxygen.

She gave me some medication to ease the altitude sickness, and possibly my brain swelling. My lips were swollen, white from the cold. They strapped me on an oxygen tank and one of the guides had to drag me down to camp immediately. 'But I'm so close...the sun is coming out now. I can make it,' I'd said shivering. I still felt

drunk and had no control over my words.

'I'm so sorry Ale. You're going down...' said the doctor.

That was it. I felt so defeated. At that moment, I felt like collapsing. I didn't want to accept it but I had to. I knew I couldn't argue about continuing on even if I had the energy to speak up, because my life was at stake now.

18,400+ feet

I shed some tears trying to accept defeat as I stumbled back down the mountain, supported by the guide who gripped my arm tightly. I stared down at my feet watching my footsteps, ensuring I didn't slip further down the mountain. I was really confused at what had happened over the last few hours. I was slowly waking up from a nightmare. But it had really happened.

And then I saw it.

A shaft of brilliant sunlight broke through the low lying cloud. I hadn't noticed the coming dawn and I looked around to see that the darkness was disappearing and I could see my surroundings. I told the guide to stop for a minute so I could take in the moment. The sun, peeking up through the sea of clouds and lighting up the surrounding mountains with its powerful, radiant streaks of red, oranges and yellows. When I looked down, I saw how high we were from the cloud level. *Wow*. My breath was taken away by the magnitude of the mountain.

I felt alone on Kilimanjaro, but at peace and a sense of absolute gratitude. Mesmerized by the beauty, I closed my eyes and finally felt the warmth I'd been waiting for. I thought it was a moment of defeat. But that moment, brought me back to life. The sun, telling me I had made it. I looked behind me at the top and saw the summit glaciers shining so beautifully. It was so clear and so close, I felt like I was already there. I was at the top.

When I realized where I was standing, almost 5600m (18,300 feet) above sea level, less than 1-2 hours from the summit, I realized I had conquered Kilimanjaro. I was standing on the rooftop of Africa with the most spectacular sunrise and most unique and breathtaking moment I had ever experienced. Suddenly my sadness turned into a blissful happiness. It was strange feeling so sad and so happy at the same time. This is it. This is my journey. This was my summit.

I was alive. And as weak as I was, I smiled.

15,287 feet

When I was brought back to my tent in Barafu Camp, I could feel the difference with the oxygen and slight change in elevation. I already felt much better than when I was up there, but I was still weak and in such a haze. Some of the porters and cooks brought me some toast and eggs and gave me more water.

I sat alone in my tent, thinking about the others who were still up there and those who had gone back down before me. I just wanted to hug my loved ones. I still felt a bit delusional, confused, my head still spinning like a terrible hangover, wondering what happened up there. The sun was now shining so strongly that I was shedding layers off and at the same time passing out in fatigue. It took me about five hours to feel slightly normal but I still could barely have a regular conversation.

Slowly, I heard the others coming down the mountain. When Sara came back to our tent, I was happy to see her. Despite how out of it

I was, I congratulated her. After that, I recall us having a very delirious conversation about life. Altitude had gotten to both of us. But there we were, emotional yet laughing. I surprised myself when I kept my spirits high after what had happened.

I was grateful to be alive and to have gotten that far. I remembered how much I was suffering slowly each day but how I kept walking. One foot in front of the other. To even try was enough. I remembered the sunrise and how it became one of most special moments of my life. That was my summit. My realization. Not a photo near the summit sign but standing where I was feeling the deepest appreciation for life, the journey and it's beauty.

Altitude is mysterious. You can be an ultramarathon runner and be the fittest person in the world and not make it to the top. You can be the most unhealthy person physically and still make it to the top. Altitude sickness may hit you, or it may not. It affects everyone in different ways. The important thing is that you recognize it, pay attention to your body and understand when it's time to turn back down. If you can't walk yourself alone, you shouldn't be attempting to continue on.

I learned that all the training and preparation in the world can't guarantee an easier path to success. This applies to any challenge in life. The important thing is your attitude. How you approach the challenge and what you take away from it. Attitude is everything.

Kilimanjaro was my 'Everest'. My internal challenge. Constant battles of giving up and pushing through. And if you're like me, you'll want to push through no matter the pain.

But it's also important to recognize your limits. It's very common that you will face unfortunate circumstances at some point in your challenge; poor weather conditions, lack of supplies or feeling extremely ill and that's when you have to say 'It's time to turn back'. And that's okay.

In this society, it is believed that only when you complete

something to the end, you should feel accomplishment. This mentality makes it harder for dreamers. To the ones who try. People forget to recognize the important of the journey. Our mentality can get the best of us. But you have the power to make your own decisions.

I had learned all the symptoms of altitude sickness, and I was aware of all the facts, but I was too 'out of it' to understand, in that moment, what was happening to me. I was lucky that my guide found me in my weakened state and the doctor evaluated me and had that spare oxygen tank. I was lucky to be brought down safely. Otherwise, I wouldn't be here today writing this story.

I spent many days after, wondering what I could have done differently, if I had drank more water or taken the altitude sickness tablets. But the truth is, I'll never know and there's no reason to question it so much. I had taken away something beautiful from this mountain and that was enough.

Before climbing Kilimanjaro, I heard people say things like 'I wouldn't be able to live with myself if I didn't summit' or 'What will I tell people if I don't make it to the top?' I realized people had different reasons to climb Kilimanjaro. For me, it wasn't about bragging or proving someone wrong. I did it for myself. I wasn't just conquering the mountain, but conquering myself. The mountain just helped me get there.

When you invest so much energy, money and time preparing for a challenge, it's really easy to feel disappointed when you don't reach the summit. But the summit is just a small segment of the experience. Don't be so hard on yourself if you have to turn around. Being able to turn around is a bold move and will only make you stronger and more prepared for the next challenge. Say 'yes' to challenge but also 'yes' to taking care of yourself. It takes courage to prioritize safety over ego.

The summit will always be there.

I had never pushed myself as hard as I did on Kilimanjaro. Mentally and physically. I climbed out of my comfort zone and I was still on top of the world. I learned more getting to where I did than if I would have summited.

Climbing these mountains make us vulnerable and allows us to feel a different sense of being alive. It allows us to transform ourselves, to move beyond our perceived boundaries. For me, it's all about the challenge, the fear. This challenge became a life-changing, growing, and enriching experience. I believe on the other side of fear, there's always something beautiful. You come out the other side a stronger, wiser, transformed person. Some may not understand that the adventure brings such beauty, joy and satisfaction. That the struggle makes you stronger, and then, make you feel reborn.

When I close my eyes and think of Kilimanjaro, it wasn't just that moment where I reached my summit. Those torturous, long hours of dragging my legs. It was seven days of unstoppable laughter, stunning scenery and unique mesmerizing skies. Seven days of forming bonds with people, singing and dancing while trekking through diverse landscapes. You realize, wow, the Earth is pretty amazing! I'm proud of everyone and everything we experienced together. And I'm grateful for the patience, encouragement and all the support. It was heartwarming to come back down to the gate and see the crew welcome and celebrate with us with the Kilimanjaro song. They even took our boots off and washed them along with our trekking poles. Everyone was so friendly on this journey and it's them who contributed in making the journey great. When I look back now, it's those moments that really make me smile.

Mount Kilimanjaro nearly defeated me but I had an amazing journey getting there. Moments where I caught myself completely immersed in the now. In complete serenity. Experiencing things I never have before. This is what life is about. These moments. The experience.

The journey.

Instagram: **@fearlesscompass**

Website: **fearlesscompass.com**

Chapter 10

The Sober Fish Story

by Dawn Comolly

In 2014, I turned forty. I wasn't overly fussed about it; age is just a number in my opinion and my life wasn't so bad. I had everything I needed; a home, a car, a job, friends, a couple of decent holidays abroad each year and a decent social life. OK, I was single, and dating was a chore but apart from that, I was happy with my lot.

In the years preceding the big 4-0, I hadn't really thought about how I expected my life would look once I hit the milestone, but my vision would've been a skinny, coiffured, solvent, non-smoking, possibly married with at least one dependent, employed, comfortable, happy, sex bomb.

The reality couldn't have been more different. OK, I was employed and solvent and believed I was the ultimate sex bomb when drunk, but apart from that, I was a single, Tinder obsessed, childless, overweight, unfit, overemotional, argumentative, cigarette smoking, binge drinker.

I tried half-heartedly to be fab at forty. I stuck myself on yet another diet and signed up to an early morning fitness boot camp to try to release my inner Skinny Minnie, but it turned out my Skinny Minnie was a stubborn old mule and didn't fancy coming to my party. Plus, despite being an intelligent person, I was still in denial that binge drinking to excess on a regular basis was making me fat. In my humble opinion, anything in liquid form didn't stick to your hips like a donut would and so I happily quaffed away, blaming anything but the booze for the size of my not so pert backside.

From a young age, I remember alcohol. I have memories of my parents drinking wine with Sunday dinner or going to the pub on a gorgeous Saturday afternoon, the adults drinking beer in the sun while my brother and I ran around the large garden, high on a bottle of Cola and a packet of ready salted crisps. I remember wanting to be grown up, to drink this magical liquid only reserved for adults, it's exclusivity fascinating to me. I had already started exhibiting traits of a party animal; I didn't like going to bed if we had guests, I didn't like to miss out on grown up conversations and I didn't like to leave a party. At all. Ever. I have a vague memory (and photographic evidence somewhere) of refusing to leave the 1977 Silver Jubilee street party, remaining defiantly in my chair, in a mood, after everyone else had left. I was aged 3.

As the years went by, my reluctance to go home at a decent hour didn't improve. In fact, it got progressively worse with the more freedom I gained. By the time I'd left home and was living with friends, the off switch was well and truly jammed into 'on' mode.

In my twenties, I worked in Greece for a few months. My best friend and I booked a one-way ticket to Athens and spontaneously jumped on a ferry to the islands with no idea where we would end up. We settled on an island called Paros and soon realised that we weren't going to make our millions that summer. We both got jobs quite quickly but barely earnt enough to pay our rent. We existed on a diet of alcohol and little food, saving our wages for cigarettes and sugary drinks to relieve the hangover.

My thirties continued along the same theme. While my friends were getting married and having babies, I was still partying like a rock star. Whilst they would leave a gathering at a sensible hour to relieve the babysitter, I could be found sharing highly inappropriate stories in an outrageously loud voice or alternatively, crying ridiculous crocodile tears onto some poor unsuspecting soul's shoulder before unceremoniously passing out on the sofa in an alcohol induced coma.

The difference in hangovers between decades was quite astounding. There were a couple of reasons for this; age, amount of poison devoured and length of time indulging in said pursuit. The older I got, the more I drank and the longer I did it for. The hangovers were killers. All consuming, debilitating and long. In my late thirties to early forties, drinking to excess on a Friday night would render me useless until at least Sunday with no mercy.

With each awful hangover I inflicted upon myself, a little voice inside my head got louder. Is this what you really want? Is this how you want to feel? Is this how you want to live your life? Is this what it's all about? Is this it?

Alcohol doesn't discriminate. It isn't fussy whose life it takes hostage. It sneaks in, slowly at first, but soon spreads like poison ivy, damaging everything in its path. Before I realised, I was under its spell and to escape was no easy option.

But something had to change, and that thing was me.

I was drinking for many reasons, but pleasure had been pushed way down the list. At the top was stress, self-loathing and unhappiness. I was working in a highly toxic, stressful environment, was involved in a damaging relationship, was morbidly overweight, had zero self-confidence and above all else, I didn't believe there was any alternative. I mean, why would anyone consider sobriety unless you were a proper fully blown alcoholic?

Despite much debate, I choose not to label myself. I wasn't physically dependent on alcohol, but, without doubt, I had a massive issue with it. If I must be labelled, I prefer to categorise myself as the ultimate binger. I binge drank, binge ate (still do in some circumstances) and binge smoked. Nothing could satisfy the beast.

I didn't drink or smoke every day and could go for substantial periods of time without both. I believed, naively, for many years that I was ok, that my drinking was normal. I ignored that I drank/smoked/ate my quota in one sitting rather than spread over a period of time. I ignored that I was physically sick most weekends, wasting time lying in bed, waiting for the waves to subside. I ignored that alcohol was damaging my brain to such an extent that I was blacking out. I ignored that alcohol made me do things I wouldn't dream of doing in the sober light of day.

In short, I was in complete alcohol fuelled denial. I was in my own self-inflicted hell.

My relationship with alcohol was horrendous; it was a form of self-harm. It was a perpetual cycle of self-sabotage to such an extent that I just didn't care about the physical effects; damaging my liver, killing my brain cells, destroying my stomach lining and sucking the life out of my skin. The eczema I had suffered from since I was a child was sore and out of control, my tummy was constantly irritated, and I endured repetitive ear infections from smoking. I was always tired, moody, emotional, overweight, self-loathing, anxious. My body was screaming out for me to stop but I just carried on regardless.

And then it happened. In the summer of 2016, aged forty-one, an article randomly popped up in my Facebook feed, showing before and after photos of people who had stopped drinking for long periods of time. I was intrigued. The difference between photos was astounding. I mean, they looked like entirely different people. And suddenly I knew what I needed to do. This was it. I needed to get sober.

I began by researching sobriety online. I needed to know exactly how someone would go about giving up the biggest crutch of the 21st century. Was it possible? Could I do it? Could I do it alone? Can one survive without a glass of wine to sort them out after a hard day? What were the alternatives? How did sober people celebrate a special occasion? My pickled brain was spinning.

I read a variety of articles by a range of people from all walks of life. The key advice was to break time into small chunks, taking one day at a time. For most people who'd been guzzling the strong stuff for most of their adult life, forever was way too big to contemplate, however a few days or weeks at a time was far more manageable. I also needed a target to work towards, after all this wasn't forever. I needed to know there was an end to my challenge when I could retreat to my old life and pick up where I left off. I decided on a year, convincing myself that 365 days wasn't that long. I mean if pregnant women managed to go without for nine months, I could do this, no problem.

Once I'd made my decision, I started telling my friends and family about my idea. My reasoning was that by making myself accountable, I was more likely to succeed. Ironically, this became the fundamental basis for my continuing success. If I put it out there to the world, there was no going back.

I received a mixed bag of reactions to my quest. I could tell that some people thought it was a pipe dream, others thought it was a joke. Some were curious, and some were indifferent. Most were supportive, some were silent. Some just disappeared.

As the news leaked among friends, I was busy leaking the news online. I set up a Facebook page named 'Sober for 2017' and a friend set up a website for me. The intention was to use these facilities as an online diary about the pitfalls of sobriety. I imagined it would mostly be about moaning how unfair life was without my old friend Sauvignon but as I hoped I'd lose a few pounds along the way, I planned on using my own 'before and after' shots as an inspiration to carry on. I honestly thought no one would care.

The plan was to have my last glass of Prosecco at midnight on New Year's Eve 2016/2017.

The aim was to be stood by a clock, glass in hand, my last sip caught by the camera.

The vision was to document the highs and lows of my journey for the year and my intention was to get absolutely slaughtered on the following New Year's Eve to celebrate my victory.

The stage was set. Dawn was saying yes to sobriety. Dawn the party animal was going Sober (and smoke free) for 2017.

After I had decided that 2017 would be all about the abstinence, I was headhunted in October 2016 for a new job. The offer was too good to refuse but came with its share of alcohol fuelled fear. What if I hated it? What if I regretted my decision? What if it was the worst move I'd ever made? The fear was eating me up inside, stressing me out, but to the outside world I was doing just fine.

As well as a massive change in my work life, my love life was also taking a hard hit. I had been involved for the best part of 18 months with someone who had been playing me for a fool. I knew that, for as long as I was drinking alcohol, I would allow him a place in my life and that the only way for the contact to be broken was for me to get sober.

It was another nail in my alcohol coffin.

Most of my stress was internalised but slowly started spilling to the outside. I was massively overweight, which was causing pain in my hips and knees. My face was bloated and blotchy. I had suffered from eczema since I was a child and whilst it had mostly been under control for 40 years, it was now spreading uncontrollably across my body like a wild fire, popping up in places it had never been before. No amount of scratching would satisfy it. No amount of cream would stop it. I wasn't sleeping well, and I was mostly tired, irritable and emotionally drained. I was a sad, sorry mess.

After leaving my former job, starting my new job and getting rid of my relationship, I got ill. Not just a common cold but proper, full blown ill. Bedridden, hallucinating, dying ill. My ears went deaf, I couldn't move, I couldn't stay awake. I couldn't eat. But most of all, I couldn't drink, and I couldn't smoke. I now believe it was no coincidence that my body was finally turning in on itself, after all I'd been hammering it for 25 years, continually poisoning it, feeding it rubbish food, drowning its obvious warning signs and filling it with smoke. No wonder it had had a gutful.

By default, my 'experiment' to become sober had started earlier than I thought. My sparkly new sobriety date was 27 November 2016.

It was nerve racking putting myself out there for the first time, admitting publicly that I had a problem with a substance, especially when that substance is considered socially acceptable and was intrinsically linked to every part of my life. It still amazes me to this day that if you decide that you're smoking too much and want to give up, you're applauded and supported and encouraged with your quest. You're not asked when you're going back on the fags; it's assumed your decision is forever, not a temporary whim.

Soberdom is not for the faint hearted. It is a destination with an uninspiring reputation. It's considered dull, boring, lonely and no one choses to go there willingly. In fact, the only people who do go there are considered to have no hope and usually don't stay long. However, if by some miracle they choose not to return to the normal world, you'll probably never hear from them again as they retreat into a world of water, kale and misery. After all, everybody believes there is no joy in sobriety.

Surprisingly, despite its bad press, I started receiving private messages from people curious about my temporary destination. My public admission that I had a problem was starting to encourage my friends to question their own habits, their own consumption, their own demise. People I'd thought drank little or handled their drinks well, were saying they were struggling. Party animals were agonisingly regretting their past. People told me about their family members who had been affected by drinking or about relatives still in the throes of addiction.

I was beginning to understand that alcohol was a far bigger problem than I ever could have imagined, that no one's life goes unscathed from the drug we are led to believe is so innocent, all wrapped up in a shiny glass bottle with a pretty label. It transpired that there are thousands of us sat at home at night, looking for the answer at the bottom of a bottle when ironically, the answer couldn't be further away from it. I learned that I was not alone, that there was a whole big massive gang of us, unhappy and drunk, wishing there was another way. I decided there and then, my mission was to find another way.

Christmas 2016 arrived. I had been sober for four weeks. I felt a bit of a fraud as had mainly been in bed blowing my nose and hallucinating, but I was also pleased that I had started well ahead of my original start date of 1 January 2017. For a brief, fleeting moment, I did consider drinking 'just for Christmas' but soon dismissed that thought as just plain crazy after all, my rationale was that as I'd started early, I could finish early, guaranteeing a boozy Christmas for the end of my experiment.

The first sober Christmas was hard. It is only once you stop drinking alcohol that you realise just how entrenched it is in our society. It is advertised morning, noon and night, on TV, radio and magazines, not to mention social media. It is served for breakfast, lunch and dinner. It's injected into crisps and soaps and candles. It's subtly dumped into mince pies and desserts.

To attempt to 'fit in' and to convince my inner child that we weren't missing out, I bought myself an abundance of treats ranging from alcohol free wine and cordials, to boxes of Lindor Balls, chocolate and ice cream. At each Christmas event I attended, I arrived with my bag full of my sober options, the bottles rattling louder than when I was drinking, and left high as a kite on sugar.

But, things didn't feel the same. The party animal was struggling. I felt quieter, less engaging and no fun at all. I was impatient with my friends once they'd had a few beverages, their drunken happiness a niggling irritation to my sober state. I felt antsy, frustrated and despite my best efforts, like I was massively missing out. Overwhelmingly, I felt like I didn't belong.

Slowly but surely, I started to understand that sobriety was not just about swapping my drink for a non-alcoholic version. Alcohol had influenced absolutely every part of my life from morning until night for the last 25 years, and to remove it meant huge change. Its removal would dictate what I did to relax, for fun, who I hung out with, what I enjoyed. It would change the foods I ate, my daily routine, my sleep patterns. Sobriety was about a lifestyle change, not just a choice of refreshment.

The early days of sobriety are not easy. I'd be lying if I said they were. It's akin to trying to do your morning routine backwards or landing in a foreign country where you don't speak the language. You have a constant feeling that you're wearing the wrong clothes or turned up to school on the wrong day, that something is wrong or missing. You have an intense internal nagging, a tiny voice reminding you of what you think you need to survive. The reason for this is due to stepping out of your comfort zone and discarding the trusty old comfort blanket of booze.

It was also interesting how much everyone else cared about my sobriety, as if it affected their drinking habits directly. They still do. People were intrigued, inquisitive, interested, in awe. It appeared to matter much more to everyone else what I had in my glass than it did to me. People also like to justify their own drinking habits to me 'oh I've only had a couple' or 'I don't drink in the week', unaware they were halfway through a bottle, on a Wednesday.

By spring 2017, the blog had started to gather momentum. I began to share my ideas and my journey with the outside world, not just within my friend zone. I had found some online groups that were and still are, fundamental in my recovery. The support received from these groups was phenomenal. They were happy for me to share my musings and as a result, my gang of sober stars grew daily. I started Slimming World in the New Year to prevent me becoming one big giant Lindor Ball, started doing a couple of long walks each week (for the same reason), made lots of virtual sober friends and as the alcohol fog began to clear, began to see just how much alcohol had disrupted my life.

My health however, had other ideas. My dedication to sobriety was rewarded with a stinking cold every month and my eczema showed no signs of getting better. I tried taking a selection of vitamins, added hemp to my diet and changed all my beauty products to natural and organic. I bought a new duvet (hypoallergenic), a new mattress and, out of sheer desperation, considered swapping my sofa after becoming convinced I must be allergic to something I was spending a lot of time with. Despite these minor health issues, I was euphoric when I hit 90 days sober. It felt like such a massive achievement as it was the longest time I'd spent on my rickety old wagon during the whole of my adult life. The overwhelming tiredness of the first few months had passed, and I was now sleeping better than ever. My eyes were brighter, my clothes were looser and due to an abundance of energy, I was far more productive during the day.

June was the month of change. I happily celebrated being alcohol free for 6 months by booking myself a solo trip to Thailand in 2018, I bought a new car and I employed a cleaner with my redundant wine money. I entered an online challenge called 'Walking Challenge' and pledged to walk two hundred miles in thirty days. I attended my first sober meet up in London and had the overwhelming feeling that I had met my tribe, that I could finally socialise sober in a sober environment.

I also made the final decision that I wanted to remain sober for life.

There were endless reasons why sobriety was the only valid conclusion for me. My skin, hair and eyes all shone with health and vitality. I was happy. I was content. My moods were stable. I wasn't making stupid, uninformed decisions. Overall, my life was just better, and alcohol had no part in it.

In July, I went on my first sober holiday and admit I was apprehensive. For me, alcohol had always been a massive part of a trip away, starting with a large glass at the airport and finishing only hours before I came home. I was going to the South of France to stay at a friend's holiday home where I'd visited many times before and I was concerned that the triggers would be high.

I found the airport was far less stressful without a hangover or the need for a goblet of the white stuff. I weirdly enjoyed being present and alert and my flying time was used to sleep, not guzzle.

What I didn't find so stress free was arriving in Toulouse, blissfully unaware it was Bastille Day, a public holiday like Christmas Day, and that there were no trains running to my destination. Using google translate and my pidgin GCSE French, I managed to understand that I needed to get a bus and that it would take several hours to get where I needed to be. 'Drinking me' would've had to deal with all of this with a stonking hangover from the night before, followed by a top up on the way there. 'Sober me' took it all in my stride, remaining calm and positive that everything would be ok in the end.

On previous holidays, lie-ins were a necessity mainly due to atrocious hangovers, however one of the massive changes that comes with sobriety is your body clock reverting to a child. 'Party animal me' used to only see sunrise when the soiree had gone on a tad too long, but now they were a staple part of my sobriety armour. On every day of my holiday, I awoke fresh, before the sun, got changed and headed out to the beautiful French countryside for my morning walk. My overwhelming feeling though, was that in all the years I'd visited this stunning part of the world, I'd never actually left the safety of the house (and the fridge) to explore. I vowed that, never again, would a substance stop me enjoying the natural beauty of our world. It was the first holiday I returned from refreshed and without needing another holiday to detox.

In October, I celebrated my first alcohol free birthday. The previous year, my birthday had been a mammoth session starting at lunchtime and ending in the early hours the following day. I remembered very little about it. This year, I booked a table at an expensive restaurant I had been wanting to try for a long time, reasoning that if I was only drinking sparkling water, I could eat what I liked. Unfortunately, while out walking that morning, I'd hurt my back and spent most of the day lying on my floor, unable to fathom how I was going to make it to the restaurant which was 20 miles away. But I did, and despite my back pain, it was an enjoyable evening, however I was happy to get home, take some pain killers and hopefully sleep.

November came, and I was both excited and apprehensive. I couldn't wait to celebrate the end of my personal challenge, but I was also growing increasingly sad that it was over. I had enjoyed setting myself mini targets, was ecstatic at how the blog had become so popular and how many chums I had made and relished the support I had received. But what if this was it? What if I just became another alcohol-free statistic once it was done?

But I needn't have worried. I hit my Soberversary, a whole 365 days without booze, and marked the occasion with my first ever tattoo. I was inundated with messages of congratulations, received cards, flowers and gifts and went to the pub (shock horror) to celebrate with friends and family. I had completed the biggest challenge of my life however instead of my life being over as I had imagined at the start of the experiment, my real life had only just begun.

The saying goes 'you only have two lives. The second begins when you realise you only have a one'. This is one of my favourite quotes and sums up how I feel about sobriety beautifully. Once I stopped knocking back alcohol like it was the freshest water from a Highland spring and decided to halt the damage I was doing to my amazing body and precious brain, my wonderful life began to unfold in front of me.

Sober people have always been considered as the outsiders, the oddballs and the minority, because their choice is to refrain from swallowing a lethal substance. How utterly random is that? Can you imagine the same scenario with another drug like heroin for example? If you could only fit in with your social circle if you injected it on a Friday night? Or your ideal night in was with your friends and a load of needles? Or imagine plastering what a great night you were having on social media whilst shooting up a syringe? No? That's because we've all been conditioned that drinking ethanol is perfectly acceptable, that exhibiting what you are drinking on a weekend like a strange kind of trophy is normal and that drinking to oblivion is 'just what we do'.

I sometimes feel like sobriety is like a secret club, a bit like a cult or a religion, which until you fully embrace it, you can't quite understand.

I believe that in the future, society will view sobriety as the norm, rather than the outcast place it is deemed to be now.

I hope that in time, alcohol will become as taboo as smoking has in the last twenty years, that it will be recognised for the harmful toxin it really is and that there will be more low cost help available for those affected.

I pray that it will become socially unacceptable to drink until you're sick or unable to move, that this behaviour is seen as an externalisation of damage being done inside, rather than someone in this state becoming a YouTube star whilst their friends hysterically laugh at their plight.

Saying YES to sobriety is a freedom like no other. For me, it is a blessed relief not to have to think about a substance constantly or plan to drink something that was killing me slowly, like an insane drip feed suicide.

Alcohol clouded my judgement about myself. It gave me false hope that I would feel better, that I would be a happier, shinier version of me. Instead, it made me feel a failure, unworthy, fat, unlovable. It was a fun sponge. It made me sad, depressed & distorted my view of the world and myself. It stole all the good bits of me and replaced them with bad.

Alcohol made me believe it was my friend, that I needed it in my life to be more confident, funnier, sexier, a better person.

Alcohol is a lying bastard.

Saying YES to sobriety has literally given me my life back. I love the person I have become, and I have no intention of going back to where I came from. Saying YES was the best gift I gave myself and for that I will always be truly grateful.

Website: **www.soberfish.co.uk**

Facebook: **soberfishie**

Twitter: **@soberfishie**

Instagram: **@soberfishie**

Chapter 11

The Choices We Make

by Jon Doolan

Making The Bike Decision

'So you buy the bike, yes?'

I was stood in a bike shop. That's a pretty good place to buy a bike I suppose.

The difference was that this bike shop was not your usual bike shop. I mean it *was* a bike shop. It didn't sell flying broomsticks or anything. It's just that this bike shop was in Phuket in Thailand and I was planning to cycle from Phuket to Bangkok.

'Wow! That's incredible!' you might say. You might be in awe of people who embark on epic cycling adventures. Maybe you think they must all be exciting and courageous individuals. Good for you.

But that's not me. I'm not a cyclist. I haven't sat on a bike since I gave up my paper round when I was fifteen.

In fact, I actively detest cycling.

It's not the cycling itself. It's the fact that I'm petrified that I'll get a puncture. Absolutely terrified. I'd say my mechanical skills are akin to a monkey with a monkey wrench. If ever I got a flat tyre on my paper round as a kid I'd pay my younger brother to fix it for me.

So what was I doing choosing a bike in a bike shop in Thailand?

The plan hadn't even been to buy a bike. The plan had been to purchase a rickshaw, a pedal-powered three wheeled contraption, and cycle half the length of the country with my best mate Harry. He was far more mechanically minded than me so I felt that I was in safe hands. However, his fitness left a little something to be desired. I'd taken him on two ultra-endurance events the previous year and he had DNFed both of them. He was about as physically fit as a jar of marmalade.

So, my cunning plan had been to combine our two talents, his vehicle maintenance with my superior aerobic fitness, and we'd ride a rickshaw north along the coast.

It was a genius idea. We could take it in turns cycling (with myself doing the lion's share) while the other person sat in the back relaxing or running ahead to get awesome video footage to later turn into an award winning adventure video.

The only problem was that I'd forgotten that Thailand had moved on since the 1920s and no one rode rickshaws anymore. In fact, the only 3 wheeled vehicle tended to be a motorbike with a sidecar and a family of 12 hanging off of it.

So the alternative was to buy a pair of bikes. Only with the idea of cycling the entire way now on the cards, Harry was far less enthusiastic about the idea.

'Mate, I'm not getting one,' he said as he stood next to me in the bike shop, his arms emphatically crossed against his chest, 'but if you really want to get one, you should.'

The bike guy casually picked his nose as he eyed me suspiciously. 'Where you go on bike?' he asked.

'I'm cycling to Bangkok,' I told him confidently.

'No way!' he said, his mouth dropping open and his itchy left nostril forgotten. 'You no get to Bangkok on this bike.' He stepped away from the mountain bike that he had been showing me. The cheapest bike in the shop. 'This bike, you go to Bangkok, maybe.' He rested a hand on a high-end piece of advanced machinery. Just with a simple lift of the cross bar I could feel the price rise.

He told me the cost and I was flabbergasted. I didn't even know bikes *could* be that expensive. I could have bought a small car for the fee he was asking of that bicycle.

'No, no, no,' I said lifting my hand off of the bike like I'd burned myself. 'I can't afford that.'

'So are going to buy the bike or not, Jon?' asked Harry motioning toward the cheap mountain bike.

'Umm.'

Starting off

Half an hour later I was £170 lighter but was riding down a sandy country road with the wind whistling through the holes in my helmet and a grin spreading across my face like the Cheshire Cat.

The guy in the shop, once he'd finished rearranging his bogies, had thrown a helmet, water bottle, bike repair kit, under-seat bag and a frame bag into the bargain as well. I'm sure he thought I was going to be found underneath the wheels of an articulated lorry so had appeased his conscience by flinging random pieces of kit at me that would aid my journey. I didn't mind at all.

The best thing he gave me though was a little bell for my handle bars. The bell itself wasn't special and the only time I ever used it was to get an errant chicken out of the my path. The thing that was special about it was the fact that it housed a tiny compass. I took great pleasure in following the little N northwards.

I whizzed away from the bike shop and headed back to the resort that I'd been staying in with Harry.

I pulled my bike up to the reception desk and demounted (Unmounted? Dethroned?). Within minutes I had changed, dragged my bag out of my room and found Harry in the beachside bar.

'Mate? What are you wearing?' said Harry wryly.

'Don't you like it?'

'Yeah, I love it. But what actually is it?'

'It's a Union Jack morph suit,' I said, as if that's something that everyone wears.

'You look like a complete doofus,' said Harry, unhelpfully.

'Are you sure you're happy lugging my bag around the country?'

'Yeah, yeah. Whatever.'

'And you're *sure* you're going to be ok?'

'Yeah, mate. I'm going to go surfing for the rest of the week. Are you going to wear that for the whole cycle?'

'Yes. I'm not taking a change of clothes with me. Anyway, I better be off now. I'll see you in a few days.'

Harry came out to the front of the resort to see me off. He embraced me in a long man hug. 'Be safe,' he said.

'Yeah, I will,' I said taking my first pedal away from the only person I knew in the whole country.

I was off.

About 50m down the road I stopped my bike abruptly. I'd just had a horrific thought.

'HARRY,' I shouted back to the floppy haired dude as he stood in the middle of the road waving. 'DID I LEAVE MY MAP WITH YOU?' Then I remembered that I'd packed the map in my small rucksack with my DSLR camera. 'AH, DON'T WORRY. I THINK I'VE GOT IT.'

'YOU'RE A MORON!' he yelled after me.

Wat a Brilliant Start!

I was heading north. The sound of the sea roared like a stadium crowd heard from a few streets away. I couldn't see it beyond the hotel resorts and the thick jungle that ran along the coast but I knew it was there. I could smell it.

I knew I couldn't get lost. I was heading north, following the little compass on my bike bell.

I'd also memorised the map the night before. This wasn't as challenging as it might sound. There was only one road that went my way. The number 4 highway.

Very soon though, the fast and direct highway 4 lost its appeal to me. I quickly grew tired of the trucks and cars that zoomed past within metres of my handlebars. This wasn't the Thailand cycle I had envisaged for myself. I took the first opportunity and, at an old, dilapidated bus stop near a junction, I gratefully turned off the main road and headed towards the coast.

It was idyllic. It was exactly what I had expected it would be. Exactly what I had dreamed of. I was slowly pootling along a sand strewn road surrounded by jungle letting the heat of the sun warm my back and the breeze cool my skin.

All of my responsibilities were 7,000 miles away. I had all I needed with me: the clothes I stood up in; a camera to record my adventure and a bottle of water to quench my thirst. Even my phone had stopped working, which could have stressed me out but actually made me feel even more free. I had not a single worry in the world. I felt like Baloo singing 'The Bare Necessities'.

I breathed the sea air deeply and whooped with delight.

I sucked the last of the warm liquid out of my water bottle as I freewheeled down a hill into a heavily forested stretch. Sweat had started to trickle down between my shoulder blades and my tongue felt warm and furry. 'I'm going to stop at the next roadside café that I see,' I promised myself as I rolled past some ramshackle houses.

Soon I spotted a massive ubiquitous Coca Cola sign outside a building and I rolled my bike under the awning.

I spied an older lady who was bent double over a washing bowl scrubbing some dishes. 'Is this a restaurant?' I said using the international language of speaking slowly and loudly.

She looked at me with mix confusion and terror in her small eyes, like a rabbit caught in the headlights. Other small faces appeared at the windows like baby rabbits.

The old lady barked an instruction at the children and one of them, a well fed lad in a Real Madrid football shirt, came out of his house, walked bare-footed to the end of the block and shouted something.

A young man came around the corner, pulling a white shirt over a tightly muscled body.

'Hello, how can I help you?' said the beaming man in near perfect English.

'I'm sorry to intrude,' I started, removing my helmet politely. 'I'm looking for a café?'

'Do you want something to drink or eat?' he asked.

'Yes,' I said. 'Do you have any fizzy drinks? That would be perfect.'

'Please, sit down,' he motioned to a white plastic garden chair. He spoke quietly to the elderly lady who bustled over to a fridge, removed a bottle of Coke and brought it over to me.

The man in the white shirt introduced himself as Bam. He sat smiling in a chair next to me and started asking about where I was from and what I was doing cycling along his road. I told him my intention to get all the way to Bangkok in 4 days and he seemed suitably impressed.

'So, whose café is this then?' I asked Bam as the old lady found a clean glass and placed it in front of me.

'This isn't a café,' said Bam. 'This is our home.'

'Oh, I'm so sorry for intruding.' I stood to go, ashamed at my invasion of their personal space, but Bam motioned for me to sit, his smile expanding broadly.

'So you want to see the real culture of the Thai people?' he asked. 'Would you like to see our temple?'

'That would be amazing,' I said. 'Is it close?'

'We'll go on my moped.'

'Oooooo Kay!' I said. Immediately my thoughts were to what my wife would say if she knew that I was about to climb aboard a moped with a stranger with nothing more than a flimsy bike helmet to stop my brains getting smashed in on the sandy road.

At least I had a helmet. Bam's black hair tousled with the wind as we sped along towards the coast.

Soon we pulled up in front of Bam's temple. The carved wooden wat towered above the palm trees as the surf gently rolled against the beach nearby. It's intricately etched eaves and panels depicted different scenes from Buddhism. Probably. I don't really know what the carved figures were doing but you'd assume it's got something to do with the religion, right?

'The temple was carved by hand,' said Bam puffing his chest out proudly.

'Incredible,' I said, genuinely awed as I gazed up at the painted gold flames that danced across the portico.

'Would you like to come in?'

'I would love to,' I said grinning.

We removed our shoes and stepped over the threshold to find a solemnly dark and cool room. I was strongly aware of my apathy towards religion but I couldn't help but be inspired by the tranquility that seemed to descend on us as we entered. A lone man sat cross legged on the carpet in front of a collection of marble deities surrounded by floral offerings. We daren't disturb him so we quickly exited and Bam filled me in on his religious commitments as we walked across the temple compound.

'We come to the temple once a week but it's important to meditate every day. We are vegetarians and we eat only one meal a day.'

'Wow!' I said impressed. Not about the vegetarianism. I reckon that's pretty standard, but only one meal a day. That's commitment.

'It helps us appreciate our food.'

'I bet it does! What about the monks? What do they eat?' I asked as I noticed a bald dude in an orange robe exit a nearby building.

'Yes, they are vegetarian too.'

'No, I mean, where do they get their food from?'

'Offerings,' said Bam. 'We give them, what is the word...' he waved his hand as if he was physically grasping for the words from thin air. 'Alms.'

'Wow!' I said, once again impressed, this time with Bam's impressive English vocabulary.

Soon we were back on the moped and skidding along the road towards Bam's house. Black clouds had suddenly appeared overhead like a really bad magic trick and big plops of rain started pounding the ground like tiny watery napalm bombs. Just as the heavens really opened we bumped down off the road and under the awning in front of his home. It was like the Buddhist gods had been unhappy with my ignorance about their religion.

Rain hammered off of the tin roof like a thousand tiny steel drummers had moved across from the Caribbean and taken up a residence on the top of Bam's house. We collapsed back onto the plastic garden furniture water dripping onto the concrete floor.

'Have you had any lunch?' said Bam, jumping to his feet.

'I haven't, no,' I said.

'I'll get you something,' he said disappearing into his house quicker than I could say 'no'.

Bam's three young boys came to investigate the bike and the idiot who was riding it. I busied myself by showing them my camera and letting them snap photos of each other. Soon Bam was back with a steaming bowl of rice and stir-fried vegetables. 'I'm sorry I don't have any more,' he said as he placed it in front of me.

'No, no. This is perfect. Thank you.' I chowed down gratefully as we discussed how his wife worked as a maid in a local tourist resort, how his boys were on holiday from school and how two of his buffalo had been struck by lightning the previous year. You know, the usual banter.

It was partway through my fourth mouthful that I realised that I was the only one eating. Bam was sat politely nearby his hands folded demurely into his lap. Bam's three boys were a little less obvious, their jaws pretty much lying on the floor, their tongues rolling out and their hungry eyes bulging like a gaggle of cartoon characters.

'Are you not going to eat?' I whispered to Bam, while I kept my eyes glued to the boys as they sat watching my bowl like three salivating labradors.

'Oh, no. We've already eaten our meal today,' Bam grinned.

The rain eased off and I was soon climbing aboard my bike to search for horizons new. Bam had shunned the idea of me paying for my food or drink or even offering anything for the impromptu temple visit. He was just pleased that he had had a chance to show me a tiny snippet the real life of the Thai people and not just the sterilised, westernised insides of a holiday resort.

I turned and thanked Bam and his family for their kindness and hospitality. Bam and the boys waved with enthusiastic smiles as I cycled away into the rain. Even the old lady raised a wrinkly arm in farewell.

I faced into the last of drizzle and cycled on, dodging puddles with a belly full of rice and the warmth of humanity. I thought of Bam a lot as the rain eventually stopped and the wet road quickly dried in the tropical heat. He didn't have much in life but what he had he shared. He gave offerings to the monks and to the temple. He supported his family and that old lady (whoever she was). He even fed a stranger who appeared on his doorstep riding a bike and dressed as a flag. I wondered whether his generosity came as a result of his Buddhist religion and how much of it came from just being an awesome guy? How much of it was enforced by some long dead prophet and how much was simply the 'kindness of strangers'?

About an hour later the country lane I'd been cycling along spat me unceremoniously back out on the number 4 highway. As if to emphasise the fact that I was leaving the tranquility of rural Thailand, a massive lorry carrying construction waste rumbled past within a hair's breadth of my front wheel kicking dust up into my face.

'Oh well,' I thought resigning myself to my fate of sharing the road with these carbon monoxide belching beasts for the most of the rest of my journey north. 'But at least you just leapfrogged a whole length of the highway by riding those country lanes.'

I looked back down the road. What was that I could see just a hundred yards away? Hold on. That looks very familiar.

It was a dilapidated bus stop. Exactly the same dilapidated bus stop I'd seen some four hours previous.

'You're kidding me!' I moaned out loud as I stared up to the gods.

I'd been aware that the little compass on my bike bell had danced around like a hyperactive ballerina as I'd meandered down the country lanes. I hadn't realised that I'd just ridden randomly around a peninsula for the best part of the afternoon.

Fudge nuggets!

I glanced down at my watch. I was going to have to get a shift on if I was going to reach my night time stop before sun down.

I put the pedal to the metal and put my head down and all those other phrases that mean I cycled faster than was strictly healthy in the heat.

The day wore on and finally, exhausted, I found a hotel for the night. And not just any hotel. For the price of a Big Mac meal I had an air-conditioned room with a shower that had warm running water and a double bed all to myself. I didn't know that adventuring would be this luxurious!

I removed every item of clothing and hung it all up to dry before diving into the shower and collapsing into my bed naked.

The End of the World

I left before dawn and headed north into the mountains. A whole day of cycling passed and I found myself on Highway 4 about 6km from Kapoe, my destination for the evening. Like the ache in my bum, the day wore on and soon the sun was setting in the sky casting red hues across the jungle.

It was then that the worst catastrophe in the world happened.

This was worse than the earth opening under my feet.

Worse than a meteor smashing into the earth.

Worse than World War 3!

I got a puncture.

Move over, Aron Ralston. Here's a real adventure dilemma. Yes, you were stuck for 127 hours between a rock and a... well another rock. But at least you had the skills and knowledge in how to chop off your own hand.

Here I was stuck in the middle of the Thai jungle with less understanding of how to fix a puncture than a spaniel with a spanner.

I pulled a tiny shard of metal out of my rear tyre and stared at it in a mixture of rage and despair. I looked up and down the deserted road for help but it was obviously dinner time. Or the Thai version of Eurovision was on. Whatever the case, no one was there to help me.

Suddenly, from out of nowhere, an immense sense of calm and resignation settled over me. I was on this adventure on my own. I was the only one who could sort this situation. I was the only one getting myself out of this mess.

So I did what any sane person would do.

I began walking.

I knew I was 6km away from Kapoe because the Thai government had very kindly paced little white pillars with the distance in km to the next town painted on them. I'd manage to decipher some of the elaborate symbols and I'd learnt to recognise that 'O' 'n' 'two squiggles' 'b' q' 'l' 'o' meant Kapoe. By my reckoning it would take me about an hour and half of walking to get to the town. I stared at the darkening sky ominously.

I'd only walked about 200m when I came across a shack by the side of the road selling soft drinks. The decision to stop and get a drink wasn't a difficult one. If I was going to be walking along the road in the dark then I may as well be hydrated and full of sugar. I bought a bottle of green Fanta (I think it was pretending to be watermelon but just tasted of fizzy glucose) and a non-descript packet of biscuits.

The man behind the counter looked at me sideways. I was used to this. I was dressed as a Union Jack after all. But when I picked up my bike and started to walk away from his shack he ran over.

He pointed to my blatantly flat back wheel and beckoned me over to his house which was behind his roadside shack. A group of children and a couple of men were lounging about on the porch chatting in their wonderful sing-song language.

Sack, as he introduced himself, and another man who was clearly his brother, Bow, took my bike from me and with a couple of moped tyre irons started to remove the back tyre. I felt pretty useless as I just stood watching these two mechanics working away in the dim light of the single bulb.

In minutes they had the back wheel off, the tyre removed and the spare inner tube in place (yes, that's right. I even had a spare inner tube and still didn't know how to replace the damn thing). They used an electric pump to inflate tyre and soon I was back on two functioning wheels again.

They then offered me a bowl of thin soup with rice. It was while eating their offering (and noting that, once again, no one else ate either) I saw the piles of broken down mopeds nearby. I'd obviously got the puncture within metres of a moped repair shop, the one group of engineers who would know exactly what to do to fix my problem. Serendipity is a wonderful thing sometimes!

I finished my meal, which Sack and Bow refused to take payment for, and I was on my way once again with a cheery 'Cop-un-crap' as I left.

The Thai people are incredible!

I rolled into Kapoe well after dark to find the shop keepers closing their shutters. They pointed me towards a hotel around the corner and I cycled up an eerie road to find it. The darkness made everything seem so dangerous and my heart was in my throat with fear. A dog barking like a maniac in the near distance didn't help matters.

Soon though I'd found the hotel and a round teenager manning the front desk gave me a key and returned to the reality TV programme he'd been watching.

Once again I was blessed with a beautiful, clean, cool double room with air conditioning and a warm shower. I'd been cycling on and off for 14 hours so sleep found me quickly.

Mr. Packow

I was way behind schedule. I'd had only averaged 80 miles a day when I should have been well into triple figures. In a vain attempt to beat the clock I was up long before the sun had officially signified the start of the day.

I headed ever north reaching the outskirts of Kraburi town just before dinnertime. I stopped at the first market stall I could find and asked where I could find a hotel for the night.

I think I lucked out because the first person I asked was Mr. Packow.

Mr. Packow was not dissimilar to slightly older and skinnier Jackie Chan, massive face-splitting grin and all. He wore a crisp, white shirt, grey dress shorts and what looked like a red and black child's school cap from the 19th century. Maybe he'd represented Thailand at cycling or something because the moment I said that I was looking for a hotel said, in excellent English, 'Follow me,' and he pedaled off into the distance.

I would have thought that 3 days of intense cycling training would have enabled me to keep up with the elderly gent but he was zooming off down the road before I had even put my feet on my pedals. My tired legs rotated as fast as I could as I tried valiantly to match his superior speed but soon I was lagging behind and even more exhausted.

'How far are we going?' I asked myself as we cycled out of the far end of town along a straight and flat road. The little man just went on and on.

Some 4km later he pulled into a gravel driveway and I rolled in behind him, spent. I must have looked like an out of shape, sweating walrus next to Bradley Wiggins. Bitterly, I noticed that there wasn't a bead of sweat on him.

He stepped into the reception room and negotiated a price for me.

I wasn't 100% sure that I wasn't being fleeced in some commission scheme but Mr. Packow seemed like such a genuine bloke. His smile was bigger than a slice of watermelon. How can someone so smiley be a con artist?

And besides, we were so far out of Kraburi that I couldn't be arsed to cycle all the way back in to find alternative accommodation.

So instead me and Mr. Packow went out for dinner. He knew a lovely place just off of the main road which was owned by a battle-axe of a woman. It appeared that she had a love / hate relationship with Mr. Packow. Or she was his wife. Either way, he just laughed off her scything comments and the odd tea-towel flick with his trademark grin.

Back at the hotel Mr. Packow and myself sat out on some decking overlooking a river drinking tea.

'You know, over there,' he began pointing to the opposite bank, 'that's Myanmar or, how you say, Burma.'

'What, just over there?' I was shocked. I hadn't realised that I was right on the border of another country. I could easily have swum across the river. Hell, I could have thrown a stone across the river. I briefly contemplated a little international trespassing.

'Yes,' said Mr. Packow. 'Here we are at the Isthmus of Kra.' He waved his hands to demonstrate the surrounding area.

'Yeah, I read that on the map. What is the Isthmus of Kra?' I asked. In my mind it was a mystical weapon or a race of indigenous warriors.

'Have you not heard of an 'isthmus'?' he asked sitting up from his perch on the bannister with a look of bewilderment on his face. 'I thought 'isthmus' was an English word.' He pulled his phone from his pocket and found a translation app. 'Yes, English. It means the narrowest part of a peninsula,' he said looking up at me. 'Here we are at the narrowest point of the Malay Peninsular.'

Is that it? No tribes with poisoned arrows and war drums? No magical totems and lost civilisations? No +2 Swords of Might forged by dwarves? I was massively disappointed.

Soon the sun was setting over Burma and Mr. Packow had to go. Probably back to the old lady in the roadside restaurant to happily receive some more abuse. I bade him farewell and he gave me one final massive grin before he cycled off.

I collapsed on the double bed in my hotel room. I'd left the air-conditioning on before I'd gone to dinner and now it was icy cold inside. Once again I was surprised by how easy this adventure thing was. I turned my phone on and saw a half dozen messages from Harry. He'd finished surfing and was heading up the coast and wanted to meet up. He was about 20 minutes away so I sent him my location.

I grabbed my hi-vis vest and strode out to the road. I sat on a bridge over a brook and watched a steady stream of white and red lights head up and down the highway.

Soon a car screeched to a stop on the hard shoulder next to me and Harry's cheeky face popped out of the window. 'Hey, stranger. You look like a Day-Glo hippy. Get in.'

I climbed in the car and he gave me an awkward hug over the gear stick. It was nice to see a familiar face. The first one I'd seen since the adventure had begun... all of 3 days before.

'Mate, I'm starving. Where can we eat?'

'We could check out Kraburi town.'

It felt weird being in a car. The kilometres just flew past. What had taken me over half an hour to cycle flew past in less than five minutes. My butt relaxed into the comfy seats of the car relieved to not be receiving a pounding by the bike saddle. The air-con in the car defied the heat of the night.

Critically, although I was travelling in a car, I was retracing the route that I had already cycled so I didn't feel like I was cheating on my goal to cycle all the way to Bangkok.

We pulled over at a street stall that was lit entirely with candles. We ordered some random greasy food and sat on plastic chairs and discussed our, very different, experiences of Thailand.

While I had been slaving my way north on my bike, Harry had been lazing on sun-drenched beaches drinking cocktails and enjoying surfing in the warm sea. He had befriended an expat and his family who was running the surf school and had been having wonderful communal dinners with them.

'You would have loved it,' he said.

I'm sure I would have done and once more I questioned the sanity of spending days in the saddle riding in the heat, eating street food alone.

But then I would never have met Bam and his boys and been driven to a wat on a moped. I would never had met the incredible Sak and Bow who fixed my tyre and fed me. I would never have been given the tour of Kraburi from smiley Mr. Packow. And I wouldn't have experienced all the other hundreds of tiny pieces of joy on this ride.

I also wouldn't have the sense of achievement of having travelled the whole way from Phuket under my own steam.

'So,' said Harry bringing the conversation back to the Asian elephant in the room. 'What are your plans for tomorrow?'

I'd been putting off the inevitable decision for the past couple of days. I'd cycled over 315km in 2 and half days, which, as a non-cyclist on a heavy steel mountain bike, I was pretty chuffed with.

However, I only had two days left to reach Bangkok which was still over 500km away, most of which was along South Thailand's main arterial motorway. I didn't even know if I would be allowed to cycle on the motorway, let alone imagine how dangerous it would be.

Realistically there was no way that I was going to cycle all the way to Bangkok. My dream was a complete impossibility.

'I think I'm going to cycle across the Isthmus tomorrow and then call it a day,' I said in answer to Harry's question. 'There's a big city on the West coast called Chumphon. It seems like as good a place as any to end my adventure.'

The decision was a difficult one. I felt like I was cheating on all those people that I had boasted about my upcoming adventure with. I felt like my body was incapable of the challenge that I had set it (it most definitely was!). I wished that I had another handful of days to make the adventure complete but it was never going to happen. I couldn't afford to move the flight.

Harry could see the uncertainty in my face. 'Ok,' he said finally, nodding his head in agreement. 'I've only got one question for you. What's an Isthmus?'

Grinding to a Halt

If this was going to be my last day cycling then I sure as hell was going to make it my best cycling day yet.

I pushed myself as hard as I could, daring myself to keep cycling and not to give in on the steep hills and walk. I didn't stop once but my poor bike was taking the toll of my constant pressure. The right crank was creaking like a pensioner. Maybe it knew that this was its last day with me and it was complaining that we would soon be parting. Maybe it could sense the finish line and was starting to fall apart beneath me. Maybe it was just exhausted from well over 300km of constant riding.

Sometime in the late morning Harry zoomed past me, his horn blaring a fanfare and his face beaming like an excitable puppy. I caught him up again half an hour later when I spotted his hire car at a street café. I pulled in to find him finishing off a late breakfast.

'Hey man,' he said. 'The food here is amazing.' He finished licking his fingers with a self-satisfied grin on his face.

After stuffing my face with grub I climbed back aboard my steed.

'Hang on,' said Harry fishing his mobile out of his pocket. 'I'll catch some footage of you cycling away.'

'Yeah, good idea,' I said as I pushed down heavily on my right pedal.

There was a loud snap.

'Ah, crud,' I said looking down at the plastic pedal that had cracked all along one side.

'You alright?'

'Yeah, I bloody just bloody broke my bloody bike,' I replied angrily, forgetting my vocabulary in the process.

'Never mind. Not far to go now,' said Harry jovially as he jumped back in his car and sped off.

With my crank creaking and my pedal broken I carefully rode the rest of the way to Chumphon, thankfully mostly downhill.

On the outskirts I passed over a busy flyover. Beneath me, the country highway that I'd been following morphed into 8 lanes of busy motorway. The number 4 motorway disappeared off to the north full of rushing cars and roaring lorries. I was glad that I wouldn't be taking that route any more.

I descended into the busy streets of Chumphon. The traffic increased dramatically and my navigation became a lot of guess work but the bonus was that there were ice-creams for sale on almost every corner.

I'd agreed with Harry to meet him at Thungwualean Beach north of the city. Following my nose I eventually descended a steep hill towards the beach. Despite my best attempts at reconstructive surgery with a roll of fuse tape, my right pedal had completely given up the ghost and pedaling had actually become painful so I just stood on the left pedal and rode the bike like a scooter down the hill.

I knew I was in the right place as I could see his bespectacled head bobbing about in the waves near the shore.

I climbed aboard my trusty bike for the last hurrah. I did my best to cycle across the deep sand before ploughing the bike into the gentle surf and flopping into the warm shallow water completely spent.

And as if to really mark the end of my journey the storm that had been brooding on the horizon suddenly broke and Harry and I floated about as rain hammered down on top of our heads and kicked up the salty water around us.

The End

Of course that may have been the end of my solo adventure but that wasn't the end of the story. Harry and I spent the rest of the afternoon lazing on deckchairs drinking beer, receiving the obligatory Thai massage from a couple of ladies with VERY strong hands and generally chilling out.

I also had the dilemma of the bike to deal with. The original plan had been to give the rickshaw away to a homeless person in Bangkok to give them a potential career opportunity. Or at the very least they could sell it.

However, now we were in Thungwualean Beach and everyone around us seemed to be fairly well off.

'You could just leave it at the hotel,' suggested Harry the next morning as we walked to breakfast.

'But I really wanted the trip to make a difference. It would bring closure to the adventure.'

We continued discussing our options as we strolled down the

beachside road to a café.

Suddenly a small mewing noise caught our attention. It was coming from a deep storm drain at the side of the road and, on closer inspection, we found a small black and white puppy trapped in there. Her back legs or her spine were clearly damaged and the poor thing couldn't pull itself out of the hole it was stuck in.

To say Harry likes dogs is like saying that Winnie the Pooh might be a fan of honey. For him, seeing a dog in distress is akin to a full blown natural catastrophe. 'What do we do?' I asked him.

'There's nothing we can do,' he said mournfully. 'She's obviously broken her back. Unless you want to put it out of its misery, we'll just have to leave her.' He turned away and continued down the road silently.

We arrived at the café under a dark cloud and sat and ordered our food. A middle aged Thai lady at a nearby table started up a conversation with us. Harry answered monosyllabically, still distraught with thoughts of the poor puppy.

The lady, who we never caught the name of, was fascinating. She had grown up on the beach but had moved away to work as a lecturer at a college. Now she had thrown that in and said 'Yes' to her dream of owning a hotel on the southern end of the beach. She had bought the land but was now saving up to build the hotel itself. What a dream! What ambition!

'Are you ok?' she asked Harry after a while.

Harry sadly relayed the story of the puppy in the storm drain.

'Oh my god,' said the lady. 'I'll go and get it now.'

'Where will you take it?' asked Harry his face starting to light up.

'I'll get a taxi and take it to the vet's in town,' she said as she pushed herself to her feet. 'Thank you for talking to me.' She left swiftly. A few moments later we spotted her and the puppy in the back of a van that was heading back along the beach road and off in the direction of Chumphon.

'Mate,' I said, turning to the now slightly less depressed Harry. 'I've just had the best idea ever. Why don't we donate the bike to that lovely lady? I know it's got a knackered crank, the pedal is all but snapped off and there's probably salt water damage from where I dumped it in the sea, but it must be worth something. We could help this lady to get just one step closer to her goal of owning a hotel.'

'That sounds like an awesome idea, especially after she was so kind to that poor puppy.'

'Yeah, it's like karma or something. I've had all these wonderful people doing nice stuff throughout my journey. Here is a way that I can pay back someone who did a selfless act for someone else.'

I didn't know the lady's name but the guy behind the counter in the café said that he knew her. I wrote a note and taped it to the bike and left the bike with the café man.

I left my email address as well in case she wanted to get in contact with me.

She never did.

Maybe she's been busy building her hotel. Maybe she's been saving more puppies from drains. Whatever she's been up to, I like to think that she made some use of the bike. Or more likely sold it and used the profits to go towards her new hotel.

A Time to Reflect

I planned to ride a rickshaw from Phuket to Bangkok in 5 days. I ended up cycling from just under half the distance in three and a half days. Then I was chauffeured the rest of the way by my long suffering best mate in his hire car.

Was my adventure unsuccessful because I 'failed'? Was my adventure any less adventurous because I slept in air-conditioned hotel rooms and enjoyed the luxury of a warm shower and a double bed each night?

I spent £170 on a bike that I eventually gave away for nothing. Coincidentally, Harry's hire car cost him almost exactly the same amount of money. Did I make the wrong decision buying the bike? I mean, I couldn't have made it all the way to Bangkok without Harry picking me up to finish the journey. Was it a waste of time and money riding a bike across part of Thailand? I'll leave that up to you to decide.

But here is a question for you. What would you do with £170 and 5 days? I wonder where you will go and what you would see. I wonder what adventures you would get up to.

What would your choice be?

Website: **jondoolan.com**, Facebook: **jondoolan.505**, Twitter: **@jondoolan1**, Instagram: **@jondoolan1**

My book, *Writing for Adventure Authors*, is FREE on Amazon.co.uk.

If you want to write your own adventure story, why not join our Facebook group: **Adventure Writers' Club**

Chapter 12

Take the Ridge, not the River

by Catherine Edsell

It was drizzling. The mood was sour as cherries. I sat on the armchair in front of the cellar door, guarding its contents like a dragon protecting treasure. All the costumes for our Anglo-Bulgarian theatre collaboration were down there and Stefan claimed they were his property. I stood my ground despite feeling quite sick.

Were they his? I didn't know any more. All the edges had blurred. Rights had become wrongs. Trust and truth distorted, twisted like arms behind our backs as we winced in pain, never meaning to hurt one another.

Stefan, beside himself with fury, was thankfully a gentleman and would never harm me. He left. They all left. I glimpsed through the open door as the five Bulgarians piled ungracefully into the back of a taxi and drove into the damp November night.

Now what? The performance was tomorrow night. Our cast had just left the building (never to return). All the tickets were sold; the audience expectant.

Panic rose in my chest. If you've ever stood on a stage and had to improvise an hour-long dance performance in front of a live audience when you had, up until this point, been expecting to execute a well-rehearsed 5 person ensemble piece, you'll appreciate how excruciatingly distressed I felt - a bit like trying to breathe underwater. I held my breath, gritted my teeth and hoped I'd reach the surface before I died. Kicking my legs. Flailing my arms. Eyes wide but unable to see. Thoughts streaming through my mind in a disconnected nightmarish way.

Dying could, in fact, be preferable. At least I wouldn't have to hear that no one clapped.

To use a well-known adage, that was the straw that broke the camel's back. It was time to escape, see the world, leave the desperately dreary streets of Nottingham behind. I owned very little. I owed nothing. Nothing was stopping me. The penned-in animal pacing the length of her cage, suddenly started to dig for freedom. This was 1996, I was 26 years old.

In these pre-internet days, 'URGENT' was a first class stamp, and the only place to get information was the library. I sat leafing through the soft green pages of the 'working abroad' directory contemplating the endless possibilities; saving turtles in Costa Rica, protecting coral reefs in Belize, monitoring scarlet macaws in Peru. My thoughts were driven by conservation (for the simple reason than animals can't speak up for themselves, so someone's gotta do it!) but, perhaps not so altruistically, the further away, the hotter, the more adventurous, the better.

How had this London girl, far happier enclosed on the top deck of a bus in the warm and dry than battling the elements on top of some godforsaken mountain, (unlike my Scottish cousins), gotten here?

Truth be told, it was a desire to 'Say Yes More'*. Whilst at university my boyfriend, Sam, and I had always 'done our bit' during the lengthy summer holidays, choosing to volunteer on projects rather than sit by a pool. But the holidays always annoyingly came to an end just when you'd made friends with some Dutch guy named

Storm, who was thinking of training as a dive master and asked you if you wanted to join him on a jaunt to Egypt. Or when Pedro from Portugal invited you to his family vineyard to help harvest the grapes. It was always a big fat NO. 'Sorry, I'd love to but I can't. I have to get back...' or, 'Sorry, that sounds AMAZING, but we have to rehearse our next performance, it's already booked...'

But now, now with The Bulgarians gone, and with that disastrous performance still painfully sharp in my mind, I just wanted to go. To carry on going. To take any opportunity that came my way. To be able to say, 'YES I'd love to help you dig a well, plant some trees, meet your grandma, climb a volcano', whatever it was. I wanted to be able to say 'YES!'.

And so, sitting in this library with its wooden bookshelves and tomes of inspiration, Sam and I coined, 'The year of saying YES'.

*I was Saying Yes More decades before Dave Cornthwaite made it a 'thing', back when tribes were discovered, not created, and if someone was following you this was generally a bad thing especially if it was dark. There were no Facebook friends, just real friends, and the people you met along the way you rarely ever saw or heard of again unless one became your boyfriend for a while, or you both lived coincidentally in England and met up in a pub in London some months later. It was always inevitably a disappointing affair as it was probably raining outside, and you'd have to catch the night bus home and it was nothing like it was when you were saving turtles on a moonlit beach in Costa Rica.

* * *

I say Costa Rica, as that is actually where we went first. A beautiful hot wet jungle dripping down into the sea. A place where gigantic beasts of the deep labour up the beach to lay their eggs because once upon a time, maybe 20 years before, their mother had laboured up that same beach. Strangely when her eggs hatched, the imprint of the beach on the hatchlings belly, the magnetic field of the earth, the constellations in the sky (no one really knows how or why), draws them back. Even if it's all just hypothesis, it is a magnificent sight.

We collect her one hundred glistening ping pong ball eggs in a huge plastic bag, pulling them out just before she delivers a swipe of her flipper to my unfortunately positioned face. Then creeping off into the dark we dig a hole, an exact replica of hers, to replant the eggs. We make sure that we leave no trace, as lurking in the bushes are poachers who will steal these eggs given half a chance and sell them for a dollar a piece as an 'aphrodisiac' for drunk men in bars. Leatherback turtles unfortunately are not very discreet and leave tracks not dissimilar to those of a large tractor, giving the poachers a huge X marks the spot as to where their treasure may be hidden.

The work wasn't easy. It was all night, every night, with sandflies biting. But the sky, the electric storms that raged out to sea, the iridescent sand, caused by phosphorescent phytoplankton, and the people... oh, the people you meet!

Another volunteer, Alfonso, was so absolutely full of himself I couldn't believe his audacity. I caught him having a tantrum about the fact that he had been moved out of his private hut to a shared hut as a couple were coming to volunteer and obviously needed the privacy. He literally threw all his toys out of the pram.

The weird thing was, that it actually reminded me of a time, not so long before, when I had screamed at the lighting designer because he'd done something I didn't like. I recognised this raw ugliness, it was as though a mirror was being held up for me to have a good look at myself. I was suddenly embarrassed, with an urge to make amends to the lighting designer.

I faced Alfonso, and instead of reprimanding him for being so self-centered, I said. 'Thank you for showing me how awful I have been.' I turned my back and walked away, lighter. I was leaving the next day, so didn't really care. These first few months of complete immersion in expedition life with all its curve balls was nothing short of incredible.

So, from here on the real yeses started to flow and it was soooo exciting. Greta, a rather portly German girl told us how she had just come from a farm that had been set up as an El Salvadoran refugee camp in the early '80s when their country was systematically destroyed in civil war. Greta was going to travel around the world without using any form of motorised transport, certainly not aeroplanes. Greta was far more educated in issues like global warming and biodiversity loss than me and actually made me feel a bit stupid at times, but I thought that the idea of working on a coffee farm sounded like fun.

Picking coffee doesn't pay much. About $1 for one canasta (huge basket that you tie around your waist and put the coffee beans in). Of course if you are adept you can fill up to 7 canastas in a morning.

I was not adept. Coffee, I quickly learned, is a tricky plant to navigate. Only the red ripe beans make good coffee. But the plant doesn't ripen uniformly, so you cannot clear a whole branch by running your hand down the length of it. You have to individually pluck each bean off one by one, and this takes time.

However, the gentle beauty of being up at dawn, standing, surrounded by lush green leaves, unable to see anyone else, but hearing lilting Spanish accents as workers commune between the plants, half understanding, half off in my own thoughts, enjoying the rhythm of manual labour, changes the focus. And as if life weren't sweet enough, a scrumptious breakfast of hot thick corn tortillas and fried eggs was brought to me every morning by a young scruffy haired boy on a huge dapple-grey horse. I drank sweet coffee and listened to the birdsong for a few minutes before starting to pluck coffee beans once more. Such joy.

Months later during a sideways trip to the U.S. I noticed a sack of roasted coffee beans being sold in some designer deli for $500. The perks of the middleman. The drudgery of the labourer. The gap of inequality. But who was the richer?

* * *

It was time to move on. Sam and I had plans to work in an eco-lodge in the mountains, however, the jungle drums didn't appear to be working. As we sat in a stuffy bus station waiting room losing faith that the people from Pura Vida Eco Lodge would keep the appointment we had made 9 months earlier in the UK, a man who looked suspiciously like Sean Connery sidled up to us. He was wearing shorts and a white vest and sweating. His body hair was so thick it looked more like a pelt and I half expected him to grow claws and fangs and turn into a werewolf as soon as the moon rose. Instead he offered us a cup of water and engaged us in conversation.

It turned out that he was not Sean Connery, but an American named Al who was developing a campsite near the boundary of Corcovado National park, one of the most biodiverse, beautiful, tropical nature reserves in the world. He needed some assistance. 'Could you help me set up a camp ground, dig a well, build a bar and act as guides into the forest?' Hey, if ever there's a yes to be had, this was it! 'Pura Vida' could wait. We instead followed 'Jungle Al' to his scarlet macaw palace facing west over the Pacific Ocean.

Ever since I was a child I've loved to watch sunsets (my first camera roll of 24 exposures was only sunsets, nothing else). With a place to stay, food in our bellies, a cold beer in our hands our true payment during these next few months was the gloriously dramatic daily ritual that brought us from whatever we were doing out onto the beach to stop and breathe and watch the light show-fantastic.

Have you ever built a bar from bamboo, dug a well, made chocolate, rigged up a jungle shower, led people through the jungle during a solar eclipse? No? Well, neither had I until all of these situations presented themselves.

Tips (in case you ever do):

1. Bamboo shrinks as it dries, so if you are going to use it as a building material, make sure you have cured it first. We didn't know this, so our beautiful bar soon wizened to look like witch's teeth and we had to start over.

2. If you ever get the chance to dig a well expect to feel like you are being buried alive and might even be drowned in the process.

3. Chocolate making is really easy and so much fun – who knew? Roll over Willy Wonka.

4. Jungle showers only work if your water source is much MUCH higher than the shower head. It also helps if dead tree branches don't fall and continuously break the rather flimsy pipes you have rigged up.

5. NEVER attempt to guide a group of people through the jungle during a solar eclipse without a very strong torch and an excellent sense of direction!

It started fine - we'd made our pin-hole cameras and awaited with anticipation, as we trekked through the dense undergrowth, for the solar eclipse that was forecast for around 2pm.

I was taking two American guys into the Corcovado National park via the back door. The 'front door' involved a hefty fee and lots of documentation via the Rangers station - my entrance was a direct route to one of the most stunning waterfalls in the world. I'd walked there several times in the last few months, and now gave myself the grand title of 'jungle guide'.

Tom and Davey, a couple of 25 year olds from Minnesota knew no better, and were happily following my lead. We chatted about the leaf cutter ants that crossed our path carrying the equivalent of a windsurf sail in leaf fragments, wobbling towards their nest in the base of an enormous buttress rooted tree.

Tom narrowly missed stepping on a coral snake and went quite white with the shock. I sat him down (in case he fainted and fell over), and then explained to him that it was a false coral - red next to yellow could kill a fellow, red next to black venom lack. "Red next to black - now remember that one!" He looked relieved. To tell you the truth it moved away so fast that I couldn't actually see what type of coral snake it was, and strangely, it was getting rather gloomy.

Suddenly, our ears were bombarded by a cacophony of sounds. Howler monkeys roaring, spider monkeys screeching, a galloping herd of peccaries rumbling across the forest floor.

We stepped into a clearing and found it glitteringly full of all kinds of butterflies, blue morphos (my absolute favourite), swallow tails, red ones, black ones, orange ones, like a fairies' ball. We stepped back under the canopy and the penny dropped - the animals KNEW that something was happening. They could sense the eclipse, the changing light, the apocalyptic darkness in the middle of the day. Now I understood how the earliest humans may have felt – the end of the world seemed nigh!

And then silence.

The crescendo of noise abruptly stopped, the butterflies disappeared and it was actually quite dark, dark enough for me to not really be able to see where I was going. And definitely dark enough not to be able to see whether the snake in my path was a false coral or a real coral or even see if there was a snake there at all.

I could feel a mild panic rising in my throat - oh my God, of course! All the diurnal animals were quietening down, and all the nocturnal animals would be coming out - including all the snakes!

I've never particularly disliked snakes. My childhood best friend could be scared out of her wits simply by being shown one in a book (something that I took great glee in doing), but now with the possibility of a writhing mass coming to find me I was quite overwhelmed.

'OK let's go!' I shouted, and quickened my pace to the one place I knew we'd be safe - the waterfall. The only problem was I could hardly see my way. 'Make lots of noise! Stamp your feet! Scare them away!'

Tom tried to ask a question. 'Not Now!!!' I barked. 'Can't you see we have to keep moving?'

My heart was beating like the clappers and my speed and gait increased as I squinted in the darkness trying to see the trail. I knew there was a fork coming up soon and really didn't want to go the wrong way.

By now it was completely black. Even though it was still not 2pm, the leaf cover was so thick that each tiny shard of light was struggling to get through this natural pin-hole camera.

Finally the sound of the waterfall could be heard in the distance and eventually we broke out into open space. The weird amber/grey light was eerie but welcome and the gush of the water filled the silent void we had experienced in the forest. Panting, we lay down on the smooth rocks. I couldn't help bursting into laughter.

'I'm so sorry guys,' I apologised. 'I had no idea it would be like this!'

They forced a smile, but I think they thought I was a little bit crazy, and were wondering what they were doing in the middle of nowhere with this strange British girl.

We waited until normal service had resumed and made our way back home to the sound of chattering capuchins. At the gateway to their lodge I waved a cheery goodbye. I never saw or heard from them again.

* * *

Sam and I had to go to Panama to do a visa run. We'd done a couple before but always come back to our idyllic adventure hideaway. Eventually though, surfing giant ocean waves, navigating through the jungle and even swimming with crocodiles becomes samey, so we decided to move on.

We had heard that the Panama Canal had opportunities - opportunities to get passage around the world if you were prepared to crew. We had zero sailing experience, so it seemed like a perfectly brilliant idea.

We knew we had to go to the yacht club and hang around making contacts, so we jumped in a taxi and clearly asked in clipped English to go to 'THE YACHT CLUB'.

The driver didn't understand and we didn't know the Spanish. 'THE YACHT CLUB?' we enquired.

Still blank.

After a while of us repeating the words yacht and club over and over, his face changed from frown to smile, 'Ahh, you mean da yoot cloob.'

'Yes!' He wasn't Spanish after all, more Creole.

We quickly learned that the best thing to do was write a note saying you were willing to crew and pin it up in the yacht club laundry. No one had mobile phones, and everyone washes their clothes, right? A simple space left at the bottom of the page where yacht owners could write the names of their boats and where they were moored was all the communication we needed.

While we waited for passage to unknown shores we fell into the lucrative business of line handling. By law, each yacht that passes through the Panama canal has to have four line-handlers. A line-handler has the important job of stopping the yacht from crashing into any other boats or the sides of the lock as the water gushes in from one part of the canal to the other. The reality is that yachts often get rafted together, like a pack of sardines, so only the outside boats have to do any line handling. The inner boats just tie themselves to each other and crack open the bubbly!

It is an amazing sight though. Each movement through the lock was jammed packed full and the little yachts were dwarfed by massive cruise ships who loomed over them using their bow thrusters to stabilise themselves. The water frothed like a massive jacuzzi for half an hour or so and then we were all spat out into the lake in the middle to spend the night and inevitably have a huge party. There are crocodiles in the lake but no one seemed to care as they dived drunkenly in between the party boats.

I was tasked on one occasion to go and fetch a sack of ice from the shore and almost got mown down by a huge oil tanker when my tiny outboard motor phut phutted and died.

The morning after, with bleary eyes and aching heads, we passed through the second lock in much the same fashion and were dropped off at the other yacht club on the other side of the canal. With $50 in our pockets and a bus ticket to return to the first yacht club, we were ready to start all over again.

One time, after a brilliant party with a crazy Dutch couple and a girl who had been at university in Nottingham at exactly the same time as me, and had actually seen me in a performance (fortunately not the last solo disaster), confirming the fact that it really is a very small world, we returned to find that our note in the laundry had the names of three boats on it - Segue, Harmony and Lands' End.

Segue was headed for Alaska - lovely crew but it was going to take about 3 months to get there. Big commitment, and did we really want to end up in Alaska?

Lands' End was bound for the Galapagos, a dream destination, but there was something about the skipper that I just didn't trust.

Harmony was headed for Pensacola, Florida. The catch was that the skipper Don, his wife and two small children had a second boat that they wanted us to crew. For some reason we kept up the facade that we knew how to sail, and so got the job. It was then that we discovered that Seahorse, our boat, was a bucking bronco!

It soon became apparent that Sam suffered badly from seasickness. It also became apparent that we didn't know how to sail a 40 foot ketch.

We had left the harbour in the dead of night and, because our skipper's papers were not in order and he needed to make a quick getaway, Don couldn't turn around.

A hastily cobbled Plan B emerged. He would tow us... all the way to Florida.

I can clearly recall that entire journey - Sam throwing up for three days. Having to have the motor on to keep up our speed. Willing the motor to break as I hated the noise so much. The motor breaking. Spilling diesel all over the crisp teak deck, then hearing Don over the radio saying, 'You're not trying to fill up in these conditions are you? Whatever you do, don't get diesel on the deck!' Cleaning the deck with bleach. And finally, learning to sail!

I was so excited when I caught my first fish ever in my life - a huge mahi mahi that we then proceeded to butcher and eat. Despite being a vegetarian, our rations of rice, beans and cabbage were not only boring, but dangerously difficult to cook on an un-gimbaled stove.

We went swimming in the deep blue sea with no sight of land, getting freaked out by the enormity of it after about 10 seconds and having to climb back on board. We watched sparkling phosphorescence during the night shifts. We decided that naked sailing was fun and it was raining anyway, so a good excuse for a shower. We were very VERY scared as massive waves tossed us around like a small and insignificant cork.

Strangely though, as dry land came into view, I desperately wanted to head back to Panama with all its lush beauty. Pensacola Florida. Where even IS that?

It turned out that 'dodgy Don' as we now liked to call him had not only escaped in the dead of night because *his* papers were out of order, he had omitted to get the proper exit stamps for us too - be careful what you wish for!

As we were a private yacht, there was no queue at the border. There was no border. We had just landed but we were not allowed to leave our vessel until a member of the United States immigration facility had boarded and authorised us to enter the good ole US of A.

A huge ginger headed official-looking man clambered on board. My palms began to sweat. My throat tightened, What if he didn't let us in? What would actually happen?

Time to turn on the charm! I literally didn't take my eyes off him. I looked him square in the face and engaged him in sweet British conversation to the extent that Sam thought I had completely lost it. But I needed to do this. I needed to make sure that this man didn't look too closely at my passport. That he didn't see that we were missing an all-important exit stamp.

And it worked! Thank you ma'am!

* * *

I soon decided that the U.S. was not for me, and actually Sam wasn't either. I said goodbye to Sam and to Mabel, the 1979 Champlain II RV (Recreational VeeHickle) that I had thrown half my savings into. I'd loved her even though she only did 6 miles to the gallon and had to be fumigated as she was full of cockroaches.

Instead I flew to India, for the very simple reason that someone asked if I'd like to go to India - obviously I said 'YES!' Why wouldn't I?

India is not like any other place on the planet. As soon as I walked out of the airport a strange smell of hamster cages and sweet rotting fruit tickled my nostrils. I looked for a bus to take me into town, but could make no sense of the squiggly Hindi writing so just got on one and hoped for the best.

Chennai is a sprawling city, so eventually I just got off and checked into a guesthouse and tried to sleep. Mosquitoes lurked in the dank corners of the room. Someone was throwing up next door. Mmmm, so this is how it's going to be?

I made a break for rurality and headed south – Kerala, the waterways. I found a boat and took to the canals watching the villagers swim, wash their clothes, defecate all in the same area. I headed west and soaked in the monsoons in search of VERY well camouflaged tigers. I headed north to the chaotic capital, but now I had a fever. I only knew I had a fever because I happened to rub up against a man in a cafe and his skin felt ice cold. I was in Delhi and the temperature was in the high 30's, but my temperature was way hotter than that.

In my delirious state I decided that the only option was to take a two day bus journey into the mountains. It would be cooler up there.

The journey was deadly. Actually really deadly. Not for our bus, but there was a bus that had got stuck on the highest pass, people were dying. Small children. Old monks. Through a wry twist of fate our bus was suffering from a failed clutch, making the climb to 5050m rather a slow process. So although our journey took four days and involved a trans Himalayan bus exchange (after a whole day of going virtually nowhere, the smell of burning cables not really adding to my feverish recovery, I had the inspired idea that we should swap our bus with one that was coming down - I told the driver who though it a great idea, so the exchange took place, we were on our way once more. Genius!), it meant we stayed alive.

Leh proved to be just the recuperation I was looking for. Fresh apricot juice, straight from the orchard. Little fried dumplings stuffed with yak cheese. Even the tsampa tea, an acquired taste reminiscent of a stock cube, seemed nourishing.

Health restored, my housemate at my home-stay Benny, and I, decided to take a ten day hike up the Zanskar valley. We were joined by Pat, an American I had met on the bus, bonded by our need to crouch behind rocks after eating tainted samosas at a roadside stall. Benny had a stove, Pat had a walking stick, I had a reflective piece of foam previously used to keep the sun off a taxi driver's window, a pair of second hand boots and a 1980's ski jacket that I'd bought from a market in Delhi for £1. Pretty well equipped for high altitude trekking I'd say!

Within two days the stove packed up, we crunched raw spaghetti and then drank water waiting for our bellies to swell. We picked apricots from the trees, eating the sweet flesh then cracking open the kernels careful not to crush the almond-like nut in the centre. Some of them were foul, (too much cyanide), but some were palatable, and frankly, there was nothing else - uncooked rice was not an option.

We were tired and hungry and according to the moth-eaten guide book, there was a village not too far away. The problem was, we would have to first climb over a substantial mountain, only to come down the other side before we could cross the river. Feeling demoralised by this information I looked up from the book and spied a clear path leading around the side of the mountain. My spirits lifted! 'Hey, what about THIS path', I exclaimed. 'It must go to the same place and this way we don't have to climb.'

The boys must have been feeling as weary as me, as before long, we were all trotting off like goats along the track. Soon, but not quite soon enough, it became clear that it was in fact just a goat track, made by goats.

The trail was getting narrower, the shale more unstable. We thought about turning round, but our weary bodies and empty stomachs won over the nagging logic that this may not end well. There is an expression, 'Always take the ridge, not the river'. I hadn't heard it, much to our detriment.

The Zanscar river raged 500m down to our left. The mountain towered 1000m up to our right. The path in front disappeared!

There had been a landslip and two metres of path had literally slipped away. There was nothing to walk on. I could see the path ahead, but my stride was just not quite wide enough...

And then I had a brilliant idea. 'Pat, if you just give me a push I can make it to the path over there.' Pat grabbed my backpack and launched me into the air. Woohoo! This was going to work!

What I hadn't considered in my cunning plan was that when I landed I would land hard. Very hard! Suddenly the mountain started to move - Oh my God. I had started a landslide! We tumbled down in an escalator of scree heading for the mighty Zanscar.

I screamed. I scrabbled. I tried to grasp anything that wasn't moving. Everything was moving. Benny having the heaviest pack tumbled past me, speeding up as he fell. Pat dug his stick in and surfed to a halt. The ground eventually stopped moving.

I pressed my body as close to the mountain as I could, imagining that I was somehow magnetically attracted to it and could fall no further. I tried to sink my nails into the sand beneath the scree, to gain a little more purchase. I twisted my neck and looked down to see Benny upside down but still. Pat was above me his stick providing anchorage that neither me nor Benny possessed.

I called to Benny to take his pack off. We had to try and work out a way to get out of this mess. Slowly, slowly we crept a little sideways until we reached some sturdier boulders. We hardly dared breathe as we inched our way up towards the goat track. Pat helped with his stick, giving us something to hold onto. A lifeline.

Benny's hands were bloody. He'd lost most of his fingertips in the fall, and needed medical attention. The only option now was to retrace our steps to the base of the mountain, clean Benny's hands in the river then bandage them up, walk OVER the mountain that we should have climbed in the first place, and then try to get to the village by nightfall. This we duly did mostly in silence, the echoes of our screams and clanging rocks still loud in our ears. I re-enacted the disaster with a different more chilling outcome and wondered how my parents would have heard of our deaths. Would the military have posted them a letter, a phone call maybe, or would they have read it in the newspaper - headline "Stupid foreigners think they know better and die because they can't be bothered to take the ridge not the river".

We arrived back at the river late in the afternoon. The heat had gone from the day but we were exhausted. We could see the village in the distance, but between us and them was a tumultuous raging river 300m wide. In Ladakh, there are few bridges, instead, a thick metal cable akin to those used in cable cars is suspended across the river and a small wooden box and a tangle of ropes is the only means of getting across.

The box was on the far side, and there was not a soul to be seen. I suggested we made camp where we were. We had water and I'd found a couple of apricot kernels in my jacket pocket. Benny shrugged, but Pat didn't agree. 'I think I can shimmy over there and get the box and bring it back.'

'Really?' I said in disbelief.

But he was adamant, so I helped him construct a rudimentary sling using his emptied backpack and watched as he hauled himself the 300m to the other side. He must have suddenly gained some 'He Man' energy. Maybe he was so hungry that he had gone a bit mad. 'By the powers of Greyskull!'

He untangled the box and then slid down to the middle where the cable bowed, then had to again haul himself arm over arm up the 150m towards us. We clambered in and slid back down to the middle, it was a tad cramped as these boxes are only built for two small Ladakhis not the three of us and our backpacks. The spaghetti jumble of ropes were more of a hindrance than an aid, and we were making slow progress - heave, heave, HEAVE.

In that moment it did strike me that we were completely ridiculous, but so incredibly human in a 'We must get there whatever the cost' kind of way. Frankly, I would have been happy to do this in the morning, but sometimes you just can't argue with testosterone.

We wandered into the village at dusk looking as though we had just walked off a battlefield - our clothes were ripped and bloody, our faces streaked with dust and sweat, our hair full of grit, and Benny's hands bound like a lepers. The villagers, wide eyed and hushed, poured us tsampa tea (stock cubes never tasted so good), and showed us to an earthen floored room where we could lay down our things. My eyes welled at their kindness, their care.

It was time to go home. Time to get some training, time to say no, just for a little while.

* * *

Post Script

As you can probably tell, these were not planned adventures. They were the product of nothing more than simply saying yes. And while these stories may seem haphazard and random, (and believe you me, there are many more), looking at them retrospectively there is a pattern, a pattern of my life. Pivotal points. Cyclical journeys. Lessons learned.

I can say, hand on heart that every experience forged a strength within me, a confidence, a trust that I really could create my own reality. This understanding of life has been a wellspring during the times I have felt beaten and low, the wellspring of true freedom.

So what happened next? If I were to write about it, (which I haven't yet, but now seems like a fun idea), I would tell of more 'Adventures in YES'. Many solo, pushing the boundaries of my own personal exploration. Navigating uncharted rainforests. Helping scientists discover new species in Indonesia. Tracking wild desert elephants in Namibia. Stumbling across opium dens in Laos. Searching for sink-holes in Belize with my trusty hammock and machete on my hip. Until I discovered I was pregnant.

At this point, the story takes a swift detour via a parallel universe, but as my husband once insightfully said, 'You can take the girl out of the jungle, but you can't take the jungle out of the girl!' With his help I have clawed my way back, revisiting the energetic waypoints of my life. This ocean, that jungle, those leatherback turtles and desert elephants, encouraging others to join me on extraordinary adventures.

Definitely, to be continued...

Website: **cathadventure.com**

Check out my **TedX Talk** by searching for it online.

Chapter 13

Wonder on the Wye

by Samantha Ahern

And so, it begins. It is only Tuesday and I am already dreaming about Friday's trip. What am I taking? How am I packing it? Will I fit in? Am I up to the challenge?

A little over a year ago I wasn't even sure I would renew my canoe club membership. It had taken a number of attempts before finally joining the club. Every time I would do a pool session or two, or get ready to re-contact the club, I would injure my knee and plans would have to be put on hold and now I wasn't sure I wanted to continue.

For as long as I can remember I have struggled with a sense of belonging when it comes to social groups. This is part of the reason I got involved with the canoe club in the first place.

I've had an ongoing issue with anxiety for a number of years. I was signed off work with anxiety for 6 weeks a while back. I'm still very conscious of my mental state at times.

My physical state isn't much better. I dislocated my left knee during my first ever attempt at bouldering. This resulted in a visit to A&E and a fixed splint for 6 weeks. I was devastated. It turns out this wasn't the first time I'd dislocated it, but the fourth. Ever since I've been plagued by a recurring knee injury that has severely limited the activities I can do.

I can paddle an open canoe to roughly 1* level but we are <u>not</u> friends. Ideally you should kneel in a canoe but that is just not physically possible for me. I struggle to bend my knee to an acute angle and also find it extremely painful to put pressure on my left kneecap. Kayaks are my boat of choice.

In July 2013 I had my Medial patellofemoral ligament (MPFL) reconstructed, this involved drilling through my patella and femur. It took a long time to recover from the surgery. I was unable to weight-bare for the first month, wore a hinged splint until the December, and was unable to cycle without pain or hitching my hip for a year. I had a stable knee joint, but I was extremely grumpy and unhappy for a while.

That first summer with the club was hard. I'd done well in the pool sessions over the winter but being on the lake was completely different. For the life of me I couldn't paddle in a straight line. Hours were spent constantly going around in circles. I was always at the back in group paddles, scared and feeling very alone. I felt extremely frustrated that I wasn't making progress and decided that I definitely didn't like boats without a flat bottom.

My mind races, and eventually I find sleep.

It's Wednesday evening. I stop by the club to arrange the loan and transit of a club boat and paddle. I collect my preferred club helmet, leave some money in the honesty box and head home. I feel much calmer. I've borrowed the Pyranha H3.

I like to have things organised. It's Thursday afternoon. I start to pack my kit for the weekend. I have three bags. Is it too much? Have I packed enough? Am I sure I've got everything I need? Will I be able to keep up or be a hindrance? A last minute online purchase of a new dry bag and karabiner means I won't be having soggy sandwiches at least.

Friday lunchtime; I'm nervous, excited and impatient. I hate having to wait to go somewhere or do something. My preference is just to get up and go. But, be patient I must.

I run through what I need and what I've packed in my head. I've bought some new canvas pumps. I'd rather take my trainers but they're likely to smell. Do I wear or pack the pumps? The weather isn't looking too good and I don't know what the conditions will be when we get there.

My phone beeps. Time to go. Jim from the club is outside and there are two bright yellow boats strapped to his car's roof. I throw my kit in the back and we're off.

I don't think I've ever seen so much rain. Endless spray from lorries as we make our way westbound on the A14. There have been reports about delays on the M6, thankfully we need to detour via Coventry and seem to skirt around the problem area. I am yapping incessantly, and we inadvertently end up turning-off when we shouldn't have done. A return journey to the next junction required. It's not as bad as it could have been.

I'm feeling nervous as I spot the road signs for Ross-On-Wye. The last time I was in the Wye Valley I was in Year 5 on a school camping trip. It wasn't the best of trips. My first attempt to pee outside wasn't a success and one evening I even wet the bed. The worse thing about it was that everyone else sharing the tent knew.

The kayaking trip on the Wye didn't go too well either. We were in doubles and synced paddling is hard at the best of times. It's a lot more work when you're 10 and it's your first time in a kayak. I persevered with the trip and was awarded The Best Camper tent peg at the end of the trip. I still have it.

The Inn at Symonds Yat West is at the end of a narrow road and down a steep hill. There is a very tight turn into the car park. There are a few other cars with boats on the roof. It's likely a few other club members are already here. I'm looking forward to seeing the others, but nervous I won't fit in. My head hurts. I've not drunk enough, and I'm hungry. I'm glad we've arrived.

The Inn has two fireplaces, one near the bar and the other at the far end. This is where we find some of our crew, sat on one of the big sofas next to the wood burner. A wild boar's head hangs above the fireplace. I sink into the sofa opposite the others, whilst Jim opts for the armchair between the two sofas. Dinner is scampi and chips washed down with a glass of lemonade. I also take the opportunity to sample one of the Wye Valley Brewery's ales. Everyone is on fine form; lots of jokes and free flowing conversation. As the evening goes on other members of the group arrive. Although it's a bit of a struggle, all of us crowd around the fire. It's nice to be surrounded by other people when everyone's focus isn't on me. I relax and enjoy listening to the stories of others.

The entrance to the bunk house is a few yards from the inn. We spread ourselves out over the adjoining rooms that are accessed via a flight of stairs. More people will be joining us tomorrow so I opt for a top bunk. All the beds are a bit wobbly and creaky.

Anxiety starts to creep in again. This my first time sharing a room with these people. Will I be able to sleep? Will I snore and disturb others?

I sleep surprisingly well and wake a little before my alarm. I even mange to successfully extract myself from my sleeping bag and visit the bathroom in the early hours. The trickiest part was navigating the bunkbed's ladder and few stairs between the rooms. Putting a light on wasn't really an option. Thankfully the bathroom light has been left on, spilling out light from the slightly ajar door.

I'm not one for make-up or spending hours on my hair, but I do like to be clean. I have to have my daily shower and wash my hair. I also like to know that my clothes are ironed before leaving the house, even if they get crumpled immediately after. I've been known to start a day's trekking with wet hair hidden under a beanie.

There's nothing I can do about my clothes, but there is a shower. My first attempt at using it doesn't go well, it only seems to be pouring out cold water. I give up and opt for the sink. I need to wash my hair, but there's no plug and I have nothing to use as a jug. The water from the hot tap is annoyingly hot, and the flow keeps changing. I try to mix the water in the middle and throw it over my hair with my hands. My hair is a bit too short to dunk in the sink, but I try nonetheless. It's a bit of a faff but I manage to get my hair clean and give myself a full body wash.

Happy Birthday to me.

We take a group walk to see the rapids. I'm glad I wore my walking boots. The road section was fine but once we take the steps down towards the river, our path turns into a mud track. I'm relieved that I don't slip. This is where the river splits around a small island. On the left are rapids and, on the right, usually much shallower and slower water. Today's paddle will end at the inn but tomorrow morning, we will need to opt for one or the other. There may be an option later today to test my skills on the rapids.

Breakfast is in the inn. We have one long table for the nine of us, I opt for a seat between the table and window. It is organised chaos as we try to cook toast and get coffee or pass around the tea pot. I don't really know what's going on. The cooked breakfast is good but there's a lot of it. I'm initially a little confused by the hash brown as its shaped like a fish finger. I eat it anyway. Ian's ate too much and is now unwell.

The weather forecast isn't looking great, rain expected. Might be a good day to test the dry suit. I've never worn one before. I switch out of my breakfast clothes to swim leggings and a tech tee. I'll put the dry suit on when we get to Ross-On-Wye.

My phone beeps, its other group members checking to confirm the meeting point.

We are almost there. It is very busy when we pull-up. There are vans and trailers from the local canoe hire company. We start to unload the boats and place them on the green between the road and the river, trying to keep our equipment separate from the hire company's. Somehow, I manage to get myself into the dry suit and zipped up without assistance. My wetsuit boots even go over the feet with relative ease.

I love and hate my spray deck in equal measure. It's very effective at reducing water intake but I just cannot fit it myself. At times it's a three-person job. I decide to give it a dunking in the river, this may help getting it onto the boat. I clamber down the steps to the water's edge, dodging families and open canoes.

Once we're all ready, we queue to get onto the water; 5 kayaks and 3 opens. We take it in turns to slide our boats down the steps to the water's edge. Unsurprisingly, my spray deck won't go on my boat. It's embarrassing. Two of us try and it still won't go. My heart is in my throat. Everyone is watching me, waiting for me. The awkward girl with the awkward kayak. I can feel my cheeks flushing.

Ian offers to loan me his. His tummy is still playing up from breakfast so he's decided not to paddle today. I pull my deck over my head gratefully and throw it on the bank, replacing it with Ian's and stretch it over the boat's cockpit and I'm good to go. I think.

I'm not comfortable, I've barely paddled in 6 months, and not for more than an hour at a time. My legs are killing me, and I'm hot. Almost immediately I am at the back of the group.

I'm the least experienced paddler of the group, and I'm at the back. Again. Mentally I'm back to that first summer. I feel isolated and alone, like a small child slowing the group down.

And then we see the swifts, swooping down to the water's surface from each bank, like a choreographed dance. I am in awe as they spin and twirl around our heads, flashes of darkness across the sunlight reflecting on the river. They surround us completely as we paddle, yet never making contact. With a mesmerising sweep they brush away my concerns and I start to relax. This is not an experience I will forget.

Goodrich Castle sits by the water's edge, closer than I expected, the curved towers clearly visible from a distance. It looks stunning as we paddle around it, the medieval stone glowing yellow in the light. I feel very small on the water next to the towers. It's not long now until lunch.

The original plan was to stop at Kerne Bridge but unfortunately due to hire company boats this isn't possible. There's a suitable stopping spot a little further on, but some faster moving water needs to be navigated first. This is my toughest test of the day so far. I follow the line of more experienced members of the group and the instructions I am being given.

I struggle to extricate myself from the boat. I am extremely stiff, especially my hips. I climb up the bank to the benches where we are gathering to eat. I'm not too worried about food, but I desperately need a drink. There is no shelter and I quickly start to cool.

In my infinite wisdom I have left my paddle in my boat. Getting back down the bank is much harder than climbing up. I think I've successfully navigated back down, and I'm on my bottom. It might have been easier just to slide down.

I point my nose upstream. I am paddling but still being pushed downstream. The water is moving much quicker than I'd realised. I suddenly realise the power of the water. I now feel unsettled and nervous. I'm glad to turn around and be facing back downstream.

After lunch feels like a bit of a slog. The water slows and there was a head wind as we paddled around two large bends in the river. Initially pheasants then geese are visible on different sections on the river bank. At least these pheasants aren't going to scare me by jumping out from behind a bush. Unfortunately, we cannot see any of the peregrine falcons that nest near Symonds Yat Rock.

Every part of me aches. The inn comes into view, we reach our get out point sooner than I expected. I am so tired. According to someone we have paddled over 25km. The cars need to be retrieved from Ross-On-Wye before any runs on the rapids can be undertaken.

Myself, Sophie, Linda and Nicola talk to Ian and keep an eye on the boats whilst the others go to retrieve the cars. Most of the kayaks paddled today are Pyranhas. Different models of creek boat, but all in the same yellow and orange colours. We line them up for a photo or two. Our collective love of these boats has become a bit of an in-joke within the club. I share the photo on the club's Facebook page. I ask Linda to take a picture of me in my gear so that I can share it with friends and family. Reviewing the picture, I seem to be smiling. Today is definitely type two fun – fun after the event, but not at the time. We also pose for a group shot of female paddlers. Really pleased that on this trip that female paddlers are outnumbering the males.

We've paddled for 3.5hrs, the longest I've ever been in a boat. I am too tired to attempt the rapids section. With almost certainty I would end up going for a swim. It's not worth it. I am starting to get cold, I need to get changed, so make my way to the bunkhouse. The stairs are hard work.

I remove my wetsuit boats and sit to undo and get out of the dry-suit. My tee and swim leggings are damp from sweat. I need a shower. The shower doors are a little awkward and the water wants to be either scalding hot or freezing cold. I persevere. I don't think a shower has ever felt so good. A cup of tea is most definitely required.

The inn is very busy and I opt for a seat at a normal table. I respond to birthday wishes on my phone and add to the notes on my phone about the trip. The fireside sofas become free and I quickly move to a seat by the fire. The waitress is initially confused when she brings out my tea.

It's not long before I'm joined by some of the other members of the club. Some Uno cards appear and we play a few rounds. As always with Uno we start to double up the +2 and +4 cards. Thankfully I'm not on the receiving end.

Tea in streaming out the bottom of Dave's cup as quickly as he pours it in. It has a large crack in the base. Everyone is laughing. Some friends have joined us after a day of walking. We are now a group of 13.

We hadn't reserved a table early enough, dinner is ordered and eaten in shifts. Rotating between a table and the sofas. The bar manager has allowed me to bring the chocolate cake I brought with me into the bar area. The group sing me 'Happy Birthday' as I prepare to cut the cake. I am touched and embarrassed at the same time.

It's still quite early in the evening. A group of us decide to go for a walk. We walk up the zig zag roads, pausing to take photos of the sun on the trees opposite and a rainbow over the valley, before joining a woodland path. Anna is at the front of the group and I'm not far behind. It's more of a climb than I'm used to but we continue.

We are chatting and spotting the bluebells. Suddenly it is suggested that we are quiet. Stood in a glade nearby, some deer are quietly eating the grass. Unlike the Muntjac that I've seen at home, these are proper deer. Full size, elegant and grey. We stealthily take a few steps forward careful not to spook them. I try to take a photo but only have my mobile phone. I left my camera at home. I've never seen deer other than Muntjac in the wild before. There is always something magical about seeing animals in their natural habitat.

After a few minutes we move on. We loop round and start to head back towards the inn. We have another opportunity to view the deer as they graze. There also a couple of stunning horses in a paddock on the other side of the path. It is quite a steep descent back down to road; my left knee isn't liking it much but my footing remains sure.

The pub seems even busier, and really hot when we return. Myself and a few others decide to have our drinks outside. It's ok for a few minutes, but we quickly cool and make a move inside. I have predominantly been drinking lemonade but have heard good things the last two days about the rhubarb gin. It wasn't oversold; this stuff is gorgeous, even though I've drowned it in a whole bottle of Fever Tree tonic. It's not the cheapest drink option and I'm paddling again tomorrow so have just the one. There's a final opportunity to chat around the fire, then it's time for bed.

It's 6am. I'm awake and staring at the peeling ceiling just above my head. For some reason I slept really badly. Everyone else seems to still be asleep. I try to doze but to little effect. There's bits of ceiling on the mattress.

Maybe I'll try the shower again. I leave the shower to run a little bit and find that the water is nice and warm. I get can't quite get the shower doors to move properly and inadvertently take them off the rails. Somehow trying to be quiet I am making far more noise than I wanted too. Hopefully I've not woken anybody. It feels good to be showered and to have clean hair.

I pack as much of my kit as I can. I won't be using the dry suit today. I will need to leave space at top of kit bag for my change of clothes. It's about 8am, people start to wake and it gets crowded in the dorm room.

I walk down towards the inn and stop at the partially submerged ferry. Listening to the birds chattering in the trees, I stand almost perfectly still looking at the river. Without a word I watch the ducks and swans glide effortlessly across the glassy smooth surface. A feeling of calm washes over me. Water is a weird thing. Watching it, I can see the speed at which it is moving but on the water itself it feels so much slower.

Breakfast is even more hectic, but somehow, we're a little more organised serving out hot drinks and toast. There are more guests for breakfast today, we try to keep the breakfast orders as simple as possible. Service is a little slower but we don't mind. Helen says something that makes me laugh, I try not to, my abs hurt so much.

I put on my usual paddling gear; semi-dry cag, rash top and wetsuit leggings. Feel much more comfortable. My spray deck is still a challenge. Ian is paddling today, so I return his to him and end up borrowing an old one of Jim's. I really need to get a new spray deck.

I feel much more comfortable in the boat. It's a nice gentle paddle to the rapids. It's been decided that some of the group will take the right-hand side. I've lulled myself into a false sense of security. Our friends wave at us from the bank as they head out on their second day of walking.

The water is fast, the boat bounces over the big waves as I try to make sure I take proper strokes. I listen very carefully to the instructions being shouted at me. I need to avoid the rocks. If I wasn't awake before, I am definitely awake now. Pretty much feels as though I can take on anything now.

This section of the Wye is moving a little slower than yesterday. However, I am much more comfortable in the boat today and my paddling technique is much better. Proper strokes instead of half-strokes. I am starting to pre-plan my responses more to upcoming hazards. I find myself towards the middle and front of the group.

It's not long until we reach Monmouth Rowing Club. There is a set of concrete steps that lead down to the water's edge. I 'park' the kayak on one of the steps. We're only stopping for a 5-minute leg stretch so I decide not to get out of the boat fully. Instead I sit on the back, have a drink and look out to the river. I'm enjoying just sitting and relaxing.

I continue to watch the more experienced paddlers. As we approach a faster moving section I point my nose left under bridge. I'm expecting the water to push me right. The water isn't pushing me right! I'm too close to the bridge support. I'm caught in a squall. I can't seem to paddle right. What do I do?

I take a deep breath. I use a backstroke to slow the boat, giving myself some time to think. I correct my course and paddle on.

I'm feeling really proud that I've resolved the problem for myself and not had to seek help. I'm starting to feel more like a peer than a babysat child.

We're at Redbrook sooner than I expect. I'm instructed to go left and eddy out. There isn't a nice portage like Monmouth or Symond's Yat. Like yesterday lunchtime there's a steep exit up the bank. We take it in turns to get off the river and help each other with our boats, placing them on the green at the top of the bank, before carrying them around to the car park.

Where has that wind come from? An unpleasant surprise after being in the river valley. I start to feel cold as we load the boats onto the cars. Unlike the others I need to get changed.

Suddenly a kayak falls off the roof of a car, narrowly missing Jim who was strapping our boats to his roof. We all initially jump, then laugh.

I head to The Boat Inn with Sophie. It's in Penalt on the other side of the river. A footbridge has been built next to an old railway bridge. I really like it, and you can still see the sleepers. It sways slightly like the Millennium Bridge over the Thames. I don't mind but Sophie really dislikes it.

The inn is really small and the toilets are in an outbuilding. There is only one of each, so I need to be quick in getting changed. I'm the only one that wasn't in a dry suit and feel like I'm inconveniencing the group. I try to get my cag off but the rubber seals are stuck to my wrists. I manage to release my left wrist, but in my rush, I put my thumb through the right-hand wrist seal. I am gutted and it dampens my mood.

Most of the rest of the group are waiting for me by the inn's picnic tables. We were going to stop here for lunch but there's a 30 minute wait on food. As most of us are still full from breakfast we decide to just have a drink.

The bar is small and most of the tables are in use, however there is a little table near a wood burning fire. I try not to place my kit bag too close. I join the queue at the bar for a drink. The inn has various botanical wines that you can try but I opt for a pint of lemonade.

The group heads back to car park, ready for the journey home. As we drive we can hear a rattling sound; the strapping between the two boats is tapping against the roof. It must have been doing the same on Friday but because of the rain we didn't notice.

I'm feeling tired now but happy and proud of what I've achieved this weekend. The H3 is rapidly becoming my new best friend on the water and my confidence has improved greatly. The return journey seems longer and I struggle to stay awake, doing nodding dog impressions for the first part of the journey. Jim drops me off and I give him my share of the fuel costs.

My Mum is in the kitchen. Instead of being greeted with a 'How was your weekend?', I walk through our back door to be greeted with 'You didn't do...'. Welcome home.

Until this point I had avoided club trips. I didn't believe that I was a good enough paddler and didn't want to be perceived as an added risk to the group. I also didn't want to be a nuisance in needing a lift and borrowing a club boat that someone else would need to transport.

This trip was important. I have much more confidence in my own ability and have a greater sense of belonging to the club. If I hadn't pushed myself to attend despite my fears I would not have improved and I'd still be wondering if I truly belong.

It's scary, but sometimes you just have to say "YES"!

Website: **2standandstare.wordpress.com**

Chapter 14

How to Leave a Country in 30 Minutes or Less

by Andy Madeley

My big yes moment came in 2011 when I set off to cycle to Sydney, Australia from Trafalgar Square with my best friend, Matt, to raise money for War Child UK. The journey took us through 23 countries over 16 months and raised £35,000 for War Child.

What I learned is saying 'yes' to an adventure means saying 'no' to a whole lot of other things. I was saying 'no' to working in the 9-5 until I retired. I was saying 'no' to my fear and doubt that told me over and over I couldn't complete such and audacious feat. I was saying 'no' to my comfortable life and my own laziness.

Saying 'no' to the office job was easy and I relished writing my resignation email. I worked for an IT support company who pimped me out to one of their clients. It was the monotony of working in the same role for 2 years solving the same problems by turning computers off and back on again, plugging things into other things and repeatedly answering the same questions about why a laptop DVD tray is not a drinks holder (quite often to the same people). I spent most of my days underneath desks plugging keyboards, mice and internet cables into machines for users who barely noticed me. I assume they thought their computers worked by magic. I remember a customer suggested tying a balloon to me so I could be located at all times. It was funny and only 50% serious. It would have been ineffective though as they wouldn't be able to see the balloon from the disabled toilet where I'd sometimes while away several minutes of each day.

My job paid well and I had made some great friends, yet I couldn't shake the feeling that there was more to life. I believe that we only have one life to do all the things we're ever going to do, so if there are any ambitions that burn within us it is only prudent to attempt to accomplish them. Some people called us crazy at first, but they were quite often the same ones complaining loudest about their lives. This cycle ride was part of trying to make life extraordinary. To be able to look back and say that I experienced the world in a liberating way. To learn about myself and push my boundaries.

The freedoms we have are often overshadowed by the obligations we feel. The idea of leaving my girlfriend and comforts of London life were unsettling and tugged at my sense of duty and of obligation. By undertaking this adventure, we would reject those comforts for the unknown with no guarantee of success, having no income, no permanent abode and only each other to rely on for the duration of the trip.

The truth is that those comforts - the internet, the pub, Netflix and Facebook, chilling on the couch with a takeaway - are a bit of a prison or, at least, the feeling that we need them is. They end up owning us. As we pedaled along the backroads of France, through rolling hills and green pastures reveling in a newfound sense of freedom, the gaps in the prison bars got larger until we barely noticed them. By the time we reached Albania we didn't miss TV, Facebook, the comfort of a sofa.

Hell, I didn't even miss pizza.

Well, maybe I did miss pizza. Sometimes, on long barren stretches of desert or mountains when exposed to icy winds or baking sun, we would discuss which food we'd eat first when we reached civilization. It was usually pizza.

I missed my girlfriend. She understood my drive to go on this adventure and was supportive, until about 10 months into the ride when our time apart really began to bite. But had I stayed and not left her to cycle to Sydney she would have been dating a ghost; someone who was never present.

My laziness stemmed from a childhood spent growing up on a farm in Shropshire. My mum and dad worked so hard to provide for me and my siblings, hardly taking a day off all year. My dad would always say, 'You've got to make hay when the sun shines, son.'

'But dad,' I said, 'what about my hay fever?'

'MAKE THE HAY!' he'd tell me.

So I'd spend summers literally making hay. At the end of each day my face and arms would be as red and swollen as salami and my eyes and nose would be streaming and itchy. Ever since I have experienced a similar reaction to hard work. Planning and carrying out such an epic cycle ride was bringing me out in hives.

Overcoming such deep-seated inertia proved tricky. I soon grew immune to Matt's eye rolling and stern words at the lack of my progress in preparing the website, planning the route, visas and inoculations.

My approach was to take baby-steps. I'd try and do only 5 minutes of a task at a time, breaking things down to such ludicrously small chunks that even a corpse would struggle for an excuse not to do them. More potently I'd remember why we were cycling the planet in the first place. The plight of the children of War Child still stirs anger in the pit of my stomach. I used that energy to get things done and keep Matt happy.

The unknown was our biggest thrill and concern. The road ahead was blank, and my imagination was keen to fill in the gaps with axe-wielding maniacs, murders and thieves. I knew these ideas were fanciful, but that didn't stop them scaring me.

Even my rational mind chipped in with worries about whether we could actually do this at all. Did we have enough money? What would we eat? What if we got sick or the bikes broke? The real dangers were likely to be the ones that were hidden which we hadn't considered. And those are the ones that scared me the most.

To overcome these fears, I'd ask myself 'What was the worst that could happen?' Then 'How could this problem be mitigated or solved?'

I found most problems could be solved with one phone call home to arrange a flight back to London within a couple of days which made me feel incredibly blessed. Children growing up in war zones don't have that luxury, there's nobody for them to call. When times got tough and I felt like giving up, I called that to mind.

The fear about money was largely misplaced because we were spending so little. We ate simple meals of bread and burek - a delicious greasy snack of cheese wrapped in a flaky pastry. In China, rice and a tofu dishes large enough to feed a family of five cost little more than a dollar. Nights in Europe were mostly spent in tents or peoples' homes. We had contacted several people from WarmShowers.com, a couch-surfing site for touring cyclists, and slept in their homes for a night or two and, more importantly, used their showers. Meeting a stranger on the internet to spend the night with them seemed a bit strange back then. Now we have Tinder.

Our few splurges consisted of nights in hostels, coffee and beers, all taken in moderation. On average we spent around £200 per month over the 16-month duration of the journey. Living from bicycle bags is simple and inexpensive. Certainly way more so than the average month in London.

All the other fears we had at the planning stage of the trip failed to materialize. The major problems we did encounter were mostly of our own making...

...like getting deported from Uzbekistan.

It started out as a venture to avoid trouble for our wonderful hosts, Emma and Anders. They lived in the utilitarian and concrete capital city of Tashkent.

Uzbekistan used Soviet-era tourist registration, called OVIR. It worked through hotels, authorized to host foreigners, giving you a slip of paper which recorded your stay. These slips would be totted up at the border when you left, any gaps would likely be met with an under the counter fine.

We were worried our hosts might face similar fines for letting us stay. So, to avoid getting them into trouble, Matt went to get fake papers from an Uzbek hotel. Our intent was pure. Our idea was bad. So bad.

While Matt went to the hotel to get the fake OVIR documents I went to the Kyrgyzstan embassy to get my visa for the next country on our itinerary. The embassy was more informal than I was used to. It was missing the bunches of CCTV cameras, iron bars and queuing that earmarked other embassies. In a wood-paneled office two gentlemen helped me complete my application. They were quiet yet cheerful. The younger of the two stuck the visa into my passport with Pritt Stick while I picked out our intended route over the 5 mountain passes we'd have to take before getting to China on a 3D relief map of the country mounted on the wall. As I ran my finger over the bumps I felt a twinge of trepidation (Kyrgyzstan is one of the most mountainous countries in the world). I seriously doubted crossing them would be easy at 1:1 scale.

Matt was supposed to meet me outside the embassy at 2pm. He is a stickler for being on time and after 20 minutes of standing around in the February snow I decided to walk back. Wondering what had happened to him I jokingly said to myself, 'I bet he's been arrested' and gave a little laugh.

40 cold minutes later I arrived at Emma and Anders' place. Anders, a tall and thin Uzbek octogenarian opened the door. He was a dour chap who couldn't speak English and there was an air of extra dourness about him that afternoon. He lead me into the kitchen where I was met with a blast of warm air from the gas furnace at the centre of their home.

The normally chatty Emma quietly pottered around in the kitchen. Sat on one of the benches surrounding the small kitchen table was Matt, head rested in the crook of his elbow, as I entered he raised his head and with bloodshot eyes, told me, 'Mate, it's all over. We're going home!'

After getting to the hotel and requesting fake papers he had been led by the receptionist to a small police station. 'I thought I might have to bribe them,' he told me. The receptionist spoke to the officers in Russian for a short time, then promptly left. Matt suddenly realised she had just turned him in! The officers arrested him, took him to the police station where he was questioned and his passport confiscated. Anders was asked to collect him and he was placed under house arrest. He had to tell them about me, so I had to go in to the station the next day.

Matt was in a state of shock and disbelief. Of all the things that could have ended the journey it was a stupid decision we had made.

'It's no big deal mate,' I said. 'We land in Heathrow and get the next plane out to Kyrgyzstan.'

This did cheer him up a little but not as much as Emma and Anders's neighbour, Sergi, inviting us over for what he claimed was 'the best plov in Uzbekistan' and 'the best wine in Uzbekistan' followed by some Russian folk music. The song was apparently about a mountain climber. It was probably the best Russian folk song in Uzbekistan.

Sergei's floppy hair bounced along with the rhythm as he strummed his battered guitar. I watched Matt as Sergei sang, the stress that showed through his body language seemed to have been undone by the music. Even Anders was smiling.

The next day Anders took us to the police station for further questioning. After a long wait we were met by a tall and broad-shouldered man in the green police uniform. He introduced himself as Sergeant Sangerbeg. He took us to his small office with pale green paint peeling from the wall. Matt was collected by a plain clothed officer and questioned for nearly an hour.

When he came back in he turned to me, 'Mate! They think we're terrorists!' We looked at each other and burst out laughing. I don't think we were supposed to. Sergeant Sangerbeg didn't look happy, his monobrow frowning so hard it almost touched his chin. I escaped the uncomfortable silence by attending my interview.

I was led to another small room with the same peeling green paint and a small oblong table. Sat opposite me was my interrogator a plain clothed police officer, his .38 pistol in a shoulder holster poked out of his leather jacket as he motioned me to sit down. Next to him sat a tall, thin man with close-cropped dark hair, he introduced himself as the translator, no names were given.

The feeling in the room was serious. Although it felt a little out of place I kept smiling. I thought my winning smile has got me through a few scrapes before, speeding tickets mostly, so continued grinning inanely.

My interrogators remained unmoved. Damn!

The questioning began with why we were cycling. It was something we had been asked in less austere circumstances a few times along the way. Cycling was often viewed as a means of transport for the poor and cars were a status symbol to some, particularly in Albania where everyone drove a Mercedes. To the inspector we were rich white boys from Europe, surely we should be driving!

I explained how cycling was more of a challenge and that we were raising money for a good cause. Which raised the concept of charity. The officer struggled with the idea of giving money to people we had never met. 'This is going to be a long interview,' I thought. I tried to explain why we thought it important to pay our good fortune in life forward.

Abandoning the notions of challenge and charity the inspector moved on. He'd seen our Iranian Visas in our confiscated passports and wanted to ask about our time there. Specifically, he wanted to know about the Iranian nuclear program. At this my smile broke into laughter. 'I know that they have a nuclear program, but I got that from the BBC news channel,' I told the translator.

The officer continued to stare at me as the translator explained. He also wanted to know if I was aware of any terrorist organisations in the UK or was, in fact a member of said organisations.

I considered this, like the green card for entry into the US, a litmus test for stupidity. 'Why, yes officer, I am a member of an illegal group. Please imprison me at your earliest convenience and let the waterboarding commence!' I didn't say. I always think it best to avoid sarcasm when dealing with people who have the power to administer a body cavity search.

I scanned the room for a box of latex gloves and lube (would they use lube? Are they that considerate to suspected terrorists?). I instead replied that, again, the BBC had informed me of terrorist organisations in the UK, but I assured him I wasn't a member of any of them.

He looked dubious, it could have been the straggly beard and unkempt appearance.

'Look,' I said. 'What kind of terrorists are going to use a bike as a getaway vehicle? Have you seen how slowly we travel?' The officer conceded this and almost smiled. He left the room at which point the translator explained he was actually an English teacher from a school and apologised profusely for the trouble.

The officer came back and said I could go. The powers that be must have finally realised we were not in fact international terrorists or spies, just two idiots on bikes.

We didn't avoid punishment completely and neither did our hosts. Anders and Emma were fined for harboring unregistered tourists (a fine which we paid, they refused the cash, so we left it on their coffee table the day we left) and we were still to be deported.

The next day Sergeant Sangerbeg and his friend who he called 'Big boy' came to deport us. Big boy was an accurate description. He was about 6'4" and chubby. Sangerbeg was also a broad-shouldered fellow, taller than Matt and me.

Unfortunately, our warning that we had 2 bikes and 12 bags went unheeded and they arrived to take us to the Kyrgyzstan boarder in a small family saloon car. Colin and Doris were unceremoniously put in the boot with their wheels hanging out. We padded them as best we could with cloth to prevent damage to their frames then piled into the car ourselves. The officers crammed our luggage in on top of us.

Emma and Anders were there to see us off. Like so many people we met on our adventure their hospitality had been amazing. Emma, who was born in Kyrgyzstan and so knew how harsh the winters were, was worried about us. She had plied us with food including pig fat, delicious dumplings and Anders fed us honey from his collection of beehives. Her round face wrinkled with a broad smile and tears glistened in her kind eyes. Even Anders cracked a toothy smile as he waved us off.

We got going on our 200km road trip the Kyrgyz boarder. Every jolt of the pockmarked road made Matt and me flinch with concern over our bikes. A crack in the titanium frames would require special welding skills uncommon in more populated parts of the world, never mind the barren and snow-frosted landscape we now travelled across. Coupled with the officers being unhappy at having to spend their day off by driving to the boarder with two strange men from England meant the atmosphere in the car was tense. Sangerbeg popped a tape in the cars cassette player and we cruised towards the border to the sounds of Status Quo's classic, 'You're in the Army Now'.

Two hours into our bone shaking travel though the rocky landscape and a weird compilation of The Quo, Enya and Yah Kid K tunes we approached a service station. 'Food?' Sangerbeg suggested. Our bodies were aching from 2 hours cramped up underneath our bags and we wanted to check on Colin and Doris, so we agreed.

We entered the diner. It was unlike most we had encountered on our journey which usually consisted of a few petrol pumps and a small cafe where we would sometimes be allowed to sleep. This one was large and had a lot of plastic tables and booths for our fellow road users. Sangerbeg looked at the menu, 'Vodka?' he asked, flicking his neck in the way we had seen done when suggesting alcohol in Uzbekistan.

Matt and I looked at each other. 'Fifty fifty,' Matt replied, we also flicked our necks and 2 bottles were delivered to the table.

Vodka in Uzbekistan was extremely cheap. I remember seeing 500ml bottles of the stuff for $1.50. At lunch we'd see plates of dumpling soup and the rice dish, plov, with a bottle sitting on the table too. We also saw a lot of drunk Uzbeks, one I remember staggering along a main road, weaving around the traffic. I tried to move him onto the side of the road, but he got aggressive and pushed me away.

After 2 bottles of vodka we were all friends. Sangerbeg, our driver, only had one bowl of the stuff. We arrived at Sangerbeg's friend's home for one last send off before being deported the next day. We were strangers being paraded around but we were enjoying the spectacle and all the plov and brandy too.

The following morning Sangerbeg and Big Boy took us the last few miles to the border with Kyrgyzstan. The sergeant led us past a queue of people hundreds of metres long straight up to the border desk where a smiling official took our passports and a form from Sangerbeg. He swiftly stamped our passports with a inky splodge that said we were barred from re-entry for 5 years. It was over very quickly. Certainly if you need to get out of a country rapidly then deportation is the way to go.

Sangerbeg and Big Boy looked kind of sheepish and said that if we ever needed to come back just contact them, and things would be ok. We shook hands moved through the border controls and onto our next adventures among the frozen peaks of Kyrgyzstan.

All the gory imaginings of murders and thieves had failed to materialise when we planned the trip but deportation had never even been considered. There were of course many more problems that we faced on the road, like our Iranian friends getting arrested or the time we had a gun waved at us in a Turkish brothel. But these are stories for another time, perhaps check out **www.thecyclediaries.com** if you'd like to know how we overcame those tricky situations.

I want to stress that for almost the entire journey the people we encountered were amazing. We met and stayed in people's homes and it was a privilege to share a small chunk of their lives. Whenever we needed help, it was never far away. This opened my eyes to a wider world in which people, on the whole, are good and highlighted the almost limitless possibilities each of us has to create our own niche within it.

I sorely miss that feeling of freedom I had when unzipping my sleeping bag each morning to face an open road. We never knew what lay ahead and there were times we were both scared, but the fear of never having lived proved greater and this is what pushed us out of the front door. Ultimately each mile pedaled increased our faith in ourselves and other people too. When you consider going on your own adventure, I hope that you take the chance. After all, you'll never go back and do things differently, so say 'YES'.

Website: **andymadeley.com**

Instagram: **@agmadeley**

The Push: Overcoming Obstacles to Adventure – **Available on Amazon**

Chapter 15

Rooted in the Wild

by Miri Rudo

My Yes story begins during childhood. I was lucky enough to be born on an island close to Australia and to spend my formative years living in Africa. It was in Africa, in particular, that my love for simplicity, Nature and wild open spaces began.

Following my return to the UK in my mid-teens I struggled with a feeling of busy-ness, lack of space and overwhelming choices. In the African town I had just left, we went to school from 8am until 1pm (it was too hot to be in school during the afternoon). As children, this gave us opportunity for down time, exploration and play with friends, and further activities arranged by parents within our expat community. Our local supermarket stocked only one type of toothpaste and would often only have toothpaste, toilet roll and marmite. Much of our food shopping was done at the local market, and we grew our own.

Despite being a normal middle class family, we were aware of our privilege in relation to many. We also saw the resourcefulness and skill of local children in making their own toys, and experienced the exquisite treat of a stalk of sugar cane or a juicy mango in a world without sweets.

One thing I yearned for most upon my return to the UK was the wide open skies of Africa. The closest I have come to experiencing this in the UK is on Dartmoor on a clear day. This is one of the reasons I love the moor so much. Another reason is the freedom, friendship and sense of being at home in myself I found through walking for miles and miles over its bogs, tussocks and Tors as a teenager, in all weathers and all manner of visibility.

The main purpose for these excursions was expedition training for the Ten Tors challenge and the Gold Duke of Edinburgh's Award.

The Ten Tors challenge is an event held annually on Dartmoor for young people within the South West. It is a significant adventure challenge that involves teams of 6 young people navigating a two day route across Dartmoor without adult assistance. They must carry everything they need to be self-sufficient, including clothing, camping and cooking equipment, and food and water. All navigation must be carried out without the aid of electronic equipment. Routes are of three distances in length, trained for and walked according to age. The youngest participants (13-15 years old) walk 35 miles, the middle group (15-17 years old) walk 45 miles and the oldest participants (17-19 years old) walk 55 miles. The event takes place in May, and training occurs throughout the winter, with the associated inclement weather that Dartmoor is well known for being generous in providing.

I trained for and completed the 35 and 45 mile challenges. I loved it, and I thrived. Here was a return to the open skies (sometimes!), space, wild nature and simplicity of my early childhood. I was pretty academic, and being out walking and needing to respond to the immediacy of my environment gave great balance to my otherwise cerebral life. I was also with like-minded folk, and even though we now live many miles apart I still consider my teammates from those expeditions as friends for life.

I was yet to discover just how much I would come to rely on the resilience, perseverance and self-awareness I gained through taking part in Ten Tors and the Duke of Edinburgh Award challenges, and how integral returning to Dartmoor would be in my life.

Following completion of the 45 mile Ten Tors event I decided not to go for the 55 mile event as I was in the final year of A levels and working towards getting into veterinary college.

So, I did go to vet school, in Glasgow, and spent five years feeding my passion and fascination for animal medicine and surgery and enjoying everything that the city had to offer. Just before I returned for my fourth year I discovered I was pregnant with my daughter. Her father had just graduated and got a job in Yorkshire, so I returned to Glasgow a little scared, bewildered and full of love for the small human growing inside me. The following year was a rollercoaster of feeling ill and then feeling very well, telling my parents (my dad didn't believe me to begin with!) and finding a great doctor and amazing support from my family, friends and the university.

Ultimately, after the initial 12 weeks, I loved being pregnant and felt incredibly strong and empowered. I also had a handy little internal heating system during the Glasgow winter. Towards the end of my fourth year my daughter's father moved back to Glasgow and got a job locally. Three weeks later I gave birth to my beautiful son, Jonah, and it was one of the best experiences of my life. If you are a first time mum and anxious about giving birth I am a good person to speak to ;)

I was blessed with my own mum's genes for a short labour, and I think it also helped to not have much of a plan, to be prepared for any intervention if necessary and to trust that my body was made for this. I was also extremely lucky to have had a wonderful midwife who allowed me to move around as much as I wished. Everything was kept quiet and the lights dimmed which allowed me to relax.

Two weeks after he was born I sat my fourth year exams. It was hilarious looking back, as much of my revision involved her father reading my notes to me as I learned how to breastfeed.

All went well and I had most of the following summer with her back at my family home in Devon. I became a mother at 23 -

biologically an ideal age, but emotionally I felt like I had not even begun to learn to look after myself properly, let alone another completely dependent human being. I went through a lot of self-doubt and feelings of overwhelm whilst at the same time loving being a mother and knowing I wouldn't change it for the world.

In many ways having Jonah then saved my life. I was incredibly academic and career driven and much of my identity was built around being intelligent and getting good grades. He helped to open my eyes and remind me that there are more important things in life, such as love and laughter, spending time with family and appreciating the little things. Once I accepted that I didn't have to have being a mother 'all worked out' and that the goalposts would always be changing, I began to relax and combine learning to look after Jonah with learning to look after myself.

When he was four months old I returned to Glasgow for my final year. The university nursery was brilliant and I had a lot of support from my parents, particularly my dad, who would travel up from Devon to help look after him when I was required to have extended time in the animal hospitals. At one point, when he was approximately eight months old, my dad would bring him out to me four times a day so that I could feed him! I definitely couldn't have done it without my parent's support.

Final year was completely lecture free and involved moving around different small and large animal rotations dealing with actual live cases on a day by day basis. I would always need to arrive later than other students and leave earlier due to nursery opening times. There were occasions when I felt overwhelmed again and guilty both because I wasn't 'pulling my weight' as a student and because I wasn't at home looking after Jonah full time when he was so young. Add to this the big debate within the profession at the time around the high proportion of females within veterinary schools who would be leaving to have children after a lot of investment had been put into training them, and I felt pretty useless for a while.

Then, when Jonah was about six months old, a large animal clinician who was teaching me asked my advice about his newborn baby. This made me realise that what I was doing was pretty amazing and worthwhile, and that Jonah was a happy, healthy baby with many people involved in his care. We were both very lucky.

I also started to take the pressure off myself and reminded myself that I was doing my final year with a baby and it was ok to not be able to be such a perfectionist both as a vet student and a mother. Once this happened I could enjoy my time with Jonah more, my patient care became more heartfelt again and my grades went up. This whole process taught me a lot about letting go of things that really don't matter and appreciating the things that do. I was also building more resilience, resourcefulness and self-awareness that would help me later in my life.

Some people have asked me why I didn't drop out of vet school or take a year out, and to be honest neither really crossed my mind. I had never been a mother before, and had never done final year before so it was all new territory. I also thought it would be just as tricky, if not more so, with a one year old than with a younger baby. Looking back, there was also some small part of me that had self-belief, probably helped by my adventure experiences a few years earlier. That summer I graduated and Jonah was guest of honour.

Following graduation we moved to a nearby town and I got a part time job in a small animal practice. Jonah went to a local nursery, learnt to walk and it was the autumn that the Twin Towers fell. However, we never really felt at home there, and by Christmas we had all moved back to Devon and got jobs in the practice I'd been going to as a student since I was at school. We bought a house and me and Jonah's father got married. It seemed that our life would finally settle into some ideal plan involving marriage, a family, a mortgage and good steady jobs.

Slowly, this began to unravel...on the outside it looked as though everything was 'perfect' and on the inside Jonah's father was becoming more and more stressed. We were both experiencing some fallout from the effort and change that had gone on in the previous two years, and our responsibilities with having a child, mortgage and high demand jobs seemed overwhelming at times. Almost without realising it Jonah's father dropped into a lower and lower mood and would become increasingly angry and impatient. From my perspective he became increasingly negative and hopeless, and would shout...a lot. I often felt that I had to walk on eggshells around him and keep Jonah quiet so that he did not get shouted at too. I would try to make things better by having the house clean so as to not give him a reason to get angry. I became scared. I knew he was struggling and wanted to help him but nothing I did or suggested made any difference.

It became normal, and I came to believe that his anger and unhappiness were my fault and I just needed to figure out how to change myself to make this better.

Of course, nothing worked. He refused to see a doctor or let anyone else know about his anger and low moods. He seemed happy for things to be my fault and wouldn't, or couldn't, take responsibility. Either way, this developed slowly over 3-4 years up until a point where bad days far outnumbered good days and I felt increasingly scared of his moods.

Most days I would freeze when I heard his car pull up outside. Our neighbour called the police to check on me as she'd heard him shouting and I meekly told them that I was fine and nothing was wrong. My parents and siblings became increasingly concerned about me and Jonah.

It had become so normal and I was so used to feeling to blame that I would make excuses; 'He couldn't help it.' 'He needs help.' 'I need to look after him.' 'I need to try harder.'

Then, he started to have seemingly serious suicidal thoughts. I realised I could no longer deal with this on my own and he agreed to see a doctor. He was whisked away to crisis support and I hit a brick wall.

After years of effectively being his carer and being the target for his anger, negativity and blame, I no longer knew who I was or which way was up. I was exhausted. He began to get medical help, and my head began to stop spinning.

Although many areas were showing improvement, he would still get angry at home and blame me for his moods. To me his behaviour now seemed selfish, and although he was feeling better in and about himself he still seemed to direct responsibility, anger and blame towards me. Initially, although this is how I felt, I couldn't listen to myself, and continued to believe that I was to blame and needed to improve myself so that he would be happy.

Gradually, little by little, and with the help of my sister, I began to see that his behaviour was unreasonable and a form of mental and emotional abuse. Although I could empathise with his suffering, I could also see that mental illness was not an excuse to be abusive. I moved out of our home with Jonah and moved in with friends. Again, I didn't know which way was up. I had a very low opinion of myself and felt extremely vulnerable. I also berated myself for having allowed this to happen as a seemingly intelligent woman and felt a lot of guilt for having allowed Jonah to be put through the experience.

Whilst I was fortunate to have friends nearby to take us in, I knew that ultimately I would need to start standing on my own two feet. I felt scared and vulnerable as a single parent and also exhausted and completely lacking in any confidence.

I knew I would need to leave my job, partly because Jonah's father still worked there and no one else was aware of our home situation. On the outside he was charming and a pillar of the community, and everything seemed fine. Additionally I knew that if I stayed in practice I would need to put Jonah into childcare a lot due to the working hours. After everything that had happened I chose to prioritise being a mother and having time with Jonah as he grew up.

I had at this point developed an interest in pain management and had completed a postgraduate course in veterinary acupuncture. I decided to leave general practice to set up my own pain management service that could fit around times when Jonah was in school. I also found us a place to live still fairly local to my friends.

The following years were a struggle. I felt pretty broken, and stupid, and still blamed myself. I knew I had to remember who I was, and to believe in myself, and I didn't have a clue where to start. I felt like a terrible mother. I'd also lost a lot of weight and stopped menstruating. I had control issues around food, developed as a coping strategy. I didn't know where, or how, to ask for help. It was still up to me to make everything better.

Jonah's father also moved closer to where we were and wanted to see him regularly. For me his behaviour was ongoingly bullying and degrading to me. It felt like every step I took to stand on my feet was knocked back to keep me down. I was too exhausted to fight and felt like I was existing in a fog from moment to moment. Although I had started to offer my pain management services, my confidence was low, I was exhausted and I didn't believe that I was of much worth to anyone. I knew I needed to keep going, for Jonah's sake.

I met some great clients during this time, many of whom are still good friends today. Although it didn't feel as though my business was as 'successful' as it could be I was still helping some animals and their owners, and was giving time to mine and Jonah's healing. I still had some issues around food, and these would take a few years to dissipate and I was exhausted. Hopefully Jonah knew that he was loved unconditionally.

After a year or two Jonah's father and I were divorced. We moved again and found a supportive school community. As well as my veterinary work I took on other work in Jonah's school that would fit around his school hours and holidays. I also had the opportunity to undertake a diploma in Playwork, through some volunteering work I'd done within a play scheme.

The combination of being further away from Jonah's father and embedded within two communities of people that valued me helped me to feel alive again. I started to remember my worth.

I loved Playwork and all that it offers to children (and adults) in terms of development and wellbeing. Playwork recognises that the need to play in an unstructured and diverse way is innate in all of us. Play encompasses a variety of play types that involve a range of states from quiet contemplative time and engagement of imagination to physical activity, connection to our primal selves and risk taking.

Gradually, my confidence grew and I began to remember and rediscover my need for Nature and wild spaces. I would take myself for walks by the river and on Dartmoor as often as possible and I would swim in the rivers and the sea. This was all absolutely the beginning of me saying 'Yes' to myself and to life more than I had done for years.

In Nature I find a true belonging, a sense of being a part of something much bigger than myself and a pragmatism that humbles me and helps prevent me from taking myself too seriously. I believe, more than ever, that we need Nature and the Wild to ground us, to see our place within a much bigger whole and to feel grateful for all that life offers us for free.

I discovered that once I began to follow what I loved, opportunities would come my way. This was eight years since I had left Jonah's father, and I could, for the first time, feel myself truly coming back to life.

Jonah was now at a small secondary school. The school wished to offer the opportunity for students to take part in the Ten Tors challenge. I jumped at the chance to become their outdoor education leader and Ten Tors trainer and Team Manager. I completed my Walking and Wild Camping Leader qualifications and outdoor first aid certification and applied for a place on Ten Tors for the school.

To my surprise we were offered a 35 mile place in our first year of applying and I began to train my first team. I loved it and I was in my element. To be able to pay forward all that I had got from taking part myself to a new generation was a real privilege and pleasure. I have now just completed my fourth year as a Team Manager and I still love it as much as ever. I get so much out of watching a group of young people grow and develop and discover that they are capable of much more than they thought possible. They will each develop their own relationship with themselves and wild spaces and I appreciate playing a small part in facilitating this more than I can say.

Jonah completed the 35 and 45 mile Ten Tors challenge events with me, and went on to complete the 55 mile event with another Team Manager. Now that he is 19 I feel so proud of the man he has become, and feel so grateful for the time we have had together as he was growing up. In the summer of 2015 we went to Spain on a ten day expedition to walk a part of the Camino Pilgrim trail. We walked 240km in ten days. This was quite a big jump for Jonah, who had previously only walked on a one to two night expedition, and it was an amazing experience to have together. Saying Yes to the simplicity of carrying everything we needed, eating wild foods, and walking each day until we felt like looking for somewhere to sleep was refreshing.

We laughed a lot, and met some incredible and generous people along the way.

Following on from my role as a Ten Tors Team Manager, I have also had the opportunity to run environmental Playwork sessions for the younger students at Jonah's former school. It is so good to be able to facilitate the opportunity for children to experience free play in wild spaces. We are lucky enough to have a variety of wild spaces, including woodland and riverside areas within walking distance of the school. Students have the opportunity to experience a diversity of self-led play or to spend quiet time in Nature if that is what they need.

I work freelance for the school and have set up a second business aimed at helping people discover and fully say 'Yes' to Life. My wish is to facilitate the development of people's relationship with the Wild and with themselves and what makes them feel alive. This could be through adventures of all sizes, through expedition training and skill development to build confidence venturing into remote areas safely, through play and through carefully crafted wilderness experiences. I particularly wish to work with women, families and young people, and my ultimate intention is to build funds and collaboration to offer wilderness experiences for women recovering from domestic abuse and their children.

Earlier this year I said 'Yes' to something I had thought about for years and had previously not had the confidence to pursue and completed my Mountain Leader training. I am now on my way to being able to develop my mountaineering skills and lead people in a greater variety of wild spaces.

Much of my recent steps forward in terms of exploring ideas, setting up my new business and finding the confidence to move forward with my training is down to the love, support and encouragement of my new partner. I met him through following another great Yes to myself and applying to join my local Mountain Rescue team within Dartmoor Search and Rescue. I waited five years from when I first felt the draw to apply, until I had developed the confidence and Jonah was old enough to be left during the night should I be called out. I became a trainee towards the end of 2015, and a fully-fledged hill member just before Christmas 2016. The team are my tribe; a great and varied group of individuals with a common love of outdoor adventure and helping people in distress wherever possible. I really enjoy learning new skills and being able to use my existing skills and experience, including my medical background, in the context of search and rescue.

I did not join the team with any thought of finding a partner but by following something that I dearly wished to do for myself, there he was. I appreciate him more than I can say, and he makes me laugh every single day.

Now that Jonah is older and looking beyond home himself, I have also looked at expanding my veterinary pain management practice. This has led me to reconnect with the simplicity of good pain management and the value of taking time to observe and listen; qualities that spending time in Nature help to develop. I have also come to see the importance of animals, and people, spending time in Nature to facilitate pain relief and wellbeing.

I can see now that what I love are Wild spaces and helping people and animals to feel alive and suffer less. I still have times when old demons return, and when I look back to how things were even three years ago, life is now completely different. There were many years, even after I'd left my ex-husband, when I still felt lost and as though things could never really change.

For me it was, in particular, spending time on Dartmoor that brought me back to life and connected me with what I love. For others it will be something else. The point is that we allow ourselves to take the first step towards following what we love and what makes us feel alive.

I now feel much stronger and in a place to be able to offer the fruits of my experience to support others. If any aspects of my story can offer hope, comfort or encouragement to women, or men, going through domestic abuse then I gladly share it.

For me, what I am, and whatever I do is always rooted in the Wild.

If you would like to get in contact please feel free to email me at mirirorudo@gmail.com.

Chapter 16

What's the Worst that Could Happen?

by Hannah Cox

On the outside. I looked like I've got it all under control.

At 23, I was running a successful business, working full time and studying at University. My boyfriend and I shared a large two bed flat and we had a large group of friends.

The reality though was very different. I'd created a lifestyle I simply couldn't afford. By the time I finished University I was in nearly £20,000 debt.

Partly due to stress, my relationships also started to fall apart. I'd like to say I was a good person. But often I wasn't. I'd spent the last five years in a haze of too many nights out and toxic relationships and it'd started to catch up with me.

I'd justified my reckless and bad behaviour as typical student life, but I was beginning to see that for the lie it is. I needed to grow up and figure out what I was doing with myself, because the current situation wasn't working.

When I think of that period I don't recognise the person I was. Perhaps it was the lack of knowledge of who I was that lead me to making bad decisions, and my self-esteem was nonexistent, despite having a loud, gregarious outer shell.

Every highlight of that five year period was accompanied by a crippling low. I had made money as fast as I had lost it. I'd been so unhappy in who I was as a person I'd pushed away the people who are good for me and instead reveled in the mess of other messed up people.

I had a complete lack of respect for other people's feelings, especially romantically, because I was terrified of falling in love. Even a decade later, I cringe in embarrassment at my actions.

My parents had split up when I was at Primary School, and while I was at University my relationship with my had Dad suffered. When it came to my Graduation, I couldn't be bothered with the difficulty of inviting both parents, so instead didn't go and met my friends at the party afterwards. As a result, University ended covered in a black cloud.

The few relationships that survived this period are strong and will continue throughout the rest of my adult life. At 24, I didn't know this yet. At 34, I'm happy the ones that survive did.

In an attempt to start fresh, I dropped everything and move to a new city. But the cycle continued. I was working in a bar and out every night of the week. My debts were continuing to spiral out of control.

Not even sure why or how I got there, I ended up bursting in to tears at the doctors'. I can't even remember if it was a man or a woman I spoke to. They passed me some tissues and suggested some time off work and wrote me a note for my boss.

Within 24 hours I'd handed in my notice, my Mum had driven up, packed the car and had whisked me back at home.

Working at the same pub I worked in before University, falling back into local life is easy. But the reality was that I had had a taste of what it was to be independent and I was itching to go on an adventure. My gut was telling me London, so the job search began.

Unfortunately, as we all know, things don't always run smoothly. When I started to look for somewhere to live I'd expected things to be more expensive in London (aren't they always!). I was struggling to find a single room for the same rent as my old two bed flat.

Coupled with the fact that my new 'junior role' job wouldn't cover even half the rent, I start to realise that the dream of moving to London and making it in the Music Industry was about as likely as winning the lottery.

I could see all my mates on Facebook landing their dream jobs, living in fun looking house shares and updating their profile pictures weekly, sharing another great night out. It did not lift my spirits.

The problem was that even though I have been working in events through University, I didn't know what I wanted to do. Without any huge drive or purpose, I found myself searching through Gumtree.

The internet at that time was a clunky, confusing space beyond my social media pages and email. Gumtree was the only site I really knew. When I couldn't find a room to rent in my price range I started to look slightly above my budget, and then within hours I found myself looking at holiday villas in Spain with swimming pools.

I spent hours looking at cars. I still can't drive, but at 24 I could tell you the market value of a Vauxhall Corsa.

My only goal was to get out of my Mum's house. I had been given a very clear time limit on how long I was welcome for, and the contributions I was making towards rent were making it more and more unlikely that I'd have any savings to move with.

I was reaching a critical point, but where that was going to take me, I had no idea.

After applying unsuccessfully for months for jobs in London, I eventually managed to get an interview for a music marketing company. The money was terrible, but it's in the centre of London and has the promise of a new start so I said 'Yes' and grabbed the opportunity with open arms.

But as I mentioned before, despite having a vague plan (move to London, get a job, worry about my debts and career path later), I couldn't even seem to make that work.

I started to look at alternative jobs, searching the job ads on Gumtree for something that would jump out at me and say 'YES, PICK ME, PICK ME....I'M PERFECT FOR YOU'.

And then it did.

You know how if someone says 'Don't think of Pink Elephants' then that's the first thing you will do?

Well, imagine a tropical island.

Let me guess: golden sands, high tropical palm trees, all rising up in the middle to a jungle of lush greenery.

And there was a picture of it – along with the headline 'Would you like to live on a tropical island?'

Now, I know what you are thinking. Scam.

And so was I.

The problem with Gumtree is it is a mecca for scam artists. The few places to live I had seen advertised (that didn't look like they were owned by murderers) had all asked me in various ways to send them money in advance of viewing as they lived abroad...

That to me had been quite an obvious scam, and one that I felt a small sense of pride that I had outwitted after the initial email back and forth between my potential landlords and I.

Which is why I had given up and wandered onto the jobs overseas page. As I look at a picture of what can only be described as Paradise, I thought 'sod it – sending an email costs nothing' and within minutes had outlined my skills and work experience in an email and sent it.

So it was to my great surprise a few days later to get a phone call asking if I was still interested and available for a job interview that week. The venue was the rather odd choice of Peterborough Train Station café. Again, another reason for alarm bells to start ringing, but the guy on the phone didn't sound like he wanted to kill me, and I reasoned that a public place was probably safer than an office in the middle of nowhere.

I can't drive, so the journey took two trains, of which I can't remember much and to this day, it was the first and last time I have ever been to Peterborough. That's *if* going to the Train Station and then leaving again even counts.

I was met by a guy called Alex, who on first impressions I liked instantly. He was only a few years older than me. A tall skinny guy with a sleeve tattoo and deep tan sat at the table with a moleskin notebook and pen. I have always been an avid lover of good quality stationery, favouring a fountain pen and moleskin notebook above all. This I took to be a good sign.

I opted for a cappuccino, which at the time I viewed as the height of sophistication, and after a half hour chat or so, of which I can now remember nothing – we were done.

Alex told me he would ring me and let me know.

And that was it. I went back to Royston, and spend the weekend working in the pub. I had only mentioned my interview to a few close friends (nervous that it was a massive prank and not wanting to look stupid) and promptly forgot about it the way you do when you live in a small town.

But less than a week later Alex rang me.

'You got the Job'

'Erm....thanks'

The thing is, I didn't really understand what the job was. In the interview I had enthusiastically nodded when he asked if I knew where Tioman Island was. The reality was, I had never heard of it, and when he spoke about Malaysia I thought it was cluster of islands near Singapore.

My geographical skills in the rough location of Malaysia were correct. But it turns out that Malaysia is not a collection of tiny islands but a huge country – with 13 states and 30 million people. I had no idea about the culture or even what language they spoke. All those geography lessons I was kicked out of for passing notes to Robert Bootle at the back of the class had clearly taught me nothing.

I also had to break the news to my Mum that I was no longer moving to London, but to a place I'd never heard off, to do a job I wasn't sure of, with a person I had met once.

Surprisingly, I think my Mum was just happy to have me move out the house and find my own two feet. That or the fact she has three other kids to worry about anyway. Whatever the reason, she was happy to have her home back.

I scraped together what little money I had to cover my flight, and reasoned I would only get the injections I needed to get into the country, rather than all the recommended ones, to save money.

Alex had also passed me on the details of the other girl he had employed, who rather kindly came to Royston to meet me before we embarked on this quite frankly confusing adventure.

When Vicky turned up at my front door, I was immediately taken aback by how pretty she was. Coming from a small town you see the same faces every day, so it doesn't take much for someone to appear cosmopolitan.

However, Vicky actually WAS Cosmopolitan – as well as being beautiful, she was kind, funny and well-travelled. Sat in the pub having a few drinks with my friends It felt like I had bought along the person I had always wanted to be, and a slow feeling of dread started creeping in.

That night I sat in bed cursing myself. Why had I said yes to an opportunity that was only going to show me up. I'd never travelled, beyond a few European trips and a two week holiday in Bali with my Mum. I was as green as they came, and was worried I'd tricked Alex into employing me because I had bought a fancy cappuccino. I don't even like cappuccino!

I realise now, I probably had a lot to offer beyond my fancy coffee choices, but it just goes to show the stupid self-sabotage things we do when our confidence is low.

A week later, we were off.

Arriving at Heathrow I met Alex for the second time, along with Simon who was to be the dive instructor at the resort we would be working at.

Oh yes, I forgot to mention I would be working in a hotel. I had worked in hotels in Scarborough where I went to Uni, of which a lot of that involved pouring pints at weddings and birthday parties.

The resort on Tioman consisted of around twenty cabins around a small cove, only contactable via boat. There was a small beach, restaurant, bar and dive shop. That was it.

Before Uni I had learnt to scuba dive and my job was to be Simon's Assistant in the Dive shop. I didn't have all the technical qualifications I needed, but Simon told me I would have plenty of time to learn them. The job was to pay £100 a month with food and accommodation covered.

I reasoned that I needed to completely get out of the UK to gain perspective on where I was and how I was going to gain control of my life.

I was very aware of my problems with money and my relationships, but this opportunity seemed so rare, so impossible that I was unable to turn it down.

So, I found myself on a weekday morning sharing a pint with three strangers I was about to spend the rest of the year with.

Only my second ever long haul flight, I reveled in the free drinks and movies, not quite realising what I had said yes to.

We landed in Singapore and then had to cross the border to Malaysia and spend the night in a hotel, before getting the bus across Malaysia to Mersing, where the ferry to Tioman was.

I was in that slightly confused state that is bought on by lack of sleep and too many airplane drinks. I wasn't anxious, more unprepared. Pulling on my oversized backpack we stepped outside to be hit by the heat, my back immediately covered in a film of sweat.

We managed to get to the border crossing with relative ease thanks to the boys. They took the lead while we skirted the massive queue and confidently reaching the front with a crisp pile of dollar bills and got out unscathed via buses to Johur Baru.

Alex had booked us into a hotel, but not mentioned much more. What we actually got were two huge all singing and dancing suites, for around £20 each. Vicky and I walked around in shock, deciding which bathroom to use (answer, all of them) and quickly clamber into our crisp white dressing gowns and paper slippers.

To this day, I can't remember the name of the hotel, despite using it for several visa runs throughout the year. As a seasoned traveller I have now visited hundreds of identi-kit hotels like this all over Asia. Huge sprawling marble floored skyscrapers with potted plastic plants, an overuse of neon signage and incredibly polite and friendly staff.

The rooms are almost always spotless and near perfect, apart from something glaringly obvious, like a toenail in an ashtray or a lack of hot water.

But at the time it was the most exotic, amazing place I had ever visited. There was a karaoke bar in the basement, which confusingly Alex refused to let me and Vicky visit, (turns out there is more than one kind of Karaoke bar in Asia) so we instead had a night of room service followed by a long hot shower.

The journey to Mersing the next day took place on an old school bus that seemed to have left its suspension back in the 80's. I was terrified by stories of bag snatchers from reading the Lonely Planet guide Book (my only reference for the entire trip was 'Asia on a Shoe String' of which Tioman Island gets less than a paragraph – I definitely recommend more research when planning a trip)

My solution was stuffing my worldly possessions in my bra (including my passport, all my cash and a $100 dollar emergency bill) and hugging my bag holding my laptop. On a bus with no air conditioning the journey was uncomfortable, to say the least.

I, of course, remember none of the stress of the journey. My eyes were glued to the window watching the scenery fly past like an exotic movie. People were working in miles of rice fields. Water buffalo grazed nonchalantly by the side of the road. Town after town passed, all seemingly made entirely of concrete, corrugated iron and vinyl advertising banners.

It was new, it was exciting and it was a million miles from my small town of Royston.

There is nothing quite as exciting for me as the thrill of being in a new place. It makes me feel reborn, knowing that everyone I met will meet the current version of me. I strive to be a better person every day. Like most of us I have some moments of the past I'm ashamed of. Being in Malaysia opened the door of possibility for me in how I can create real change in myself and my life.

After all, if I had landed a job on a tropical island – wasn't anything possible?

After a short ferry ride, of which I was reminded of my very real, and very quick susceptibility to sea sickness (something I had decided not to share with my three new best friends), we were greeted at the ferry terminal by a small boat.

We buzzed across the waves round the coast to our resort. The sun beat down on our little craft as we splashed through the waves. We passed several resorts on neighbouring islands that were presumably owned by Bond villains. Walkways leading into the sea with 360 degree bars, tree top cabins and pristine white beaches. I half expected Ursula Andress to start walking out of the surf.

We eventually reached or place of work, a small cove with a visible small restaurant and bar area, and the cabins hidden almost in the jungle. At the end of the pier was a huge house, which turned out to be the dive shop on the ground floor, with Alex's home on the top.

Expecting a similar accommodation, Vicky and I were unluckily taken to the back of the resort, up a dirt path to our accommodation. Unlike the air-conditioned cabins decked out with fridges, TV's and hot water we had a rather different experience waiting for us.

At the top of the hill, on the edge of the jungle, was a row of some of the originally built cabins. One room, one window affairs, with a small bathroom out the back. These consisted of a simple shower of freezing cold water (no, it wasn't broken, we just weren't connected to the hot water and coming straight from the river) two beds and a wardrobe.

Our room seemed to far better than Simon's, which although bigger had a large hole in the wall where apparent 'bob' lived. Bob turned out to be a huge gecko.

Now for anyone that has been to a tropical place, geckos as usually no bigger than the size of your hand, and extremely adapt at eating everything around you that my bite you – like midges and spiders.

Bob was not one of these geckos.

Bob was, and still is as far as I am aware, a complete natural anomaly. About the size of a cat, he had an ability to crawl around the wall spaces silently like a reptilian ninja, before popping his head out and resting behind Simon's closet.

The thought was, and still is, terrifying to me, but Simon didn't seem to care so nothing was ever done about it. Vicky and I were luckier with just a few small geckos living in our room.

Simon and Alex were quick to remind us of the importance of the geckos to keep out the other nasties, but for me, this was already starting to feel like a very bad mistake.

Lying in bed that night, hearing loud thumps coming from various areas of my room, which I later found out are geckos falling off the wall and ceiling, I felt very, very alone.

I was lucky that Vicky was so lovely and life on the island was slow. Unless we had guests that wanted to dive or snorkel, Simon and I had very easy days. Often you would find us spending days lying in hammocks at the dive centre, reading from the vast library of books left by visitors.

It was pre-internet everywhere days, and I used to find it amusing when high powered executives would finish dinner and request the boats to take them out on the water to try and get a phone signal.

If Simon, Alex, Vicky or I needed to send an email, it involved a trip to the ferry port where the only internet café on the island existed. This would only be allowed if we had visitors to take home, and time between trips. As a result it would often be weeks between long rambling emails to friends and family about the experiences I was having.

That sense of aloneness has never left me, and I've been unable to replicate it since, not now Wi-Fi hotspots have popped up on every corner of the planet.

I've visited 45 countries since this trip and never been able to relive that feeling of disconnectedness. Local sim cards and Wi-Fi seems so easily available everywhere, I'm not sure how I could. Even if I choose to disconnect, the knowledge that I can, quite easily, get on WhatsApp or post a picture online takes away that magic feeling.

To pass the time I took up running through the jungle, on a roughly hacked path which lead me to the nearest village and a concrete path to a waterfall, where I would plunge into the freezing water after the hour's hike / jog to get to it.

On those runs I would have my old iPod tucked into my sports bra, until that got too sweaty and I had to carry it. I had, in typical Hannah fashion, been completely unable to work out how to load it with music, and as a result had a hodge-podge of odd music for my trip.

The memorable albums which I listening to on repeat were three incredible indie emo bands, Air Traffic, The Postal Service and Get Cape Wear Cape Fly. And for some reason, the Kanye West album - Graduation.

The result of listening to the same music, over and over again is almost hypnotic. Not only did you start to feel like you were living in some sort of indie film, but you really got the opportunity to analyse the lyrics and fall into a spiral of self-reflection.

Or perhaps it was slowly just sending me stir crazy...

Vicky was funny and a great friend, but because of the troubles I had left in the UK, I ebbed and flowed into pure elation at my situation and genuine fear about my next move.

Teaching diving on a tropical island was everything you imagine it could be. Beautiful coral reefs, and enough 'nemo fish' to make a film sequel.

I learnt magical things about the ocean, like how stingrays hide under a small layer of sand so that, if you don't spot their eyes sticking out, they will surprise you by flying out from underneath you during a dive.

Or that turtles prefer staying in the depths, so that when one decides to come up to the surface for a breath, you should stop everything you are doing and watch them slowly take a breath then dive down and swim away.

I also learnt that bananas are a great underwater snack for fish, and that I could quite happily sing under water with no one I dived with knowing!

Life on the resort was relaxing, there was regular routine with set meals on set days. I still remember Tuesdays being Beef Rendang, a deep rich beef stew Malaysian-style full of spices and coconut milk. To this day, this remains one of my favourite meals of all time.

Seafood BBQ on a Wednesday was a different story. I had grown up not as a fussy eater, but certainly from a family who's meals where traditional and, let's just say, 'budget'.

After eating Tuna Pasta for what seemed like every second dinner growing up, once I left for University I vowed to never touch the stuff again. While most students revel in their perceived sophistication of being able to cook tuna, pasta, pesto – I bucked the trend by avoiding it at all costs.

Apart from fish fingers as a kid, beyond those two experiences my experience of seafood was limited, despite being the grand old age of 24.

So when Simon sat down next to me at the Seafood BBQ with a whole crab and fish on his plate, my eyes widened. I watched him pull apart both meals with the easy manner of a man well versed in eating all manner of molluscs and crustaceans.

Rather embarrassed at my lack of marine meal skills I asked Simon to show me how it was done, and within minutes I was enjoying my first taste of crab and Malaysian white fish.

The new food experiences didn't of course touch on the cultural experiences I was having. Malaysian time seemed to work on a different level, and rather than be rushed, many jobs required careful consideration before beginning.

I remember well a rather slow few weeks in the dive shop in which Simon and I discussed the job of refilling the tanks (a task that takes a couple of hours at most) over the course of several days before we considered even crawling out of our hammocks.

Eventually the slow life of the island lost its appeal. I had done a lot of soul searching and knew there needed to be a point at which I dealt with my money problems. I'd never be truly content till I had become financially independent. I also had learnt to be kinder to myself. I had needed to slow down because of island life, but that had allowed me to give myself time to learn to be kinder to myself and others.

I wanted to start to take responsibility for myself, I just didn't know where to start.

My Grandad had been ill when I left and I found out about his death a few days afterwards via email in the internet café by the ferry. The helplessness I felt in regards to having no one close around me to share my grief ended up being the straw that broke the camel's back.

So I decided to leave, and heading back to the UK and home.

Moving to Tioman had taught me many things. One of the most important was learning to start to love myself again. If I could give a piece of advice to my 24 year old self, it would be to keep saying 'Yes' to adventures, friendships and yourself. We are all capable of so much as long as we keep being kind to ourselves and each other. Saying Yes to life is about saying yes to yourself. I owed myself the time and space to clear my mind before I could tackle some of the big issues and problems I had to face.

Losing my Grandad while I was away was devastating. However it reminded me of the importance of relationships. He was a man who treated everyone with respect and had all the time in the world for his family. Losing him was a reminder that love is the most important thing.

So when I returned to the to the UK I decided to try and improve my relationship with my Dad. We had drifted apart for too long and I was ready to change that.

Not long after my return my Dad passed away as well. If it hadn't have been for the life lessons Tioman taught me, about being patient and considerate for myself and others' feelings, my Dad would have died not knowing how much I cared about and loved him.

Shortly before he died my Dad passed on some sage wisdom. He told me to never settle and never stop improving. Each day strive to be better than the person you were yesterday.

So I started the website **betternotstop.com** I write about how travel can make you happy, and also how we all have the tools we need to create a better life for ourselves.

For me, experiencing different countries and culture is a way to discover more about myself and how to make the world a better place.

I believe we should all enjoy everyday life through our work, friendships, travel, and adventure. There are solutions for making our lives better; we just have to be willing to seek the answer and work hard! I don't recognize my old self, much preferring time alone or with my small group of friends. However the memories of that time are a stark reminder that I should to trust myself and trust that I have the power to change my situation, no matter how bad it may be.

And you know what? You have this power too. Be brave. Be bold. Be the person you were meant to be!

Follow my Writing at **betternotstop**

Instagram: **@betternotstop**

Facebook: **betternotstop**

Chapter 17

Journey to Mount Elbrus

by Scott Butler

I can say in all honesty that it was the most delicious drink I'd ever had. The battle to get the tiny plastic straw out of that irritatingly little wrapper was totally worth it. Hands down, the banana milkshake contained within caused me to close my eyes in ecstasy. I could feel the cold, full-of-flavour liquid run down my throat and cool my weary body from within. It was like a revitalising, life-giving nectar.

It's not often you wax lyrical about a milkshake but, when you've been alone at sea on a 23ft rowing boat for so many days you've lost count, it truly is something you'll always remember.

Little did I know that what started as my 'I fancy climbing a mountain' idea would end up being the most monumental rollercoaster ride of my life. That ride was called 'The Journey to Mount Elbrus'.

In life things go wrong. Plans don't always pan out the way we want them to. It may sound horribly cliché, but it's how we overcome and adapt to these bumps in the road that define us. This adventure had plenty of these bumps!

It all started when I decided that I wanted to climb a mountain. A BIG mountain! I chose Mt. Elbrus which is one of the Seven Summits and the highest peak in Europe.

A quick glance at a map and you can see that the Black Sea was right there. So very close.

'C'mon,' I thought. 'It'd be rude not to!'

The 'why the hell not' part of my brain took over and before I knew it I'd formed a plan.

I was going to cycle from the UK to the port of Burgas on the West coast of the Black sea. From there I would row across the widest part of the sea to the port of Batumi on the East coast. Then it was only a quick hop and a skip over the border into Russia and the small matter of the 5642 metre mountain. What could possibly go wrong?

Much like any huge decision, there was more to it than just 'fancying a mountain climb'. I'd been a shy and fat kid and had really only discovered the real Scott Butler when I joined the Fire Service. You can't be a shrinking violet in the service and I grew as a person. John O'Groats to Land's End soon followed and then I chose to try my hand at a bigger mission.

I endeavoured to try and do something new every day for a year. It was a tiring and mind opening year that ended after 343 days when I crashed a Speedway motorbike and smashed my femoral artery to bits. I was incredibly lucky and had it patched up with a plastic tube. It took months to get back to work and to fitness. People doubted – and I doubted – that I could ever go on and be strong. Be the animal I knew I could be. I needed to prove to the fat, shy and now bionic kid that nothing could stop me. The mission was on.

People often say that the planning stage is the most stressful. They were kinda right. I'm not a 'blagger' so most of the funding came from my own (rather barren) pocket.

Logistically planning such a multi-faceted trip can be a bit mind boggling, but with perseverance and a little belief it'll all come good in the end.

Bike? Check!

Guide for Elbrus? Check!!

Boat... um...

This was a bit trickier. Do you know how much Ocean rowing boats cost?! I was looking at an investment akin to my mortgage! But, much like the second hand cars I like to buy, I found a second hand 23ft plywood ocean rowing boat called *Pacific Pete*. Its pedigree spoke for itself; five times across the Atlantic since its first crossing in the inaugural Atlantic rowing race in 1997. So Pete was old. But I didn't care. In fact, I reveled in the fact.

Pete went into a boat yard to have a few minor dings in her hull repaired (and yes, before you ask. Pete *is* a female boat!). Or so I thought. With time running out until my departure I got the call to say that Pete was rotten from the inside. I may as well throw her away, I was told.

Expletives ensued.

Not one to be beaten I rallied some opinions and enlisted the help of someone I knew who'd tinkered with boats and we started work on Pete. A couple of days into the repair my 'boat specialist' informed me that he couldn't help anymore as he didn't want our botch job on his conscience.

'No Worries!!' I lied through gritted teeth.

I reckoned I'd seen enough and continued to repair the boat myself. I spent all my spare time trying to get the boat ship-shape even though I should have been training. When I finally stood back to admire my handiwork I felt an enormous sense of pride. I'd done the best job I could. I knew that there was nothing else I could do. The only thing I didn't know was is if it would float or not!

Rushed, unprepared and buzzing with excitement I stood on top of Box Hill in Surrey, head freshly shaved for the trip, posing for photos and waved off by my two biggest fans – my mum and my wife.

Then I was alone. And lost. The bike sat nav wasn't finding a satellite and I found niggling issues with the bike setup that I would have discovered had I actually practiced. That first day down to Dover was a huge learning curve. Not that it made much of a difference. Once onto mainland Europe I was equally lost, skirting the border between France and Belgium. The heat was ridiculous, the sat nav *still* didn't work (spoiler: It never worked!) and I was feeling massive doubts over my ability to actually get the job done.

I must have cut a lonely figure eating a kebab on the roadside in France when a lovely couple invited me in for a shower and a bed for the night. This was my first night away from Blighty. They were the first of many to show true kindness to a stranger. I'll never forget these people.

I wound my way up and down hills and through quaint villages. I'd been aiming for one hundred miles a day but was only managing around eighty five. This was no good at all as I had a boat to catch and a time limit of the visa into Russia!

I battled away stubbornly, unsure of what country I was actually in most of the time. There seems to be little difference between France and Belgium along the border and I even had to ask in some shops when I stopped for a life-giving Coke.

Luxembourg arrived and here I hit a physical low. I'd not been eating enough, just filling my gut with water in an effort to stay hydrated in the stifling 40 degree heat. I slumped against a petrol station wall gulping water filled with electrolytes while a group of suspect looking people raided a waste bin nearby. I was acutely aware of my vulnerability at that moment. I had no energy to chase them off should they have taken an interest in my bike and bulging panniers. Thankfully they moved on.

I trudged the last few miles to a campsite. I dragged my stinking corpse into the reception and had to apologise for my state... and horrific smell. The couple in line took pity and provided some washing powder so I could clean my gear. I was grateful to have a chance to remove the crusty sweatiness from my cycling shorts.

Everything changed in Germany. Here I met an English couple in a book store where I was trying to buy a map. These two cyclists advised that I should pick up the cycle route that follows the Danube River. It wouldn't be direct but navigation would be simple. Standing over a bridge looking at the great river flowing all the way to the Black Sea lifted me and I set off with renewed gusto.

Now I was setting hundred mile days and even a hundred and forty mile day. Sure they were long days but they were beautiful – especially Austria. The whole route felt like one giant valley where the lush green banks and the wide life giving river directed and mentally refueled me. I'd found my rhythm on the bike and when making camp too. Some of the spots I found along my route were wonderful; next to lakes, on the banks of the Danube itself, a waterpark/nightclub campsite that was surreal... but not the night at the rear of a superstore. Hot, sweaty, smelly, out of water and being plagued by mosquitoes I quickly pitched my tent and dove in. The lights and sounds of the shop made sleep hard to come by and it wasn't long before the early shift came to work to start baking bread. I soon gave in and wearily got back on the bike.

My major regret was that I had so many miles to catch up on that I missed out on exploring some beautiful and interesting places.

Three countries in one day was pretty cool. Leaving Austria I dipped into Slovakia before entering Hungary. It was here that at sunset, in the middle of nowhere, three spokes on my rear wheel broke and burst through the inner tube and the tyre.

I was screwed. Just as I was in the process of finding a bush to camp behind, a diamond of a fella stopped to help. Speaking little English, we managed to get my broken steed into his car and he drove in the opposite direction to his intended travel and took me to a hotel near a bike shop. What a legend.

Next up it was Bulgaria and I met a cracking fella called Doichin in a bike shop in Sofia where my wheel was fixed. He led me out of the city on his moped. I had to dig deep to keep up.

There was just so many amazing people, many whom I have not mentioned like the little old lady at the top of a devastating hill who spoke no English at all but directed me to a chair in the shade and brought me fresh Lemonade. I have no idea what her name was, but I'll always remember her.

But wait! I've missed the kicker here. My boat!

So, the plan was that two of my buddies were to tow my boat to Burgas for me. Then they'd drive to Batumi on the opposite shore with the trailer ready for my arrival and fly home.

They didn't make it. I took the call from Tim and Jason while in Serbia. My car had blown its turbo just twenty miles into France. It was knackered. Kaput. My luck with cars continued.

The row was off. As you can imagine I was devastated. All I could really do was finish the ride and fly home. Balderdash.

The pressure off, I invested in enjoying the rest of my time on the road. The further East I got, the friendlier people seemed, beeping their horns in support, thumbs up out of passing cars and many a question and photo when I stopped for more food. There were very few cyclists this far East and I think people appreciated how far I had clearly come. What didn't improve however was the lorry drivers' ability to give me much room as they passed. How I didn't get clipped is anyone's guess!

I finally caught sight of the Black Sea from atop yet another huge hill. I whooped with joy. There it was! Still, it seemed to take *forever* to get to the shoreline. I span the last few miles, partly with a local boy in tow who was fascinated by my bike.

I cycled all the way down to the water, kicked out the bike stand, set up my camera and ran into the sea. It felt AMAZING!

Take Two

Fast forward a year and with a new car, new trailer (the axle literally just snapped off the old one) and a new support crew we headed back out Burgas. With the help of Billy and Barry who had rowed the Pacific back in 2014, we launched Pacific Pete into the water at the yacht club in Burgas... and it floated!

The next few days were spent loading the boat with all my equipment, food and water. I'm obviously biased but Pete looked spectacular sat in the water at last.

I waved Barry and Billy goodbye as they set off to drive through Turkey and into Georgia (which was a mission in itself with the Turkish border police demanding paperwork that they didn't have for the trailer). But they made it across and left my car and trailer at the yacht club (which turned out to be a very grandiose term for the small marina) and flew home.

I sat and waited for a weather window. I needed the winds to be blowing out to sea in order for me to escape the mainland. My new friends, Kras and Siana, looked after me like I was family. Then the window arrived. I arose nice and early, finally nervous, and headed down to the marina... only to find yet another disaster!

At some point during the night Pete had been slammed into the marina wall and had made a hole in her side. My heart sank. We presumed that one of the passing ferries had been going too fast causing Pete to smash into the concrete.

The locals burst into action in an effort to repair Pete. And repair him they did. Head coach and local legend, Kosta, worked his magic. He patched Pete back up and made my pride and joy seaworthy once again. I was ready to go but the weather window had closed again and I had to wait another night. 'Perfect!' I thought, trying to put a positive spin on the situation. 'I can watch England's first match of the Euro's'... we all know how that panned out!

So there I was again, back at the yacht club and this time Pete was still in one glorious piece. I completed the customs paperwork and posed for photos before casting off and setting 'sail'. I was off! It felt amazing to finally be on my way and pulling at the oars. The sea was wonderfully calm, the sun was out and I was doing it. I was rowing out into the sea. Into the unknown.

What the hell was I *doing?!*

Right from the off I settled into the 'two hours on, two hours off' routine used by most ocean rowers. The plan was to row my heart out for two hours and then rest, sleep, eat and clean for two hours... for twenty four hours a day. This was fine during the day but at night this, for me, truly sucked! I hated it. I'd fall asleep at the oars, especially the two am shift.

I made pretty good progress for five days (although comically my tracker showed that I didn't exactly head in a straight line). I was getting used to my surroundings and falling into routines when it came to food prep and my 'ablutions'.

I'd spotted dolphins who swam around the boat in the mornings and the evenings, making fine company for my meals. These friendly mammals appeared on most days when the sea was calm. As you can imagine, they were a huge spirit raiser.

After five days everything changed. By everything I mean the wind.

Strong winds turned and blew straight at me from the East making rowing impossible. I had to deploy the sea anchor which, in simple terms, is a parachute that you drop into the water at the end of a line. It opens up under water and slows the boats backwards progress. It doesn't stop you though and for eight dreadfully frustrating and uncomfortable days I drifted backwards. The waves at times were huge and I often sat out on the deck, tethered onto Pete and watched us rise and fall over the watery mountains. It was exhilarating and made me really appreciate the power of the sea. Little old Pete never batted an eyelid and my repairs held true.

The boredom sucked! I tried to sleep as much as I could despite the cramped and uncomfortable conditions. I hit real lows during this period. My shoulder had become so painful that no matter what pain killers I took, the pain wouldn't go away and I couldn't sleep. I wanted to cry but that didn't happen either.

I plotted my negative progress on my paper charts and as I came to the end of day seven of no rowing I predicted that I had less than forty eight hours to go before I would be washed up on the Turkish coast. THAT would be a disaster and game over.

Luck and hope collided and with it the wind changed direction. Suddenly I was back at the oars and heading back on course. The joy of finally returning to the seat and pulling on the oars again is indescribable.

Now though I was in a race. A race against time. If you look at the Black Sea on a map it's kinda split into two at the bottom, like the shape of a W. I needed to reach the centre of that W before the winds changed again and I was blown, once more, backwards. To the oars I cracked, dispensing with the two-and-two shifts and rowed for sixteen hours straight – but for food and toilet breaks – during the day. That way I would have a day and night which suited me so much better.

The other race I was now in was the one against the Russian visa office. The visa issued was for a specific date and specific entry point. I needed to make that or I would never make it into Russia for the climb.

So I rowed.

Some of the days blur into one with the monotony of the landscape and the task at hand. That's not to say however there weren't very memorable times. There was the day of the butterfly invasion – beautiful and bizarre so far from land. Then there was the fly invasion - horrible and madness inducing. The huge cargo ships that would pass worryingly close, making me wonder if they'd actually seen me. I soon realised that they just wanted to wave and take photos of this tiny boat flying the British Flag. They didn't seem to care about what the wake of the huge cargo ships would do to me though!

The weather was very changeable. Most days I had to duck away from the midday heat, sometimes tethering myself and then jumping into the water to cool down and inspect the underside of the boat. On other days you could be gleefully rowing along singing your heart out in the sunshine when you'd feel a breath of wind on your back. Behind you (and of course in *front* of the boat) was a black wall of nature's finest.

The rain was unbelievable. It made the sea look like it was covered in snow. The thunderstorms were raging all around me, twisters reaching up into the angry sky. It was a crazy time but I loved it! On one day it literally rained for fourteen hours. I was quite wet and demoralised at the end of that one!

There was, of course, the meeting with the milkshake. It was a normal day at the oars when I spotted a boat heading towards me. Clearly towards me too. At speed. Looking through my small telescope I could make out what appeared to be a very scruffy looking boat breaking through the waves. My mind, as it does, immediately jumped to the conclusion that they were pirates and so

I tried to hide what I could find that was of value and searched for anything I could use as a weapon.

My fears were soon quashed when I realised it was the Turkish coastguard who were merely curious. They launched a rib and came over for a chat and delivered that oh-so-memorable milkshake. I'm still drooling thinking of it now.

Slowly land came into view on the twenty eighth day and I could make out the skyline of Batumi. I thought that I'd made it, but the weather had one more card to play. The sea became choppy, the wind and rain appeared once again. Police boats came out to investigate and sat near me as I helplessly bobbed around. They wanted me to just head to shore. It took quite some time and disjointed conversation to make them realise I couldn't just 'turn the engine on'.

I had one more night aboard Pete with the lights of Batumi to keep me company. On the 29th day I was able to get back on the oars and headed for the yacht club.

Again, this was a mission. There was a current that ran along the coast here and I needed to cross it. I laboured for most of the day, growing ever angrier and frustrated. I was drifting further away and was going to fail to make it into port. My contact at the club, David, was on the phone insisting that they come tow me in... but I needed to make land by own steam to claim the world record of being the first person to ever row across the Black Sea.

I aimed at a beach with a small pier and decided that would be my final spot. In fact it was a poor choice. The waves bashed Pete against the pier, the ropes I had hastily lashed around it were pulling painfully against her hull. I quickly swam to shore to fully make sure the record was mine and waited for the coastguard to arrive and pull me out of that mess.

David, along with the local news crew, buzzed around on a speed boat while I was towed to the marina. Then they cheekily asked if I could row back out and then in again for the sake of the cameras.

I was greeted like a hero. It was an unbelievable feeling. I had done it! I'd rowed six hundred and fifty nautical miles across the Black Sea... On my own. With no experience.

All I wanted was a beer, a shower and some real food. In that order. I was made to wait and sit through a comical interview translated by my new friend, David, who seemed to be lapping up the attention by association. Let him have it and let me have a beer!

Eventually I was left alone to come to terms with what had happened. David had let me stay on his yacht while I was in Batumi which I had to myself. I showered and ate, somewhat soothed by the familiarity of a gently moving boat. I was still trying to shake my sea legs so this was a gentle way of easing me back to terra firma.

Sitting back and finally relaxing, the local beer gently making my eyelids heavier, I smiled to myself. I really had done it. I'd confronted the naysayers, the disbelievers, the setbacks and the physical hardship. I'd made a plan, spoke about it and finally just gone out and faced it all on my own.

I'd said 'YES'! Yes to adventure. Yes to pushing mental and physical barriers. Who'd put those barriers there in the first place is open to interpretation, but they'd been smashed through all the same. Had it been tough? Hell yes! Had I thought about giving up? Not once, despite voices suggesting that maybe I should give up on the row and just make the climb.

That was never an option. All the time it was in my hands, I wasn't going to give up. This was my moment. This had been my opportunity to say 'YES I WILL!' This was Butler coming to the party.

Of course the adventure wasn't over just yet. There was still the small matter of 5642 metres of mountain to climb.

The plan had been to cycle from Batumi over to the base of Elbrus. This didn't happen. Time, energy and logistics all added up to this being a dumb idea. This at least gave me a few days to get Pete out of the water and then chill out. David and his friend Otto made me feel like a part of the family. We had BBQ's with what appeared to be the extended family where we had to toast after every refill of the homemade wine. Touching yet embarrassingly most of the toasts were to me. I immediately loved these people.

The trip to the airport in Mineralyne Vody to meet the guide and fellow climbers involved coaches through stunning rural Georgia to Tbilisi. I then somehow navigated the trading floor-esque melee to find a minibus that was heading to the border checkpoint. Phone calls were made and one car drove me to a minibus that had pulled over to await my arrival.

A lovely Russian couple, a Georgian woman and I made conversation during the long winding drive through the Kazbegi National park valley that in the winter was a ski resort. I was *very* glad I hadn't opted to cycle! The border crossing was a bit of an issue with me being the centre of it. My new friends aboard the mini bus explained to the KGB who I was and what I had done and suddenly I was through with handshakes and smiles. We were dropped off in a town called Vladikavkaz that honestly looked like Disney Main Street. It totally debunked any preconceived ideas of a concrete Russia I had expected.

Then I made contact with their version of Uber and arranged to meet a bunch of guys at a junction in the middle of nowhere to then drive to the airport. I was amazed at the random checkpoints that were guarded with fully loaded automatic weapons where we had to leave the car and show our documents. At the airport I met Sasha our guide and his daughter along with half the team, two of which were British. I hadn't seen a native English speaker in months. I had to apologise to brother and Sister, Richard and Rebecca, for my verbal diarrhoea! I chewed their ears off discussing pop culture chit chat for entire the journey to base camp.

Then we were there. At the bottom. At the final challenge.

In total we had ten days to acclimatise and summit. The rest of the group joined us – two separate groups of Norwegians - and slowly we all began to bond. The early hikes were warm, sunny and beautiful but we were all itching to go higher. Sasha knew better though and with who knows how many climbs under his belt, we wisely listened to his 'poly, poly' – slowly, slowly – instructions.

As we scaled higher the snow soon became our landscape and what an awe inspiring one it was too. I, of course, remained in shorts until roughly the 3000 metre mark. Sure, it was snowy but it wasn't cold. The looks of bemusement still make me smile although I didn't follow through with my threat of doing it all in flip flops. I'm not that mad!

After 3000 metres it started to get serious. Slowly you became aware of the need for your self-rescue drills, the need for thicker clothing and also the awareness that the air was ever so slightly thinner.

The acclimatisation hikes blur into two. Trudging ups and jolly, gleeful downs, interspersed with idle chat, photographic wonders and laughter at the 'long drop' toilet situation.

Finally summit day had arrived. We had a weather window so at 3am we set off with four guides to keep an eye on us. One memorable guide wore a 'V' for Vendetta mask the entire time. I never saw his face and he even walked backwards for 80% of the time! Incredible.

The ridges and the saddle, which is the U shaped section that links the twin peaks of Elbrus, became ever more dangerous. We were roped together, each sporting a walking pole and an axe that we grasped at the 'pointy end'. The mountain fell away steeply to our left and we braced ourselves against the freezing gusts of wind that tried to lift us off our feet. Each of us planting the axe handle deep into the snow to act as anchor. It's hard, at times like this, to take moment to appreciate where you are and not just look at your feet.

That sunrise was something of wonder to behold. The white tipped Toblerone landscape slowly lit. The golden hew background casting rugged and lengthening shadows culminating in brilliant, blinding sunlight that instantly brought much welcome warmth.

Breathing became harder by this point too and my snood had frozen to my beard which I had to defrost with the steam from my flask. You could see people were tired but buzzing to be so close to the summit. One final push from the saddle and we would be there.

I was full of energy, enthusiasm and confidence, trying hard to communicate my excitement through layers of clothes and a biting wind.

Then.

We.

Were.

There.

5642 metres above sea level and literally higher than every single person on the European continent. Higher than almost everyone in the world. Richard and I tore off our cumbersome clothing and posed for photos in just our trousers and boots. Wow! It was cold! But that photo of me atop Elbrus has a million emotions bursting out of it.

Relief? Pride? Energy? Triumph? They're all there.

That was it. 'Journey to Elbrus' complete. Years in the making, shed loads of personal investment, both financially and emotionally, all culminating in that ascent.

There are no adequate words.

Within days I was back to reality. Back at the Fire station ready for a day's work. Had it all actually happened? Did *I* do all that?

Yes, I had. But the time to enjoy the moment is often short lived. The question on everyone's lips is and always will be 'So, what's next?'

Whatever follows I'll find it hard to match that milkshake moment, that's for sure.

Website: **splitlipadventures.com**

Facebook: **splitlipadventures**

Epilogue

The Teddington Trust

by Nicola Miller

I have always considered myself as someone who wasn't afraid of a challenge. I have lived by the mantra since a child to 'never let my own (perceived) lack of ability stand in my way of dreaming big'.

I left school at 17 and headed straight to university to study a BSc in Architectural Technology. I had applied for an HND in Building Studies but on securing enough grades in one year instead of two I got a surprise letter from the University offering me a place on a degree course. Despite only being 17 and too young even to visit my own student union bar, I said 'yes' and I grabbed the opportunity with both hands. Four years later I graduated with a 1st class honours degree.

Subsequent `yeses` have allowed me to travel, live in London, work at the prestigious Imperial College and hold positions in two of London's top three architecture practices. I said `yes` to marrying my first love (who I met at aged 17 on my first day at university), 'yes' to starting my own architecture practice and the biggest 'yes' of all – to starting a family.

I was well on my way to domestic bliss. I had a fabulous and rewarding career, recognition within my professional institute, an amazing life partner, a beautiful baby boy and son number two on the way.

Then, like all epic tales, life hit a road bump. Without warning, the entire course of my life had changed!

Time literally and momentarily froze when my husband and I received the devastating news. Our son, then aged just 13 months, had an ultra-rare disease, the name of which we couldn't even pronounce let alone spell! All I could hear was the sound of my own heartbeat and I knew in that moment nothing would be the same again.

That afternoon as we drove home from the hospital, with our son babbling away in the back, I gave myself the mother of all internal pep talks. I wasn't going to allow fear and the magnitude of this to consume us or rob my son of living as full a life as humanly possible.

I made myself three pledges:

- to ensure my son can seize every opportunity and grab all the wonders that life has to offer

- to inspire others living with his condition of xeroderma pigmentosum (XP) to be brave enough to strive for the same

- to remove prejudice against my son and others like him who live with rare disease.

Since that day I have been dedicated to fulfilling these pledges. I gave up practicing Architecture, mothballed my practice and, side by side with my sister and partner in crime, founded a dedicated global XP charity, the Teddington Trust. Five years later we launched a global rare disease publication and movement for change, Rare Revolution Magazine.

Raising a child with a life-limiting condition keeps everything is sharp focus. The need to make every second count. To coin a phrase from my son's current favourite film, *Jumanji II*, 'We always only have one life, man'. So shouldn't we all, always, live like there might be no tomorrow because that is the reality, rare disease or not?

Adventure and epic tales come in all shapes and sizes. They may be about beating adversity and advocating for others or achieving impossible feats of human endurance. Like this book will showcase, they can also be absolutely everything in between.

So, whether you are faced with adversity or are blessed with a life of good health and fortune there is some advice that I, and all the other inspirational contributors of this book, would like to impart:

Say no to things that bring negativity into your life and that aren't truly worthy of your precious time on planet earth. And to everything else, every adventure and opportunity, especially if you don't know where it might lead you SAY YES MORE.

Live, love, laugh.

Nicola Miller

Xeroderma Pigmentosum affects fewer than 110 patients in the UK. Patients lack the DNA repair mechanism required to repair damage caused by natural and artificial source of light, rendering them 10,000 times more susceptible to skin cancer than the general population. They must spend their entire lives 100% shielded from all daylight and most types of artificial lighting to avoid death my aggressive skin cancers. 30% also experience neurological involvement from vision to hearing loss to impaired motor function and learning abilities. Due to the nature of their condition they face daily feelings of isolation and face the challenge of living life while disconnected from it by virtue of avoiding the very air around them. Please find out more about Xeroderma Pigmentosum and the global work of Teddington Trust by visiting *www.teddingtontrust.com* and please follow us on Facebook and twitter @TeddingtonTrust.

100% of all proceeds have been gifted to Teddington Trust therefore by purchasing this book of inspirational stories you have helped support us in our work providing education and protection and helping us end isolation.

THANK YOU! Xx

Please Leave a Review

We really hope you enjoyed reading our stories. If you have a minute it would be absolutely amazing if you could head over to Amazon and leave an honest review. Every review makes this book more visible to the general public, so just by tapping a few words and selecting a star rating, you are potentially raising even more money for charity. Good on you!

You can use your phone to scan this QR code and it will take you straight to the Amazon page The 'WRITE A CUSTOMER REVIEW' button should be next to the reviews towards the bottom of the page.

https://bit.ly/TBBOY1

Thanks, you wonderful human being!

The Big Book of Yes team

You want more...?

If you got to the end of this book and you haven't satisified your adventure itch, then you're in luck. These tales are just the beginning of the stories of Yes. Head over to Amazon right now to find 22 more adventure short stories in The Bigger Book of Yes and 49 stories in the Biggest Book of Yes!

https://bit.ly/TBBOY2

https://bit.ly/TBBOY3

CPSIA information can be obtained
at www.ICGtesting.com
Printed in the USA
LVHW081416130121
676373LV00019B/1059